CRITICAL INSIGHTS

A Streetcar
Named Desire

CRITICAL INSIGHTS

A Streetcar Named Desire

by Tennessee Williams

Editor
Brenda Murphy
University of Connecticut

Salem Press
Pasadena, California · Hackensack, New Jersey

Cover photo: Time & Life Pictures/Getty Images

Published by Salem Press

© 2010 by EBSCO Publishing
Editor's text © 2010 by Brenda Murphy
"The *Paris Review* Perspective" © 2010 by Catherine Steindler for
The Paris Review

∞ The paper used in these volumes conforms to the American National Standard for Permanence of Paper for Printed Library Materials, Z39.48-1992 (R1997).

Library of Congress Cataloging-in-Publication Data
A streetcar named Desire, by Tennessee Williams / editor, Brenda Murphy.
    p. cm. — (Critical insights)
    Includes bibliographical references and index.
    ISBN 978-1-58765-628-6 (alk. paper)
    1. Williams, Tennessee, 1911-1983. Streetcar named Desire. I. Murphy, Brenda, 1950-
    PS3545.I5365S8274 2010
    812'.54—dc22

        2009026308

PRINTED IN CANADA

Contents_____

The Play and Author_____

Critical Contexts_____

Critical Readings_____

Resources

About This Volume

Brenda Murphy

This collection of essays on *A Streetcar Named Desire* offers a diverse selection of criticism on Tennessee Williams's most important play. The collection is divided into two main parts. The first, which provides the context for the criticism, is composed mainly of essays that were commissioned specifically for this volume. The second consists of reprinted essays that are not only interesting and revealing studies in themselves but reflect the play's critical history as well.

As background for the individual critical studies, the editor's introductory essay and Catherine Steindler's "The *Paris Review* Perspective" present a general critical context, and Robert J. Forman provides a brief biography of Tennessee Williams. These essays are followed by new articles that illuminate *A Streetcar Named Desire* from several different perspectives. Camille-Yvette Welsch presents the play in the context of the aftermath of World War II and the threat of the atomic bomb, amid the many stresses on returning U.S. soldiers and their wives and the explosion of interest in sexuality that accompanied the Kinsey Report. Kenneth Elliott provides a revealing analysis of the tragedy of *A Streetcar Named Desire* in the context of Arthur Miller's *Death of a Salesman*. Neil Heims argues compellingly that "the volcanic forces smoldering and unleashed in *A Streetcar Named Desire* suggest that it is a play whose action is a *reaction* to repression, to suppressed inadmissible material," and its consequences. Janyce Marson discusses some of the important issues that have interested the play's critics in the more than sixty years since its premiere.

The essays reprinted in the "Critical Readings" section reflect the variety of critical and theoretical perspectives that have been trained on *A Streetcar Named Desire*, beginning with the much-discussed question of the play's complex relationship with tragedy. Verna Foster argues that the play is tragicomic, "a genre that offers its audience a less cathartic, more ambiguous and disturbing kind of theatrical experience than tragedy might" and is also "an experience better suited to the needs and tastes of audiences in mid-to-late twentieth-century America." Britton J. Harwood suggests that *A Streetcar Named Desire* begins where a tragedy has already ended, arguing that its action "transposes the elements of tragedy into ironies" at the expense of Blanche, who must experience "a version of the tragic in which no real purpose or perception is possible."

One of the most significant and productive lines of recent criticism about *A Streetcar Named Desire* focuses on issues around sexuality, gender, and sexual identity. In two articles that make productive use of the authors' studies of Williams's drafts of the play, John S. Bak examines the process by which Williams arrived at Stanley's rape of Blanche as "the sole means of providing dramatic closure to his morality play" and Dan Isaac argues that, in the contest between Blanche and Stanley, Blanche is "victorious in her defeat." Dean Shackelford makes use of the gender theories of Eve Kosofsky Sedgwick and Judith Butler to examine the central trope of the closet in the play, arguing for its subversive quality. In a poststructuralist analysis, Anne Fleche examines the tropes of spatial violation and sexual violence in the context of the relationship between realism and expressionism.

A Streetcar Named Desire has been the subject of a number of adaptations into other media, such as film, opera, and dramatic parody, which have a complex and sometimes vexed relationship with the play. Three essays here examine adaptations of Williams's work. Linda Costanzo Cahir addresses the struggle of Elia Kazan, the director of both the play's original production (1947) and its first film adaptation (1951), to adapt the play authentically in the face of the censorship efforts of the motion picture industry's censorship board, the Catholic Legion of Decency, and the film's own producers. Keith Dorwick makes use of close textual analysis of various versions of the script as well as the film and opera adaptations to examine the progressive excision of the homosocial from the play and film. Finally, in a revealing study that includes a detailed account of Lillian Hellman's unused scenario for the film, Nancy M. Tischler details the effects of censorship and the Motion Picture Production Code in the development of the screenplay. A chronology of Williams's life, a list of Williams's works, and a bibliography complete the volume.

THE PLAY
AND
AUTHOR

On *A Streetcar Named Desire*

Brenda Murphy

The Broadway premiere of *A Streetcar Named Desire*, on December 3, 1947, was a major event in American theatrical history. Not only was it the official birth of Tennessee Williams's most significant play, which went on to run for 855 performances and to win the Pulitzer Prize for drama, it was the first collaboration between director Elia Kazan and designer Jo Mielziner, an artistic combination that was to work with Williams and Arthur Miller in realizing several more of the most important American plays of the twentieth century on stage, including *Death of a Salesman* and *Cat on a Hot Tin Roof*. Kazan's stage version of *A Streetcar Named Desire* was tremendously influential, and his interpretation of Williams's play has been permanently fixed in the public imagination through the 1951 film adaptation that he directed, with a screenplay written by Williams and Oscar Saul. While Blanche DuBois was played by two different actors, Jessica Tandy in the theater and Vivien Leigh in the film, Stanley Kowalski was played with such authority by Marlon Brando both on stage and in the film that the character has become almost inextricable from the actor, even for succeeding generations of the film's viewers.

Kazan had a tendency to seek an emotional and moral clarity on stage that sometimes became melodrama. Early on in their negotiations, suspecting that Kazan might have reservations about taking on the direction of the play, Williams offered an explanation of the tragic ambiguities he saw at its heart. In an extraordinary letter laying out his conception of the play, he wrote that in *A Streetcar Name Desire* "there are no 'good' or 'bad' people. Some are a little better or a little worse but all are activated more by misunderstanding than malice. A blindness to what is going on in each other's hearts." Stanley, he said, sees Blanche "not as a desperate, driven creature backed into a last corner to make a last desperate stand—but as a calculating bitch with 'round heels.' . . . Nobody sees anybody *truly*, but all through the flaws of their own ego." The only point the play makes, he insisted, is "the point or theme of human understanding," explaining that "it is a tragedy with the classic aim of producing a katharsis of pity and terror, and in order to do that Blanche must finally have the understanding and compassion of the audience." And this must happen "without creating a black-dyed villain in Stanley. It is a thing (misunderstanding) not a person (Stanley) that destroys her in the end. In the end you should feel—'If only they all had *known* about each other.'"[1]

A good example of Williams's refusal to make a clear moral statement in *Streetcar* is Stanley's rape of Blanche in scene 10 and its aftermath in scene 11, which was controversial from the first and remains so to this day. Williams had rethought this sexual encounter continuously as he worked on the script, and several surviving manuscript versions in the Williams archive at the Harry Ransom Humanities Research Center at the University of Texas show very different conceptions of it. In a fragment of a version called "The Passion of a Moth," Blanche and Stanley seem to have made love with mutual attraction, and Blanche tells Stanley she is going on to Mobile, where she expects to meet a stranger. She also speaks of bearing Stanley's son, who will wash them all clean. At the end of the play, Blanche is alone onstage, in complete control as she says it is time for her to get packed and be going. In a later version, called "The Poker Night"—Williams's favored title for the play up until the last revisions—Blanche is presented as a helpless victim in the final scene. She is described by the doctor as "catatonic" as she sits staring out the window, and later she crouches in a grotesque, twisted position, screaming. She is taken away in a straitjacket by the people from the asylum.

In the final version of the play, it is evident that Williams aimed to steer between these two extremes. While Blanche is clearly the victim of Stanley's assault, and she is ready to twist the jagged edge of a broken bottle in Stanley's face as she unsuccessfully fights him off, the determination of her resistance is undermined by Stanley's line "We've had this date with each other from the beginning"[2] and by her moaning and sinking to her knees before he carries her inert figure to the bed. To emphasize this ambiguity, Williams, in a revision sent to Kazan just a few weeks before rehearsals began, had cut a line from the next scene in which Stella said to Eunice that Blanche told her Stanley had raped her. This was underlined visually when Stella held up Stanley's pajama top, which had been ripped to shreds, and said that his shoulders and back were covered with scratches. All Stanley would say in his defense was that Blanche was crazy. In cutting this graphic demonstration of the rape and depicting Blanche as out of touch with reality and thus unreliable as the narrator of her story in the final scene, Williams took away the element of moral certainty that the earlier version had. He also made Stella's guilt for sending away her sister less overt. When she says, "I couldn't believe her story and go on living with Stanley,"[3] in the final version of the play, there may be some doubt in her mind. There was none in the earlier version.

With Marlon Brando playing Stanley, the ambiguities—and the unresolved conflicts in the audience's empathy with the characters—became more exaggerated. Kazan and Williams agreed that the audience should be on Stanley's side at the beginning of the play, as Blanche invades his home and sets about attempting to "resubjugate Stella," as Kazan put it.[4] In the course of the play, the audience should be drawn toward Blanche. Kazan wrote in his director's notes:

> Gradually, as they see how genuinely in pain, how actually desperate she is, how warm, tender and loving she can be (the Mitch story), how freighted with need she is—then they begin to go with her. They begin to realize that they are sitting in at the death of something extraordinary . . . colorful, varied, passionate, lost, witty, imaginative, of her own integrity . . . and then they feel the tragedy.[5]

In the acting script of the play, Williams added a note at the beginning of scene 5 that identifies the scene as "*a point of balance between the play's two sections, Blanche's coming and the events leading up to her violent departure. The important values are the ones that characterize Blanche: its function is to give her dimension as a character and to suggest the intense inner life which makes her a person of greater magnitude than she appears on the surface.*"[6] This is the scene in which Stanley first reveals the threat of exposing Blanche's past through his informant Shaw, and Blanche admits to Stella that she has not "been so good the last two years or so, after Belle Reve had started to slip through my fingers. . . . I was never hard or self-sufficient enough. . . . Soft people, soft people have got to shimmer and glow. They've got to put on soft colors, the colors of butterfly wings and put a paper lantern over the light."[7] This is the point at which the audience should begin to be drawn to her side.

With Brando playing Stanley, however, this was no mean feat. The magnetism of the actor carried over to the character, and Brando was able to find points of vulnerability, humor, and vitality in Stanley that kept audience members from transferring their sympathy completely to Blanche. This bothered Kazan at first, thinking that it was a fault in his direction, but Williams reminded him that Stanley was not meant to be evil and Blanche was not flawless. Kazan finally came to the conclusion that this uneasy ambiguity was exactly what was in the play: "Was the play an affirmation of spiritual values over the brutish ones? Certainly. But that simple? No."[8]

As he became closer to Williams, Kazan came to locate the play's ambiguity in the playwright himself. Observing Williams's stormy relationship with his partner at the time, Pancho Rodriguez y Gonzalez, Kazan concluded that the moth imagery originated very close to home: "Blanche is attracted by the man who is going to destroy her. I understood the play by this formula of ambivalence. Only then, it seemed to me, would I think of it as Tennessee meant it to be understood: with fidelity to life as he—not all us groundlings, but he—had experienced it."[9] Later critics have found a deep ambivalence in the play that they see arising from Williams's relationships to his homosexuality, to members of his family, and to the South or to American values in general. There is no doubt of the play's complexity, however, or of its uncanny power to touch all kinds of spectators and readers. In the ten years after its premiere, *A Streetcar Named Desire* was staged in Havana, Mexico City, Rome, London, Paris, Toronto, Hamburg, Vienna, Basel, Tokyo, Los Angeles, Toruń, Wroclaw, and Melbourne.[10] During the latter half of the twentieth century, it became an important part of the world's collective theater experience, and so it remains in the twenty-first.

Notes

1. Tennessee Williams to Elia "Gadge" Kazan, April 19, 1947, in *The Selected Letters of Tennessee Williams*, vol. 2, *1945-1957*, ed. Albert J. Devlin and Nancy M. Tischler (New York: New Directions, 2004), 95-96.

2. Tennessee Williams, *A Streetcar Named Desire*, in *The Theatre of Tennessee Williams*, vol. 1 (New York: New Directions, 1971), 402.

3. Ibid., 405.

4. Elia Kazan, "Notebook for *Streetcar*," in *Directors on Directing*, ed. Toby Cole and Helen Chinoy (Indianapolis: Bobbs-Merrill, 1963), 372.

5. Ibid., 367.

6. Tennessee Williams, *A Streetcar Named Desire* (New York: Dramatists Play Service, 1947), 52.

7. Ibid., 56.

8. Elia Kazan, *Elia Kazan: A Life* (New York: Knopf, 1988), 349.

9. Ibid., 351.

10. Philip C. Kolin, *Williams: "A Streetcar Named Desire"* (New York: Cambridge University Press, 2000), 175-79.

Biography of Tennessee Williams

Robert J. Forman

Early Life

Tennessee Williams was born Thomas Lanier Williams on Palm Sunday, 1911, the second child of Cornelius Coffin Williams and Edwina Dakin Williams. Columbus, the eastern Mississippi town in which he was born, was still small and quite rural in the early years of the twentieth century. Social attitudes of the Old South and feelings engendered by the Civil War remained strong, and Williams grew up hearing stories about his father's volunteer service in the Spanish-American War as well as stories about his mother's numerous beaux, the forty-five "gentlemen callers" who had courted her in the years before her marriage.

His parents' marriage was never a happy one, but social custom precluded divorce. In November, 1909, after only two years with her husband and before the birth of her first child, Rose, Williams's mother left Gulfport, Mississippi, where she had lived since she married, and returned to her father's Columbus rectory. The elder Williams visited regularly, however, and a third child, Walter Dakin Williams, would be born in 1919. Williams came to feel a special affection for his grandparents, the Reverend Mr. Walter Dakin and Rose Otte Dakin, and he came to dread his father's visits. Cornelius Williams seemed overcritical, insensitive, and rough-hewn to the boy, and these tensions would increase as young Thomas grew older.

When the elder Williams obtained a managerial position with the Friedman-Shelby branch of the International Shoe Company in the summer of 1918, he was able to convince his wife to join him in St. Louis, Missouri. Williams's mother left her parents' home—at this time in Clarksdale, Mississippi—with reluctance. She feared a recurrence of her husband's drinking, gambling, and womanizing, which had separated them nine years earlier, but she was expecting the birth of another child and had hopes for a more normal life.

Her worst fears were justified in every sense. Thomas, though only nine, came to detest St. Louis. His Mississippi accent was ridiculed by boys his own age, and he and his sister often absented themselves from school. He spent his time reading until he could return home; he read several of Charles Dickens's works, the Waverly novels of Sir Walter Scott, and selections from the plays of William Shakespeare. Meanwhile, his mother also waited, often for long hours in the dark, as her husband's vices continued and worsened during the St. Louis years.

Williams found outlets for this family tension in occasional visits to "Grand," as he called his grandmother, in Clarksdale, and in writing poems and short stories. Several of these were published while he was still in junior high school from 1923 to 1926. The 1925 yearbook of Ben Blewett Junior High School contained "Demon Smoke," his essay on the factories of St. Louis. He continued to write after he transferred to Soldan High School, and his review of the silent film *Stella Dallas* (1925) was the talk of his English class.

Though he read and wrote insatiably, Williams was never a successful student, and his poor academic performance, right through his college years, was a never-ending cause of friction between him and his father. His grades at the University of Missouri grew worse each term, and his consistently poor and ultimately failing grades in the required Reserve Officers' Training Corps (ROTC) courses particularly mortified his father, for whom military life and masculinity were synonymous. After a devastating spring term in 1932, Williams's father insisted that his son take some kind of job, but the Great Depression, then at its worst, precluded this. It was not until June, 1934, that Williams spent a brief time—until April, 1935—at the International Shoe Company, his father's employer. Thus, Williams passed at least two years out of school and unemployed, though this frustrating period of his early life would in time be exorcised in *The Glass Menagerie* (1944), the most autobiographical of all his plays.

Life's Work

In September, 1935, Williams returned to school as a nonmatriculated student at Washington University, St. Louis. He continued to write, mostly short stories and poetry, but it was not until he was accepted at the University of Iowa, in Iowa City, in the fall of 1937—when he met E. C. Mabie and E. P. Conkle, who taught drama there—that Williams realized where his special talents lay. His first play, *Spring Storm* (1938), though given a cool reception in Mabie's drama production class, nevertheless inspired him to write others, and *Not About Nightingales* (1939), a play about prison life, received Mabie's praise. It was during his student years at Iowa that Williams acquired his lifelong habit of reusing titles and revising plays completely, even after performance or publication.

Williams had just arrived for the fall term at Iowa when he learned of his sister's deteriorating mental state and of his mother's decision to allow a leucotomy, or prefrontal lobotomy, to be performed upon Rose. This procedure was experimental, and at the time it was considered the only way of rendering violently schizophrenic patients harmless to themselves. Williams never forgave either his mother for allowing the operation or himself for not having prevented it. Rose imagery would pervade his works—*The Rose Tattoo* (1950); the "blue roses" of *The Glass Menagerie*; Aunt Rose of *The Unsatisfactory Supper* (1948); roses "of yesterday, of death, and of time" in *The Milk Train Doesn't Stop Here Anymore* (1963), *Camino Real* (1953), *The Last of My Solid Gold Watches* (1947), and *Something Unspoken* (1958); wild roses in *The Case of the Crushed Petunias* (1957); roses of Picardy in *Moony's Kid Don't Cry* (1946); the mystic rose of *Now the Cats with Jewelled Claws* (1981); the smell of roses in *The Mutilated* (1966); wild roses in *Will Mr. Merriwether Return from Memphis?* (1980); crushed roses in *Suddenly Last Summer* (1958), the play that deals most explicitly with Rose's operation—and Williams regularly visited his sister up until the last months of his life. She would survive her younger brother by two years.

It was after his graduation from Iowa in August, 1938, that Williams changed his first name to "Tennessee." He considered his given name more appropriate for a poet (he was indeed distantly related to the poet Sidney Lanier), and he followed the lead of classmates who for some time had called him Tennessee as a nickname. Tennessee was also, however, the state in which his grandparents resided at this time, and Memphis held pleasant associations for him. In interviews, Williams sometimes quipped that his ancestors had fought Indians in Tennessee and he often found himself in a stockade fighting off his attackers.

In the autumn of 1938, Williams found his way to New Orleans, hoping to find support for his writing through the Works Progress Administration (WPA) project there. He came to love the bohemian atmosphere of the city's French Quarter; he had his first homosexual experience in New Orleans and gave free rein to the insatiable passions that increasingly governed his life. In later years, he would say that he felt as though two elements, intellectual and sensual, were constantly at war within him, and this dichotomy appears in many of his tragic protagonists. When it became clear early in 1939 that no WPA aid would be forthcoming, Williams submitted four of his one-act plays as well as his full-length works *Not About Nightingales* and *Fugitive Kind* to the Group Theatre in New York, which was sponsoring a competition. In order to satisfy the age requirement, he gave his date of birth as March 26, 1914, thus starting a fiction concerning his age that would continue well into the 1950s.

While awaiting a decision from the Group Theatre, Williams and a companion left New Orleans for Los Angeles with the vague idea of writing screenplays, but Molly Day Thacher of the Group Theatre soon wrote to praise the one-act works he had sent under the collective title *American Blues* (1948). She also enclosed a check for one hundred dollars and sent the plays to Audrey Wood, the famed theatrical agent, who would work tirelessly in Williams's behalf.

It was Wood who would bring Williams to New York, advance him money with no sure hope of repayment, oversee his personal affairs, continue to champion his works, and, in late December, 1940, bring his play *Battle of Angels* to its Boston premiere. Though *Battle of Angels* was hardly a resounding success, it brought Williams's work to the attention of important critics who recognized the young playwright's promise. In late March, 1957, its revision, called *Orpheus Descending*, would be given a Broadway production.

Williams first took the theatrical world by storm with the premiere of his compelling "memory play" *The Glass Menagerie* on December 26, 1944, in Chicago. Though not written as autobiography, it nevertheless reflects the strains of Williams's life in St. Louis during the Depression. Tom, the play's narrator, is Williams's persona; Tom presents a subjective remembrance of Amanda Wingfield (an incisively accurate portrait of Williams's mother) and his shy, fragile sister Laura (identifiable with Williams's sister Rose). It was a painful and difficult play for Williams to write, but it was immediately heralded as a landmark of the American theater and was quickly brought to Broadway, where it enjoyed immense success.

Other triumphs followed, each more astounding than the last for its innovative realism: *A Streetcar Named Desire* (1947), *Summer and Smoke* (1947), *The Rose Tattoo* (1950), *Camino Real* (1953), *Cat on a Hot Tin Roof* (1955), *Suddenly Last Summer* (1958), *Sweet Bird of Youth* (1959), *The Night of the Iguana* (1961), and *The Milk Train Doesn't Stop Here Anymore* (1963). Not all were given enthusiastic critical receptions, and *Camino Real*, Williams's foray into political drama, has never been a popular favorite; nevertheless, each reveals some distinctive aspect of Williams's genius.

Williams was fortunate to have, from the beginning of his career, the support of both good friends and professional associates. Harold Clurman of New York's Group Theatre; Elia Kazan, famed for his direction of *A Streetcar Named Desire* and other Williams plays; outstanding actors such as Marlon Brando, Laurette Taylor, and Maureen Stapleton; and selfless friends, such as his agent Audrey Wood and longtime companion Frank Merlo, all helped to foster Williams's fragile genius, bolster his always shaky self-confidence, and control his self-destructive indulgence in drugs and promiscuous sex.

It is a tragic but undeniable fact that Williams found his work increasingly difficult and ultimately impossible as these individuals were taken from him, whether by death, other commitments, or petty disagreements. Though Williams was fabulously wealthy at the time of his death, he died a lonely man. His body was found on the morning of February 25, 1983. At his bedside was an assortment of capsules, tablets, eyedrops and nose drops, and a half-empty bottle of wine. The New York City medical examiner reported that a barbiturate safety cap had somehow lodged in Williams's throat.

At the peak of his career in the 1940s and 1950s, Williams was the image of the successful playwright: sensitive features, neat mustache, immaculately groomed in well-cut English-tailored suits and bow ties, often sporting a cigarette in an onyx holder. Significantly, later pictures often show him in white or light-tan suiting, Panama hat, and a full beard or goatee added to a fuller mustache. He appears heavier in the latest of these, and, in retrospect, considering what is now known about the unhappiness of his final years, his lightheartedness might have been forced. It is the paradox of Williams's art that he drew his greatest triumphs from his deepest pain.

From *Dictionary of World Biography: The 20th Century.* Pasadena, CA: Salem Press, 1999. Copyright © 1999 by Salem Press, Inc.

Bibliography

Bloom, Harold, ed. *Tennessee Williams*. New York: Chelsea House, 1987. Collection of critical essays carries an introduction by Bloom that places Williams in the dramatic canon of American drama and within the psychological company of Hart Crane and Arthur Rimbaud. Contributors to the collection take traditional thematic and historical approaches, noting Williams's "grotesques," his morality and irony, his work in the "middle years," and the mythical qualities of his situations and characters.

Crandall, George W. *Tennessee Williams: A Descriptive Bibliography*. Pittsburgh: University of Pittsburgh Press, 1995. An important bibliographical resource.

Falk, Signi Lenea. *Tennessee Williams*. 2d ed. Boston: Twayne, 1978. Primarily discusses Williams's plays, but also addresses many of the short stories, including "One Arm," "Desire and the Black Masseur," and "Portrait of a Girl in Glass."

Hayman, Ronald. *Tennessee Williams: Everyone Else Is an Audience*. New Haven, Conn.: Yale University Press, 1993. Discusses Williams's work with a focus on the extent to which the playwright based his plays on events that took place in his own life.

Kolin, Philip C., ed. *The Tennessee Williams Encyclopedia*. Westport, Conn.: Greenwood Press, 2004. Provides a useful guide to Williams and his work. In 160 entries, Williams scholars offer a wealth of information.

Leverich, Lyle. *Tom: The Unknown Tennessee Williams*. New York: Crown, 1995. First volume of a planned two-volume biography traces Williams's life for the first thirty-three years, drawing on previously unpublished letters, journals, and notebooks. Discusses Williams's focus on how society has a destructive influence on sensitive people and his efforts to change drama into an unrealistic form.

Martin, Robert A., ed. *Critical Essays on Tennessee Williams*. New York: G. K. Hall, 1997. Excellent, accessible collection presents criticism of Williams's works.

Pagan, Nicholas. *Rethinking Literary Biography: A Postmodern Approach to Tennessee Williams*. Rutherford, N.J.: Fairleigh Dickinson University Press, 1993. Discusses the symbolism of Williams's characters in relation to his life.

Rader, Dotson. *Tennessee: Cry of the Heart*. Garden City, N.Y.: Doubleday, 1985. Chatty biography has the appeal of a firsthand, fascinating account, filled with gossip and inside information, but lacks the virtue of notes or a scholarly bibliography.

Roudané, Matthew C., ed. *The Cambridge Companion to Tennessee Williams*. New York: Cambridge University Press, 1997. Collection comprises copious amounts of information on Williams and his works.

Spoto, Donald. *The Kindness of Strangers: The Life of Tennessee Williams*. Reprint. New York: DaCapo Press, 1998. Lively chronicle details Williams's encounters with such diverse influences as the Group Theatre, Frieda and D. H. Lawrence, Senator Joseph R. McCarthy, Fidel Castro, Hollywood stars, and the homosexual and drug subcultures of Key West. Forty-two pages of notes, bibliography, and index make this study a valuable resource for further scholarship.

Tharpe, Jac, ed. *Tennessee Williams: A Tribute*. Jackson: University Press of Mississippi, 1977. Collection presents fifty-three essays on various aspects of Williams's art.

Thompson, Judith. *Tennessee Williams' Plays: Memory, Myth, and Symbol*. New York: Peter Lang, 2002. Provides a Jungian analysis of Williams's plays, focusing on the manifestation of archetypes in his work.

Tischler, Nancy Marie Patterson. *Student Companion to Tennessee Williams*.

Westport, Conn.: Greenwood Press, 2000. A well-known Williams scholar brings together the playwright's biography and critical assessments of his works to provide students with a thorough introduction to and appreciation of Williams's achievements.

Williams, Dakin, and Shepherd Mead. *Tennessee Williams: An Intimate Biography*. New York: Arbor House, 1983. One of the more bizarre duos in biographical writing, Williams (Tennessee's brother) and Mead (Tennessee's childhood friend) produce a credible biography in a highly readable, well-indexed work. Their account of the playwright also helps to capture his almost schizophrenic nature. A solid index and extensive research assist the serious scholar and the general reader.

Williams, Tennessee. *Five O'Clock Angel: Letters of Tennessee Williams to Maria St. Just, 1948-1982*. New York: Knopf, 1990. Collection of letters sheds light on Williams's personal life.

Windham, Donald. *As If. . . .* Verona, Italy: D. Windham, 1985. This reminiscence of Williams's onetime friend portrays the writer as a man of bizarre contradictions and reveals in telling vignettes the downward spiral of his self-destructive lifestyle.

Woodhouse, Reed. *Unlimited Embrace: A Canon of Gay Fiction, 1945-1995*. Amherst: University of Massachusetts Press, 1998. Includes a chapter on Williams's gay short stories. Argues that the most astonishing thing about the stories is their lack of special pleading, that while they are not graphic, they are not apologetic for their homosexuality. Provides an extended analysis of the story "Hard Candy."

The *Paris Review* Perspective _____

Catherine Steindler for *The Paris Review*

In his 1981 interview with *The Paris Review*, Tennessee Williams characterized his work as "emotionally autobiographical. It has no relation to the actual events of my life, but it reflects the emotional currents of my life." In this sense of "autobiographical," Blanche DuBois, whose struggle for survival drives the action of *A Streetcar Named Desire*, is Williams's most autobiographical creation. After all, Williams, recalling Flaubert, is often said to have claimed, "I am Blanche DuBois." She is also his most emblematic character, for in her so many elements of Williams's other major characters converge: Amanda (*The Glass Menagerie*), an incessant talker and determined fantasist who clings to the lost genteel world of her youth; her daughter Laura, prodigiously imaginative and as breakable as the tiny glass animals with which, unable to withstand the harsh demands of the outside world, she creates a beautiful play world to inhabit; Miss Alma (*Summer and Smoke*), the proper and idealistic daughter of a minister, who makes an impassioned argument for the primacy of the life of the soul over that of the body; Brick (*Cat on a Hot Tin Roof*), who drinks to blot out his guilt for having abandoned the person he loved when that person needed him most; Alexandra del Lago (*Sweet Bird of Youth*), a self-described monster, voracious and demanding, addicted to drugs, liquor, and young men; and her companion Chance, a strikingly attractive drifter whose youthful looks are fading, leaving him alone and desperate. Blanche is maddening and admirable, fragile and ferocious, pathetic and heroic, debased and noble, deluded and clear-sighted, weak and strong. It is in these contradictions that her humanity resides.

The drama critic Kenneth Tynan once quoted Williams as saying that "the theater . . . is a place where one has time for the problems of people to whom one would show the door if they came to one's office for a job." Williams's characters would not make particularly pleasant office mates. He writes about people who exist on the edge of sanity, or just over it—the guilty, the deserted, the destitute, the delusional, and the destroyed, all roasting on the fire of their own passions. "I don't think that anything that occurs in life should be omitted from art," Williams told *The Paris Review*. "I set out to tell the truth. And sometimes the truth is shocking." Williams's plays are not for the cool or the squeamish; they issue from the sweaty, squalid trenches of Williams's own dwelling. If his audience is to glimpse what Williams illuminates, it is imperative that he or she extend toward Williams's characters the empathy that his plays demand.

"I don't believe in individual guilt," Williams told *The Paris Review*. "I don't think people are responsible for what they do. We are products of circumstances that determine what we do." With this statement, Williams offers a concise lesson in how to read *A Streetcar Named Desire*: begin with the characters' circumstances, mark how their needs and subsequent actions unfold from them, and abstain from assigning guilt or blame. When Blanche arrives at Elysian Fields, she is in real danger. She tells Eunice, "They told me to take a street-car named Desire, and then transfer to one called Cemeteries." In fact it is death that has driven her into the arms of desire and deposited her—penniless, unemployed, and homeless—on Stella and Stanley's doorstep. The quantity of loss that has marked Blanche's thirty or so years is staggering: the suicide of her husband, the illnesses and subsequent deaths of her entire family (except Stella), the loss of the family home, and finally the loss of her profession, due to her own "epic fornications." She is a woman of immense, one might say heroic, endurance who, when we meet her, is near the end of her capacity to endure.

Williams's characters often perish from their excesses—of sensitivity, of imagination, and of determination—and Blanche is no exception. From the start, and not without sexual excitement, Stanley and Blanche recognize in one another true adversaries, each of tremendous strength. "The first time I laid eyes on him I thought to myself, that man is my executioner!" Blanche says of Stanley, well before he proves her premonition to be accurate. Just before Stanley, in a brutal coup de grâce, rapes Blanche, he declares, "We've had this date with each other from the beginning." Much has been made of the nature of their conflict, Blanche being a figure of the spirit (she is first described as "a moth," a creature so delicate as to have almost no corporeal presence) and Stanley a figure of the body (he first appears lugging a hunk of raw meat). This opposition exists, but to conceive of Blanche as a purely ethereal soul is to forget how intimately she has lived with bodies (her own and those of others) redolent of sex and death. Stanley's desire to destroy Blanche is not based in any abstract existential theory but is a response to the threat she poses to his dignity and dominance. Were Blanche one of those "little birdlike woman without any nest— eating the crust of humility all their life," as Amanda, in *The Glass Menagerie*, describes women in Blanche's situation, she would pose no threat. For all Stanley fails to see about Blanche—her pathos, her sensitivity, her brokenness, and, most important, her weakness—he does sense her power, and that is why he must eliminate her.

"How strange it is that I should be called a destitute woman!" Blanche exclaims. "I have all these treasures locked in my heart! . . . beauty of the mind and richness of the spirit and tenderness of the heart." It is the power of these treasures that, by provoking Stanley, ultimately brings about her ruin, but it is also that same power that makes Blanche the richest of the American theater's heroines.

Works Cited

Tynan, Kenneth. *Profiles*. Ed. Kathleen Tynan. London: Nick Hern Books, 1990.

Williams, Tennessee. "The Art of Theater No. 5." Interview with Dotson Rader. *The Paris Review* 81 (Fall 1981).

_____. *The Glass Menagerie*. New York: New Directions, 1989.

_____. *A Streetcar Named Desire*. New York: New Directions, 1980.

CRITICAL
CONTEXTS

World War II, Sex, and Displacement in *A Streetcar Named Desire*

Camille-Yvette Welsch

A Streetcar Named Desire opened in New York City on December 3, 1947. At the conclusion of the play, the audience stood and applauded for seven minutes, calling out for the author, and a shambling, shy Tennessee Williams took the stage. His play, written primarily during 1944-1945, stays in the close confines of a small apartment in New Orleans's French Quarter, a neighborhood awash in jazz, blue light, and sex. This small corner of the city and its characters resonated with Americans newly home from a war that changed the face of warfare forever. Like Blanche DuBois, American men and women alike were returning to homes they barely understood or remembered. GIs suffered from "battle fatigue," and parents came to fear nuclear annihilation. This essay will explore the relationship between *Streetcar* and the culture into which it was delivered, first as a play, then as a movie.

Director Elia Kazan had been working on Broadway since the 1930s. He was a part of the Group Theatre, a politically left group intent on creating socially relevant dramas and a troupe of actors unified in their technique. As a result of his years with the Group, Kazan was savvy in his assessment of Broadway audiences. The social dramas of the thirties, with their broad indictments of trouble at home, had lost their appeal during the war and had begun to seem limiting to Kazan. According to drama historian Ethan Mordden, "Truth, in writing and performing, was the obsession of the 1930s" (158), but that truth required a critical view of the nation and its problems. In the early 1940s the people wanted a break from issues and didacticism; instead, they opted for farces and romances or plays that spoke to the moral superiority of democracy (Mordden 191).

The tide changed again when the war ended. This new audience was less monolithic, their concerns more varied. Historian Thomas H.

Pauly has written that "Broadway harkened to the plight of the return-ing veteran. His reintegration into civilian life became an occasion for reevaluating the past and confronting a problem-ridden present" (66). In October 1946, O'Neill's *The Iceman Cometh* brought back the pos-sibility of introspection to the American theater, paving the way for Williams's *A Streetcar Named Desire*. Mordden alleges that the play is a "brutal reply to the illusion-loving theatre of the 1930s, for Williams speaks truth to someone whose whole life is a lie, the deluded Blanche DuBois" (211).

The play introduced an ailing America to truly adult fare—prostitution, homosexuality, rape, domestic violence, alcoholism, mental break-downs, and even, some critics argue, a transvestite of sorts. Recovering from the Great Depression, World War II, and the Dust Bowl, Ameri-cans were familiar with violence in their day-to-day lives and, to an ex-tent, on the stage and screen. The violence was not the shocking ele-ment of the play. Critic C. W. E. Bigsby notes: "The shock of *Streetcar* when it was first staged lay in the fact that, outside of O'Neill's work, this was the first American play in which sexuality was patently at the core of the lives of all its principal characters, a sexuality with the power to redeem or destroy, to compound or negate the forces which bore on those caught in a moment of social change" (*Modern* 51). The moment of social change had come: thousands of Americans struggled to renegotiate their places at home after the war. Women returned from work to the domestic sphere. Gender roles were changing, and, with them, expectations about sexuality.

British author Virginia Woolf claimed that "on or about December 1910 human character changed forever." This statement invoked her belief about the power of modernism and the profound effect it was having on the world. This may have been less true for Americans, for whom many of the greatest landmark changes in thinking are linked to wartime. The Revolutionary War began with the radical idea of home rule; the Civil War tested the bounds of nationhood and the practice of slavery, pitting men against their brothers. World War I established the

United States as a world power, but it was in World War II that the United States may have undergone one of the greatest, most sudden moments of maturation in its short history.

The Japanese attack on Pearl Harbor shocked the American government out of its isolationist policies, sending thousands of men to war. In their absence, the country struggled valiantly, sending women into the workplace, planting victory gardens, and the like. As a result of the war, few households in the United States were unaffected, but Americans lived with the comfort that this was a just war, for a good end. Soldiers were saving lives. This was as moral a war as it was possible to have. As historian Paul S. Boyer states, "'Hiroshima' and 'Nagasaki' stand as signposts marking both a gash in the living flesh of our historical consciousness and a turning point in our ethical history: the concluding events of a 'good' war, the opening events of a murky era of moral ambiguity and uncertainty through which we still wander" (182).

The moral ambiguity began on August 6, 1945, when the United States dropped the first atomic bomb on Hiroshima, Japan, causing untold destruction to the city and a death toll that would eventually reach more than 100,000. Three days later, a second bomb was dropped on Nagasaki, eventually killing another 100,000 people. The next day, the Japanese offered an unconditional surrender. These acts of extreme violence, billed as necessary by the government, concluded the days of American innocence. Most Americans supported the dropping of the bombs, believing the action necessary to end the war and to save American lives, but an unsettling fact remained: "Now deprived of a clear, identifiable enemy, the moral indignation generated by the nation's war effort was turning back upon itself and growing self-conscious. The previous sense of purpose and conviction was being replaced by guilt, anxiety, and above all, troubled introspection" (Pauly 68). The nuclear age had dawned, within the span of a week. World War III, were it to come, would undoubtedly annihilate the world. What had the United States unleashed?

Displacement

During the war, American women went to work in the industrial sector, serving in factories and shipyards, aiding the war effort and supporting their troops, families, and country. Their work was no longer primarily in the domestic sphere with which so many were familiar. Women were quickly becoming skilled workers, from welders to carpenters. Those women who were not working in industry busied themselves knitting sweaters and socks for the Salvation Army to distribute during the harsh months of the European winters, kept their victory gardens, and tried to support their neighbors as best they could. The war years were united years, one nation under a common goal of defeating the Axis Powers. When the war ended, so did the unity. Men returned to ticker-tape parades and new babies, wives and forty-hour workweeks, a profound change from the all-day duty of soldiering.

With the return of the men, most of the women returned to the home, a place that for some was less fulfilling than their new work outside the home had been. Like their husbands, wives were having trouble acclimating to their old lives. To compound the problem, many soldiers returned with varying degrees of "battle fatigue," then often called "shell shock," known today as post-traumatic stress syndrome—caused by experiencing major traumatic events and often resulting in symptoms including depression, irritability, guilt, flashbacks, and extreme sensitivity to sound. Fourth of July parades became unbearable for some soldiers—the whizzing firecrackers had the sound of German bombs and gunshots. Former GIs would listen to planes overhead to hear whether they were German bombers. Those who had seen action on the Pacific front fared no better. Suddenly, newly reunited couples had to deal with nightmares and personality changes. Some men sought medical help for their terrors; for others, more physical wounds kept them at home while their wives went out to earn the daily bread. With wives who worked and husbands who needed the comfort of the home, the social order skewed, and gender roles were no longer as rigid and fixed as they once were. People were fighting hard to find a domestic status quo, a struggle that *Streetcar* reflected.

Blanche DuBois, a refugee of the Old Patrician South, makes her way to her sister Stella's doorstep. Blanche is a woman without home or country. The South of her youth is gone; her expectations for marriage and for men have been shattered. She enters into New Orleans's French Quarter, where the shadows do not hide ghosts of ancestors past; they hide intertwined couples and jazz musicians. Sex is part of the landscape, and though Blanche is certainly not without sexual experience, she is running partially from the guilt of her sexual associations. She wants desperately to leave the past behind her. Her antagonist, Stanley Kowalski, newly home from the war, wants to live as lord of his domain, in sexual union with his wife. He wants nothing to interfere with his dominion.

When Blanche sees Stella again, she experiences moments of familiarity broken by moments of complete dislocation, as a soldier might. Stella has made a life for herself in Blanche's absence. This life is predicated on sex with Stanley, a raw, masculine sensualist. When Blanche first sees the apartment, she is grossly unprepared, saying of it, "Never, never, never in my worst dreams could I picture—Only Poe! Only Mr. Edgar Allan Poe!—could do it justice!" The landscape is unfamiliar, as is the sister who wears the languid face of sexual satisfaction. Blanche's literary references signal her as an outsider.

Blanche's expectations for her sister have not been realized. She never imagined for Stella a marriage predicated on desire, nor did she imagine the violence that accompanies it. While Blanche is familiar with the feeling of desire—indeed, she is one of the first female characters in drama to be so open about having sexual needs—she is no longer familiar with being the observer of desire rather than the enactor.

Stella:	But there are things that happen between a man and a woman in the dark—that sort of make everything else seem—unimportant. [pause]
Blanche:	What you are talking about is brutal desire—just—Desire!—the name of that rattle-trap street-car that bangs through the Quarter, up one old narrow street and down another . . .
Stella:	Haven't you ridden on that street-car?
Blanche:	It brought me here.—Where I'm not wanted and where I am ashamed to be . . .

Nor is Blanche familiar with desire as a part of a socially condoned relationship. What Stella has in her marriage, Blanche had to pursue outside of marriage, under conditions that labeled her deviant rather than healthy—the hotel rooms, the troops, the underage boys. The short passage highlights Blanche's place as the outsider. She cannot understand the sexual thrall in which her sister finds herself. Indeed, she is an impediment to the things that happen in the dark, much as she was in her own marriage to homosexual Allan Grey. She cannot find space anywhere.

Blanche's displacement is physically manifested through the play's set as well. Her bed is in the kitchen, sectioned from the married couple by only a curtain. Her costumes, designed by Lucinda Ballard, were meant to help establish her as an outsider.

Blanche's wardrobe sets her apart from Stella, who's first seen in an off-the-shoulder peasant blouse, and thereafter in short-sleeved house dresses and maternity clothes. Blanche, by contrast, seems attired in anticipation of festive occasions with gentleman callers. Stella wears cotton, Blanche gossamer chiffon. These filmy outfits often have long sleeves that call attention to Blanche's arms by contrasting them with the naked arms of other, more comfortable women in the Quarter. (Staggs 190)

Blanche's lighting, the softness of the Chinese lanterns,
her appear younger, and they act as a part of the perf
her life, a stilted style of speech and appearance in stark
Eunice, the caterwauling neighbor, and Stella, the averag house-
wife.

Like sufferers of post-traumatic stress, Blanche also lives in two
simultaneous times—the past and the present. Onstage, the playing of
a Polish waltz marks the flashback to the night that Allan Grey shot
himself. The Varsouviana means the memory of Allan's death will begin to replay itself. Blanche starts at sudden sounds such as passing trains. She is irritable and on edge. In her first moments at the
Kowalski apartment, she searches desperately for a drink, telling
Stella, "I was so exhausted by all I'd been through my—nerves broke.
[Nervously, tamping cigarette] I was on the verge of—lunacy, almost!"
(21). The playwright later reveals that fraternizing with young men
was the true cause for her firing, but her claim of nerves seems real
enough whatever the alleged cause. She reveals to Stella that she is on
edge, that she cannot be alone.

The trauma caused by the suicide of her husband never left her, and
the sudden return of the memory must have looked familiar to families
dealing with soldiers who found themselves suddenly mentally transported back to the battlefield. In scene 6, she reveals the cause of her
trauma to Mitch: She fell in love with a boy who was gay, then she publicly outed him, shouting her disgust for him on the middle of a dance
floor. Williams mentions in his blocking notes that as she tells the
story, "[*A locomotive is heard approaching outside. She claps her
hands to her ears and crouches over. The headlight of the locomotive
glares into the room as it thunders past. As the noise recedes she
straightens slowly and continues speaking.*]" Blanche's sudden reactions to sound are in keeping with the symptoms of post-traumatic
stress. Her reaction, combined with the polka music, suggests the level
of trauma that resulted from her experience.

> [*Polka music sounds, in a minor key faint with distance.*]
>
> Blanche: We danced the Varsouviana! Suddenly in the middle
> of the dance the boy I married broke away from me
> and ran out of the casino. A few moments later—a shot!
> [*The polka stops abruptly.*]
> [*Blanche rises stiffly. Then, the polka resumes in a
> major key.*]
> I ran out—all did!—all ran and gathered about the
> terrible things at the edge of the lake! I couldn't get
> near for this crowding. Then somebody caught my
> arm. "Don't go any closer! Come back! You don't
> want to see!" See? See what! Then I heard voices
> say—Allan! Allan! The Grey boy! He'd stuck the
> revolver into his mouth, and fired—so that the back
> of his head had been—blown away!
> [*She sways and covers her face.*]
> It was because—on the dance-floor—unable to stop
> myself—I'd suddenly said, "I saw! I know! You
> disgust me . . ."

The use of the music was part of Tennessee Williams's plastic theater, an idea that he introduced in his production notes for *The Glass Menagerie*. He said:

Expressionism and all other unconventional techniques in drama have only one valid aim, and that is a closer approach to truth. When a play employs unconventional techniques, it is not, or certainly shouldn't be, trying to escape the responsibility of dealing with reality, or interpreting experience, but is expression of things as they are. . . . Everyone should know nowadays the unimportance of the photographic in art: that truth, life, or reality is an organic thing which the poetic imagination can represent or suggest, in essence, only through transformation, through changing into other forms than those which were merely present in appearance. (xix-xxii)

The music then becomes a way to enter the character's unstable mind without having to take the viewer out of the fabric of the play. The plastic theater and its expressionistic elements gave Williams greater freedom to express what had formerly seemed inexpressible without breaking the fourth wall. This connection with the interior of the characters, with their individual conflicts, marked a turning point for the theater. "Photographic" representations no longer had the same verisimilitude as the constructions of expressionism. Williams chased an emotional truth rather than a concrete fact. His interest in the interior mirrored the new introspection within the country.

Sexuality

This quest for verisimilitude, and the audience's willingness to accept it, also showed in the way *Streetcar* popularized a new kind of sexuality, more appropriate to its generation. Cary Grant was still a sex symbol, but he was also a symbol of a certain class, men who looked comfortable in tuxedos. Marlon Brando's Stanley Kowalski ushered in a raw sexuality, overt, predatory, and blue-collar. His sexuality on-screen gave rise to James Dean, Paul Newman, and Robert Mitchum. The rise of the sexual star coincided with the public's fascination with the sex lives of themselves and their neighbors.

Shortly after the play opened on Broadway, the newly formed Kinsey Institute published its first study, *Sexual Behavior in the Human Male*, and it hit the *New York Times* best-seller list by March. Professor Kinsey, a biologist, gathered information through more than eighteen thousand interviews and compiled data against which large portions of the U.S. population were suddenly comparing themselves (Bullough 129). As part of his method, Kinsey sought objectivity, striving merely to record his findings rather than to judge them. Unlike others of his day, Kinsey's study of sexuality was not linked to a study of morality (Bullough 127-30). It tracked the sexual habits and mores of men across social classes and situations, from prostitutes to academics. The hunger for information about sex had been whetted despite protests by any number of social conservatives. Sex was on the American mind, and publicly. Soldiers and their spouses alike were still trying to figure out who might be the breadwinner, and homophobia had increased after the war.

In 1950, Dr. Manfred S. Guttmacher, a psychoanalyst, wrote an article applauding Kinsey's effort to study human sexuality scientifically and concluded the article with a list of the findings he found most fascinating and surprising in the study. First among these was "the wide variations in all phases of sexual function and behavior that occur with great frequency in a normal population." Number four was "the direct correlation of sexual behavior with the socioeducational status—not only present but ultimate." Number five, one of the most remarked upon nationally, was "the high incidence of homosexual activity, and the relatively wide prevalence of animal contact among intellectually normal males," and number six, which often works in tandem with number five, "the high incidence of sexual practices in the United States that are in conflict with unrealistic legal enactments" (294).

The film community had its own moral watchdog: Joseph Breen, the man in charge of the Production Code Administration of the Motion Picture Producers and Directors Association. Breen was legendary for his cutting of films and the story-line messes caused by those cuts. With *Streetcar*'s incendiary rape scene and references to homosexuality, Kazan knew he had to clear the play with Breen before he invested his energies in a film version that the studios would not produce. Breen, as expected, objected to "'the element of sex perversion'; the rape scene, especially because in the play 'this particularly revolting rape goes unpunished'; the suggestions of Blanche's prostitution; and the various toilet gags and references, bits of profanity, and other 'unacceptable vulgarities'" (Staggs 131). Still, in 1949, Warner Bros. agreed to take on the film. The partnership ensured that the standards set out in the Production Code would have to be met in order for the studio to release the film and make money. Without adherence to the Code, viewers would be warned away from the film.

Breen, an archconservative Catholic, wanted extensive changes. As Philip C. Kolin notes, Allan Grey was to become merely "tender" rather than gay; Kazan would have to direct the suggestion that he was gay into the movie rather than say it outright as the play had. For Blanche's rape, Kazan cut away to a shattered mirror and gushing water (i.e., broken woman and orgasmic member). Finally, Williams rewrote the end of the play to punish the rapist. True to form, Williams, in his rewrite, followed the suggestion but ignored the intent: Stella leaves with her new baby, saying, "We're not going back in there. Not this time. We're never going back." Then she leaves for Eunice's apartment, where she ran earlier in the play, only to be called back by Stanley, her sexual siren (153). Though it may appear on paper that Stanley will be punished, the parallelism in the play suggests that Stella will return to Stanley and forget all that had transpired in the weeks before she condemned her sister and discovered her husband was a rapist. The changes, as noted, were only partially effective, particularly because the actors inflected the script with enough suggestion and cultural clues that audiences could infer that Allan's tenderness might translate to homosexuality and that Stella would return to her husband.

Still, the film had to make it through one more hurdle: gaining the approval of the Catholic Legion of Decency. In 1951, the Legion of Decency was an organization that could condemn the picture if it issued a C rating, thus keeping thousands of good Catholics out of the movie theaters. A film with an A was considered unobjectionable; a B signified some objectionable parts, but still a film that a thinking Catholic might watch carefully. A C meant the film was condemned. Sam Staggs notes that "reasons for condemning a film included suggestive dialogue, lack of moral compensation, lustful kissing, and acceptance of divorce. All Hollywood trembled before the threat of a C, and even a B might result in dire consequences for the box office" (242). Not surprisingly, the Legion condemned *Streetcar*. Then a Chicago judge called *Streetcar* "'an immoral picture' dealing with 'sex, nymphomania, and liquor'" (Staggs 245). The news made *Streetcar* sinful and simultaneously fascinating. If Kinsey had revealed anything, it was that Americans were voyeuristic. During July 1951, twelve additional cuts were made to satisfy the Catholic Legion; the need for the changes enraged Kazan, who lashed out against the League after the picture premiered. In spite of the Legion's best efforts, *Streetcar* was the fifth-highest-grossing film of 1951 (Staggs 253). Clearly audiences were interested in the kind of sex that Williams was selling.

Whatever the sexual predilections of audience members, they likely found some representation in the play. As critic Walter A. Davis writes: "Plays are interrogative acts, the public airing of collective secrets which put the audience on trial. . . . The question that *Streetcar* asks is that of our sexual identity" (91). The same kinds of questions were being asked and answered by Professor Kinsey and his studies, just as they were being asked by couples whose sexual relationships had been fractured by the war. Critic Mark Royden Winchell writes, "For men, it is a fantasy of complete domination, for women one of complete submission" (173). Carla J. McDonough observes, "Stanley's relationship with Stella is not simply romantic or sexual but also somewhat Oedipal, with Stella representing both his mother and his sex toy" (26). John M. Clum writes of *Streetcar*, "It is the quintessential closeted gay play, and Blanche DuBois is in many ways the quintessential gay character in the American closet drama. Williams himself is quoted as saying, 'I am Blanche DuBois'" (150). Clum's comments suggest that Blanche is a kind of transvestite, representing both herself and an incarnation of the gay playwright. This small selection of quotations from critics reveals an array of sexual behaviors and inclinations— dominant/submissive, Oedipal, and homosexual behavior as well as transvestism and nymphomania. *Streetcar*, unlike any motion picture before it, unleashed truly adult themes that both the war and the Kinsey Report had prepared audiences to see.

Perhaps the actor most accomplished in bringing sex to the screen was Marlon Brando. Brando was a relative newcomer when he arrived in Hollywood to make the movie. Though he had earned accolades in New York for his work on the stage as Stanley Kowalski, the Hollywood elite knew little about the actor. He trained with Stella Adler, an acting teacher who helped to develop the Method, an acting style by which actors look into their own experiences and emotions in order to become the characters they are playing. It was no longer enough for actors simply to imagine what their characters might do. Actors were to become their characters in voice, movement, and idea. If the set had furniture with drawers, the actor ought to know what was in those drawers. If the character smoked, the actor knew how many cigarettes a day and what brand. Acting had became a submersion into someone else, and Brando threw himself into the character of Stanley Kowalski.

Davis claims: "It's a hard truth for many, but sex appeal per se is a myth. . . . To be 'sexy', all one really has to do is become the screen for an other's projections" (66). With the Kinsey Report fresh in Americans' minds and homosexual identity still being hidden, audiences looked to the movies to find portraits of themselves and their particular behaviors. In this state of relative unease, part of Stanley's attraction lies in the fact that he appears to be absolutely confident in his sexual prowess. He has dragged Stella down from the pillars and drugged her with his lovemaking. As Davis notes: "The appeal of Stanley is that of a man who sees through games and knows how to call them by their right names. . . . Stanley knows when a woman is interested in him and has the sexual confidence to say so" (67). Even men are attracted to Stanley's sexual powers. Mitch reveres him even as he resents him.

Part of Stanley's sexual appeal lies in his absolute commitment to all things physical. He eats with gusto, licking his fingers and his lips throughout the play. He breaks lightbulbs to thrill his wife, and he delights in the feel and vibrant look of his silk pajamas. He is an absolute and unabashed sensualist. Critic Marc Robinson targets Williams's characterization of sex as one of his most powerful contributions to American theater:

Williams made room in his plays for a startling sexual frankness about erotic attraction: He allowed scenes to follow the course of sexual approach and retreat, the strategies of seduction. Characters no longer had only an intellectual life: They had bodies as well. . . . Gore Vidal wrote that, with *A Streetcar Named Desire*, Williams introduced the idea of masculine sex appeal to the theatre. Until then, Vidal argued, an actor was only a cardboard figure in a suit. (31)

Brando's sweaty, aggressive Stanley stood in stark contrast to Hollywood's typical leading man, all smooth and unruffled. Kazan himself likened Stanley to the men who attracted Williams in real life: "Sailors? Rough trade? Danger itself? . . . When Stanley's wife reprimands him for his table manners, he teaches her a lesson in how to talk to a man by smashing all the plates on their dining room table. I doubt that Williams found that act vulgar; he'd have found it thrilling" (350). Audiences agreed.

Stanley's sexuality is not suave or understated; it is absolutely at the surface, and the costuming in the play and the film underscored that. Costume designer Lucinda Ballard found her inspiration for Stanley's wardrobe in a work crew she saw on Eighth Avenue in New York City. She bought T-shirts and jeans, then tailored them to be skintight. She even went so far as to remove the pockets of the jeans to make them tighter still. Brando was to be outlined in all of his masculine glory. Ballard, who was nominated for the Academy Award for Best Costume Design, Black-and-White Film, for her work on *Streetcar*, later alleged that still photos from the movie started the T-shirt and jeans craze among young people in the United States (Staggs 192). She may have been right. Brando's appearance, coupled with the Kinsey Report, reinforced the notion that the blue-collar man is possessed of great sexual vigor, as in the literature of D. H. Lawrence. Brando's performance was so compelling that the style of acting he used became the Hollywood standard. James Dean idolized Brando and molded his performances in both *East of Eden* (1955) and *Rebel Without a Cause* (1955) on the work of his idol.

Sex, Displacement, and Violence

A Streetcar Named Desire was well received because it spoke to some of the basic anxieties that were circulating in American popular culture: sex, violence, and displacement. Audiences identified with Stanley. He was a kind of American power, a former soldier, an everyman, and, like America, he was capable of abuses of power. Though audiences were shocked by his rape of Blanche, they were likely to forgive him as they forgave themselves for dropping the bomb. Blanche is the enemy who invades the home and breaks up the American family. Still, there is a lingering sense of unease in audience relations to Stanley.

The last scene of the play shifts audience sympathies one last time. Suddenly it is Stella who represents the mounting public understanding of violence. In the final scene, Stella talks to Eunice before Blanche is taken away.

> *Stella:* I don't know if I did the right thing.
>
> *Eunice:* What else could you do?
>
> *Stella:* I couldn't believe her story and go on living with Stanley.
>
> *Eunice:* Don't ever believe it. Life has got to go on. No matter what happens, you've got to keep on going. (133)

As the Broadway production of *Streetcar* ended each night, Stanley was holding on to a sobbing Stella and slipping his fingers between the buttons of her blouse, ready to seduce her back to sedation and acceptance of her husband. At the end of the movie, Stella runs up to Eunice's apartment, vowing never to return to Stanley, although the audience understands that she will. One of the reasons that *Streetcar*—both the play and the film version—so compels and repels the audience is that the audience is complicit with Stanley through most of the action. His is the point of view made most sympathetic. Blanche is the intruder into the lives of Stella and Stanley. Blanche is the snob who derides Stanley as she eats his food, hogs his bathroom, and drinks his liquor. But Stanley betrays the audience as he betrays Stella. The question becomes, Could Americans live with it? Stella acquiesces and comes to accept Stanley back into her life just as Americans accepted the reality of violence into their own lives.

Stanley's violence, Blanche's displacement, and Williams's sexual frankness all spoke to a moment of national confusion when soldiers returned home uncertain as to who they were and what they had just done. Women returned from the workplace to the home, many reluctantly, and wondered about their options. The U.S. government spun tales to support the dropping of the bomb even after academics and policy makers began to question the political motives behind the rhetoric surrounding the bomb. The Kinsey Report started a national furor over sexual practices. It is perhaps fitting that Williams's play never resolves the fates of its characters. In the end, the play asks more questions than it answers for audiences. Perhaps that is its enduring appeal. As Williams once said to Kazan, "Blanche is not an angel without a flaw . . . and Stanley's not evil. I know you're used to clearly stated themes, but this play should not be loaded one way or the other. Don't try to simplify things" (quoted in Kazan 346).

Works Cited and Consulted

Adam, Julie. *Versions of Heroism in Modern American Drama: Redefinitions by Miller, Williams, O'Neill, and Anderson.* New York: Macmillan, 1991.

Baer, William. *Elia Kazan: Interviews.* Jackson: UP of Mississippi, 2000.

Bigsby, C. W. E. *A Critical Introduction to Twentieth-Century American Drama.* Vol. 2. *Tennessee Williams, Arthur Miller, Edward Albee.* New York: Cambridge UP, 1984.

_____. *Modern American Drama, 1945-1990.* New York: Cambridge UP, 1992.

Bloom, Clive, ed. *American Drama.* New York: St. Martin's Press, 1995.

Boyer, Paul S. *By the Bomb's Early Light: American Thought and Culture at the Dawn of the Atomic Age.* Chapel Hill: U of North Carolina P, 1994.

Bullough, Vern L. "Alfred Kinsey and the Kinsey Report: Historical Overview and Lasting Contributions." *Journal of Sex Research* 35.2 (May 1998): 127-31.

Chinoy, Helen Krich, and Linda Walsh Jenkins, eds. *Women in American Theatre*. Rev. ed. New York: Theatre Communications Group, 1987.

Clum, John M. *Acting Gay: Male Homosexuality in Modern Drama*. New York: Columbia UP, 1992.

Davis, Walter A. *Get the Guests: Psychoanalysis, Modern American Drama, and the Audience*. Madison: U of Wisconsin P, 1994.

Falk, Signi Lenea. *Tennessee Williams*. New York: Twayne, 1961.

Fleche, Anne. *Mimetic Disillusion: Eugene O'Neill, Tennessee Williams, and U.S. Dramatic Realism*. Tuscaloosa: U of Alabama P, 1997.

French, Walter, ed. *The Forties: Fiction, Poetry, Drama*. DeLand, FL: Everett/Edwards, 1969.

Gagey, Edmond M. *Revolution in American Drama*. New York: Columbia UP, 1947.

Goodman, Walter. "Hiroshima at 40: Grappling with the Unthinkable." *The New York Times* 4 Aug. 1985.

Gross, Robert F., ed. *Tennessee Williams: A Casebook*. New York: Routledge, 2002.

Guttmacher, Manfred S. "The Kinsey Report and Society." *Scientific Monthly* 70.5 (May 1950): 291-94.

Hayes, Carlton J. H. "The American Frontier: Frontier of What?" *American Historical Review* 51.2 (Jan. 1946): 199-216.

Holditch, Kenneth, and Richard Freeman Leavitt. *Tennessee Williams and the South*. Jackson: UP of Mississippi, 2002.

Kazan, Elia. *Elia Kazan: A Life*. New York: Alfred A. Knopf, 1988.

Kolin, Philip C. *Williams: "A Streetcar Named Desire."* New York: Cambridge UP, 2000.

_____, ed. *Confronting Tennessee Williams's "A Streetcar Named Desire": Essays in Critical Pluralism*. Westport, CT: Greenwood Press, 1993.

Kramer, Richard E. "'The Sculptural Drama': Tennessee Williams's Plastic Theatre." *Tennessee Williams Annual Review* 5 (2002).

McDonough, Carla J. *Staging Masculinity: Male Identity in Contemporary American Drama*. Jefferson, NC: McFarland, 1997.

Martin, Robert A., ed. *Critical Essays on Tennessee Williams*. New York: G. K. Hall, 1997.

Mordden, Ethan. *The American Theatre*. New York: Oxford UP, 1981.

Murphy, Brenda. *Tennessee Williams and Elia Kazan: A Collaboration in the Theatre*. New York: Cambridge UP, 1992.

O'Connor, Jacqueline. *Dramatizing Dementia: Madness in the Plays of Tennessee Williams*. Bowling Green, OH: Bowling Green State U Popular P, 1997.

Pauly, Thomas H. *An American Odyssey: Elia Kazan and American Culture*. Philadelphia: Temple UP, 1983.

Porter, Thomas E. *Myth and Modern American Drama*. Detroit: Wayne State UP, 1969.

Pradhan, N. S. *Modern American Drama: A Study in Myth and Tradition*. New Delhi: Arnold-Heinemann, 1978.

Robinson, Marc. *The Other American Drama*. New York: Cambridge UP, 1994.

Roudané, Matthew C., ed. *The Cambridge Companion to Tennessee Williams*. New York: Cambridge UP, 1997.

Savran, David. *Communists, Cowboys, and Queers: The Politics of Arthur Miller and Tennessee Williams*. Minneapolis: U of Minnesota P, 1992.

Schroeder, Patricia R. *The Presence of the Past in Modern American Drama*. New York: Associated University Presses, 1989.

Sievers, David W. *Freud on Broadway: A History of Psychoanalysis and the American Drama*. New York: Cooper Square, 1970.

Smith, Bruce. *Costly Performances: Tennessee Williams—The Last Stage*. New York: Paragon House, 1990.

Staggs, Sam. *When Blanche Met Brando: The Scandalous Story of "A Streetcar Named Desire."* New York: St. Martin's Press, 2005.

Tharpe, Jac, ed. *Tennessee Williams: Thirteen Essays*. Jackson: UP of Mississippi, 1980.

Williams, Tennessee. *Memoirs*. New York: Doubleday, 1975.

_____. *Notebooks*. Ed. Margaret Bradham Thornton. New Haven, CT: Yale UP, 2006.

_____. "Production Notes." *The Glass Menagerie*. 1945. New York: New Directions, 1999. xix-xxii.

_____. *A Streetcar Named Desire*. New York: Signet, 1947.

_____. *Where I Live: Selected Essays*. Ed. Christine R. Day and Bob Woods. New York: New Directions, 1978.

Winchell, Mark Royden. *Reinventing the South: Versions of a Literary Region*. Columbia: U of Missouri P, 2005.

Young, Jeff. *Kazan: The Master Director Discusses His Films: Interviews with Elia Kazan*. New York: New Market Press, 1999.

Uncommon Tragic Protagonists:
Blanche DuBois and Willy Loman_____
Kenneth Elliott

The late 1940s was a fertile period for serious drama on Broadway. Tennessee Williams's *A Streetcar Named Desire* opened in December 1947, and Arthur Miller's *Death of a Salesman* followed just fourteen months later. It is ironic that these plays have come to be almost universally revered as American classics, given that they both offer searing critiques of the normative value systems of midcentury America. Though they are often mistakenly categorized as realism, both are marked to varying degrees by avant-garde elements that heighten their theatricality. Both were directed by Elia Kazan. They are also linked by the extraordinary ambition of their playwrights: to bring the magnitude of Aristotelian tragedy to contemporary subjects. In a private letter to Kazan before their collaboration began, Williams stated that *Streetcar* "is a tragedy with the classic aim of producing a katharsis of pity and terror" (96). Miller went so far as to write an article for *The New York Times* trumpeting his goal of creating a tragedy of the "common man."

The relative success of the two plays as tragedy has been a source of scholarly discourse for decades. While no modern play can completely adhere to the definition of tragedy fixed by Aristotle in the fourth century B.C.E., Blanche DuBois and Willy Loman are tragic protagonists in at least one classic sense: their self-delusion (the *hamartia*, or error) ultimately leads to their destruction. Yet the dramaturgical approaches of the two playwrights are strikingly different. The themes of Williams's play emerge from the powerful conflict between Blanche and Stanley Kowalski. Miller does not provide Willy with a comparable antagonist because Willy's battle is with himself (Miller originally planned to title his play "The Inside of His Head"). A close reading of the two plays reveals that Williams, by keeping his drama focused on character-driven action, comes much closer than Miller to achieving the Aristotelian ideal.

It is generally acknowledged that, broadly speaking, Williams focused his plays on the individual, while Miller was more concerned with society at large. The original impulses of the two playwrights, however, can be understood in light of the fact that both were marginalized, as David Savran points out (5). Williams was a gay man at a time when such an identity was not only illegal but also considered abnormal and deviant. Furthermore, he was alienated from his difficult mother and his distant and often-absent traveling-salesman father. He was very close to his emotionally disturbed sister, Rose, and was horrified that she was lobotomized while he was away at college, an event that further distanced him from his family. He was a genuine outsider to the dominant culture of midcentury America, and his plays reflect a deep sympathy for the Other, for those who are different or do not fit in, for society's misfits. He claimed that the writer who most influenced him was Anton Chekhov, and this is reflected not just in his richly layered psychological portraits but in the setting for most of his plays as well: the American South. C. W. E. Bigsby notes that the southern setting, like Chekhov's Russia, "suggests a culture whose past is no longer recoverable, except as myth and whose future represents the threat of dissolution" (41).

Miller was marginalized by the economics of the Great Depression, and it was his politics rather than his sexual identity that set him apart. He was an alleged communist, "branded a radical and hailed before the House Committee on Un-American Activities," at a time in American history when anticommunism was virulent (Savran 5). He considered the Depression a "moral catastrophe, a violent revelation of the hypocrisies behind the façade of American society" (Miller, *Timebends* 115), the results of which he viewed firsthand. Miller's father was a prosperous New York coat manufacturer whose business went belly-up after the crash, completely disrupting his comfortable family life. Miller became convinced that drama should have a social agenda, "that art ought to be of use in changing society" (*Timebends* 93). Miller's models were more Ibsen and Shaw than Chekhov, and an important early influence was the Group Theatre, which was famous for its productions of such proletarian, agitprop social-protest dramas as Clifford Odets's *Waiting for Lefty* (1935).

Given the radically divergent impulses behind *A Streetcar Named Desire* and *Death of a Salesman*, the extent of the parallels between Blanche DuBois and Willy Loman is extraordinary. Both playwrights chose names with symbolic value for their protagonists. Blanche explains to Mitch that DuBois is "a French name. It means woods and Blanche means white, so the two together mean white woods. Like an orchard in spring!" (59). However, a "woods" is a far cry from an orchard. An orchard is organized, controlled, laid out neatly in rows. A "woods" is wild and connotes darkness, mystery, and danger. The idea of "white woods" implies a contradiction and also suggests concealment or deception. A "white woods" is unnatural. The connotations of the name Loman are obvious, although Miller disavowed "the heavy-handed symbolism of 'Low-man,'" and insisted that the character's name was inspired by a character called Lohmann in the Fritz Lang film *The Testament of Dr. Mabuse* (*Timebends* 179). Heavy-handed it may be, but most viewers of *Death of a Salesman* are likely to make the plausible and appropriate association of Willy as a "low-man," whether Miller intended it or not.

"I believe that the common man is as apt a subject for tragedy in its highest sense as kings were," proclaimed Miller in his famous essay published in 1949. This was considered a bold statement, given that classical tragic protagonists were traditionally from the noble or ruling classes—kings, queens, lords, and ladies. And yet neither Willy Loman nor Blanche DuBois could be precisely identified as "common" or ordinary. Like their creators, both characters are marginalized figures. Blanche is a single woman in her thirties who describes herself as "an old maid schoolteacher" (60). She is destitute and alone, with no family or support system other than her sister Stella. Willy is a washed-up salesman who is no longer able to earn a living or pay the bills, and his relations with his family are strained. Though he has a loving wife, he cheats on her. His relationship with his sons is dysfunctional, to put it mildly. The sympathetic portrayal of these marginalized characters who are outside of the mainstream is an inherent critique of the values of the dominant culture. The dog-eat-dog capitalist system of mid-century America has no place for a salesman who can no longer sell or for an unmarried woman over thirty with quaintly anachronistic manners who favors the civilizing influences of art, music, and literature over the crudeness of the marketplace.

In a broad sense, these two characters even have similar objectives. They are trying to find a way to hang on in a society that has rejected them, to be accepted. Linda describes Willy as "a little boat looking for a harbor" (76). Blanche arrives at Stella's house because she has nowhere else to go, and she grasps at the possibility of marriage to Mitch as her safe harbor: "I want to *rest*! I want to breath quietly again! Yes— I want Mitch . . . *very badly*! Just think! If it happens! I can leave here and not be anyone's problem" (95). Miller and Williams both began their writing careers in the 1930s, and this sense of being cut adrift with which they imbue their protagonists has its roots in the Great Depression. Bigsby argues that the "loss of dignity and self assurance which Miller saw as one legacy of the Crash clearly left its mark on Willy Loman" (69), and the same could easily be said of the homeless and penniless Blanche DuBois.

It is little wonder that characters so completely unmoored from any social support system would find themselves on the edge of mental stability. There is a long history of madness in tragic characters from Cassandra to King Lear and beyond, and Willy and Blanche fit squarely into this tradition. They are emotionally disturbed from their first entrances. It is clear from her scene 1 reunion with Stella that Blanche is on the edge. A stage direction notes that she speaks "with feverish vivacity as if she feared for either of them to stop and think" (10), and as the scene proceeds, her nervous passive aggression builds to the point that she is literally shaking "with intensity" (20). Willy first enters lugging his sample cases in a state of exhaustion, muttering to himself. He complains to his wife, Linda, that he has repeatedly blanked out while driving his car. His son Happy soon explains that Willy's habit of talking to himself had become so "embarrassing" that "I sent him to Florida" (21). Linda reveals that Willy has already considered suicide before the action of the play begins. By the climaxes of both plays, the characters have succumbed to the insanity that makes them vulnerable to their final tragic reversals. At the top of scene 10, Blanche is out of touch with reality to the point that she is placing a rhinestone tiara on her head while talking to a group of "spectral" gentleman callers (151). After she is raped by Stanley a few minutes later, she is unable to regain her sanity. Willy's mental breakdown in a restaurant leads directly to his ultimate suicide.

Blanche and Willy are both sexual outlaws. Incidents of sexual misconduct in the past haunt them, and in both plays these incidents become pivotal plot points that lead to reversals. Willy has had a long-standing extramarital affair with a woman he met on the road in Boston, which is the source of much of his guilt-ridden behavior toward his wife. Biff Loman's discovery of his father's dalliance is the catalyst for his rejection of Willy's world. Blanche was fired from her job as a high school English teacher for having sexual relations with a seventeen-year-old male student, and she admits that she has "had many intimacies with strangers" (146). Stanley's discovery of the truth of Blanche's past, and his revelation of it to Mitch, ends her hopes for her future and lays the seeds for her destruction.

While Blanche's sexual history is more extreme by conventional standards than Willy's, Williams is not judgmental in his treatment of it. He sympathetically depicts her many sexual encounters as an escape from the death and illness with which she was confronted in her home life. In scene 9, Blanche argues to Mitch that the opposite of death "is desire," and sex is her way of clinging to life. It is Mitch who seems brutish, petty, and unforgiving in his response (149). Miller, on the other hand, takes a much more moralistic view of Willy's transgression. His adulterous affair with "the Woman" is presented as nothing less than a complete betrayal. When Biff discovers his father in fla-grante delicto, he is overcome with Oedipal rage, sputtering tearfully, "You—you gave her Mama's stockings!" Biff's previous unbridled ad-miration of his father is shattered, and he calls Willy a "liar!" and a "lit-tle fake!" (121). In the world of Miller's play, this one sexual infraction is symbolic of Willy's hypocrisy, and the results of it are disastrous: Willy's relationship with Biff is destroyed, and Biff loses all ambition and becomes a high school dropout and a drifter.

On the surface, however, both Blanche and Willy cling to out-moded, idealized views of what society should be. Blanche professes abhorrence for "brutal desire." Her manners are old-fashioned, courtly, prim, and ladylike to a comical degree, and she is an advocate for the civilizing influences of art, poetry, and music. Willy has nostalgia for the good old days when Brooklyn was full of trees rather than apart-ment buildings and when carrots grew in the backyard garden, and he makes frequent references to a masculine ideal. Needless to say, both characters are prodigious liars—both to themselves and those around them. The tension between the ideals that these characters express and the reality of their behavior is extreme.

Despite the array of similarities between Blanche and Willy, how-ever, and despite the fact that the plays were produced on Broadway within two years of each other, these characters represent two entirely different approaches to theater. Whereas Blanche is a nuanced charac-ter with deep psychological motivations in the Chekhovian tradition, Willy is more of an archetype who represents the underdog Everyman. Both playwrights professed the desire to write a genuine modern trag-edy, and the results of their efforts illustrate their individual philoso-phies of what theater should be. Miller analyzed his approach to dramaturgy a few years later in an introduction to the published version of *A View from the Bridge* titled "On Social Plays": "The social drama . . . must delve into the nature of man as he exists to discover what his needs are, so that those needs may be amplified and exteriorized in terms of social concepts" (12). This is the essence of didactic drama.

Interiority rather than exteriority was Williams's preoccupation. His letter to Kazan reveals his intentions behind *Streetcar*: "I think its best quality is its authenticity or its fidelity to life," later adding that "when you begin to arrange the action of a play to score a certain point the fidelity to life may suffer" (95-96). Fidelity to life, for Williams, is rooted in specificity.

The unique character detail that Williams lavishes on Blanche is evident from her first entrance. He describes her as "daintily dressed in a white suit with a fluffy bodice, necklace and earrings of pearl, white gloves and hat, looking as if she were arriving at a summer tea or cocktail party in the garden district" (5). Compare this to Miller's initial description of Willy's appearance: "He is past sixty years of age, dressed quietly" (12). No further detail is offered. Blanche's first action, "shocked disbelief" at the squalor of her sister's residence, speaks volumes about her background and state of mind. A relatively full biography of the character's life before her first entrance emerges not in a long expository passage but gradually in the ensuing scenes. She and Stella come from an aristocratic Laurel, Mississippi, family who lived at Belle Reve, a large estate with an imposing mansion with white columns. When she was only sixteen years old, she married a sensitive young poet, Allan Grey, whom she adored. Not long after they were married, she discovered him having sex with an older man. After making this discovery, she publicly insulted him on the dance floor of the Moon Lake Casino, whereupon Allan fled to the lakeshore and killed himself by firing a gun into his mouth. This incident haunted Blanche, and she compensated for it by losing herself in anonymous sexual liaisons. Meanwhile, Stella left for New Orleans to marry Stanley, and Blanche stayed in Laurel, where she took care of her dying relatives and Belle Reve. The family estate was finally "lost" because of the "epic fornications" and the financial mismanagement of her forebears. Homeless, Blanche then moved into a hotel of ill repute called the Flamingo. She was soon fired from her teaching job for having an affair with a seventeen-year-old student, and not long after she was even asked to leave the Flamingo. With no other options, she traveled to New Orleans to seek refuge with her sister. This is not the story of a generic southern schoolteacher; it is a character history rich in specific biographical detail that informs Blanche's action in the play.

By comparison Willy's biography is vague, despite the frequent flashbacks that show rather than explain past events. The structure of *Salesman* alternates between an objective present and a dreamlike past. The scenes in the present maintain a reasonably strict unity of time and have the appearance of realism. The scenes in the past are filtered through Willy's point of view, as if they are literally going on in his mind, and these scenes traverse the years. Miller skillfully uses Willy's episodes of mental instability to segue seamlessly into the flashback sequences. For example, the first flashback occurs when Biff and Happy overhear their father, alone in the kitchen, speaking in full voice to their imaginary younger selves about simonizing the Chevy. There is a lighting change, and Willy is no longer a mentally disturbed old man; he is a young, vibrant father. The transition is cinematic.

The long scene that follows carefully lays out the basis of much of Willy's character, but, unlike Williams, Miller does not ground his character with minutely detailed specifics. Instead, he uses broad strokes to explain the character's psychology. Willy's first half dozen lines in the scene are addressed solely to Biff, with whom he is clearly obsessed. He has brought his son the gift of a punching bag, and he laughs when Biff brags about stealing a football from school. Fighting and stealing are masculine ideals, and the important thing is to be "well liked." Willy refers to the studious Bernard as "an anemic" (33). Intellectuals are objects of ridicule. It is appearances that are important: "I thank Almighty God you're both built like Adonises. Because the man who makes an appearance in the business world, the man who creates personal interest, is the man who gets ahead" (33). The flashback scenes are filtered through the distorting lens of Willy's memory, so realism can be jettisoned. For example, Biff is not simply popular—he is so well liked that the basement is full of boys ready to do his chores for him. We learn a great deal about Willy's subjective attitudes here, but almost nothing of the objective details of his biography.

Miller uses the flashback scenes to explore the psychology of Willy's unconscious mind, and so nostalgic scenes of delusional happiness are sharply juxtaposed with ominously dark scenes that reveal the character's deep-seated guilt. The sunny and idyllic scene described above turns sour the instant the boys exit, as Willy's massive insecurities bubble to the surface. He grossly exaggerates the commissions from his recent sales trip, revealing the disconnect between his optimistic and aggressive outward philosophy and his actual view of himself. He contradicts himself repeatedly. After having called the Chevrolet "the greatest car ever built," he refuses to pay the repair shop, adding, "That goddam Chevrolet, they ought to prohibit the manufacture of that car!" (36). He admits that "people don't seem to take to me." He is insecure about his appearance: "I'm fat. I'm very—foolish to look at, Linda" (37). Stressing appearances again, he concludes, "I'm not dressing to advantage, maybe." The catalyst for these negative feelings, his unconscious guilt, is made corporeal when the Woman from his past appears (behind a scrim—obviously in the deep recesses of Willy's mind) as a dream within the dream, just as he is expressing his love to Linda. The scene ends as a nightmare. Bernard reenters, threateningly shouting that Biff needs to study. Bernard's taunts alternate with Linda's dark complaints about Biff's theft of the football and his aggressiveness with girls. The Woman laughs. Willy explodes at the apparitions, and we are back in the present. Willy is, once again, an old man talking to himself. There is no mystery about Willy's behavior. His psychology has been methodically laid out by Miller. We have, indeed, been inside his head.

While Williams was attentive to creating a psychological portrait of his protagonist, he took an approach very different from Miller's. There are no flashbacks in *Streetcar* to explain Blanche's subconscious motivations; the action is linear and causal. Instead, there is an implied subtext that is never explicitly spelled out. As her name suggests,

Blanche is full of contradictions. Her behavior often belies the elegant and aristocratic surface image that she has so meticulously created. She is well aware that she is not entirely truthful, confiding in Stanley that "I know I fib a great deal. After all, a woman's charm is fifty per cent illusion" (41). Traumatic incidents from her past, especially her husband's suicide, shed light on her behavior but never fully explain it. In a letter to *New York Times* critic Brooks Atkinson after the opening of *Streetcar*, Williams shared his view that people cannot be narrowly defined "but are things of multiple facets and all but endless complexity . . . they do not fit 'any convenient label' and are seldom more than partially visible even to those who live just on the other side of 'the portieres'" (137). The mysterious and only partially visible interior of Blanche is what makes her such a fascinating and unique character. Williams avoids a more clinical examination of her inner psychological motivations.

Despite the carefully laid out psychological motivations in *Salesman*, the character of Willy Loman remains nonspecific. We never learn what it is that he actually sells. He is an archetypal, generic Salesman. By the end of the first flashback sequence, Miller has highlighted all of Willy's salient characteristics: his empty notions of what constitutes masculinity and success, his desire to be well liked, his insecurities, his philandering, his guilt, and his obsession with his eldest son Biff. The appearance of his enterprising brother Ben in the second dream sequence reinforces what we already know. Ben represents Success. He has attained his dream: "When I was seventeen I walked into the jungle, and when I was twenty-one I walked out. And by God I was rich" (52). Willy's dream has been more elusive, and he has not attained it.

The lack of character detail for Willy does not matter in the context of *Salesman*, because this is essentially an expressionist play that merely gestures toward psychological realism. Expressionism was an avant-garde movement that began in Germany and Austria in the decade preceding World War I. By the 1920s, some American dramatists, such as Eugene O'Neill (*The Emperor Jones, The Hairy Ape*) and Elmer Rice (*The Adding Machine*) were also experimenting with the style, so it was not unfamiliar to postwar American audiences. Bert Cardullo and Robert Knopf identify the chief element of expressionist drama as "the use of the central character's completely subjective point of view to develop the action and distort the other characters" (207). This is precisely the technique that Miller uses in *Death of a Salesman*. The multiple flashbacks interrupt the causal structure and place the emphasis instead on the distorted perspective of Willy's mind. This blending of realism with subjective dream sequences recalls the structure of one of the first German expressionist plays, Reinhard Sorge's *The Beggar* (1912). Expressionist plays tend to be message-centered, which makes the style a perfect vehicle for social drama. Miller's central theme, the emptiness of the American Dream (and, by extension, capitalism) is, as Frank Rich noted in his review of the 1983 revival of *Salesman*, "baldly stated" (310). Expressionist plays often take the form of a pilgrimage to martyrdom by a Christlike figure (see Georg Kaiser's *From Morn to Midnight*, 1916). That is precisely Willy's journey as we watch him progress through the stations on the road to the grave. Extreme plot points that would be absurd in a realistic play work powerfully here. For example, act 1 ends with Biff and Happy spinning Willy into a manic high by convincing him that Biff's bigwig former employer Bill Oliver will "stake" him to fifteen thousand dollars so that the Loman brothers can start an ill-defined sporting-goods venture in Florida, to be publicized by competing basketball (or water polo) teams. After hearing this desperate scheme laid out, Willy concludes that it is "a one million dollar idea," despite the fact that Biff has little or no business experience and has not seen or spoken to Oliver in years. All the hopes of the Loman family are pinned on an obviously unattainable pipe dream. One could argue that this is no more far-fetched than Blanche's fantasy of being swept off her feet by Shep Huntleigh. However, in *Streetcar* no one believes the fantasy but the unbalanced Blanche, whereas in *Salesman* all four of the Lomans are, to varying degrees, pathetically taken in. As realism, the scene is uncomfortably implausible. Surely someone would point out that a successful businessman is unlikely to write a huge check to a relative stranger based on an ill-conceived fantasy. As a station on the road to the destruction of an archetypal salesman, however, the scene is chillingly effective, because the audience is fully aware that the idea will lead to disaster.

In the expressionist manner, much of Willy's dialogue is telegraphic. He speaks largely in clichés, his language peppered with what seem to be excerpts from Dale Carnegie's *How to Win Friends and Influence People*: "It's not what you say, it's how you say it—because personality always wins the day" (65). By having Willy almost robotically repeat such inane nuggets of cheap pop wisdom, Miller illustrates the pernicious and pervasive influence of advertising and consumer culture on the American citizenry. He also pushes the character toward abstraction; real people do not speak in slogans. All of the other characters in the play are similarly generic and representative of abstract ideas rather than distinct personalities. D. L. Hoeveler has persuasively cataloged the types: "Linda, the devoted wife, represents that pernicious American value, security. Biff, the all-American boy turned thief, embodies the vanished frontier, the lost promise of America, while Happy, whose name is the most ironically allegorical, represents the stark materialism and sensuality that have eroded the frontier spirit" (78).

It is instructive to compare the language and syntax of these characters. Their vocabularies and the cadences of their speech are remarkably similar to each other. Williams, on the other hand, takes great care in creating highly individualized speech patterns for all his characters. Only Blanche could say, "I can't stand a naked light bulb, any more than I can a rude remark or a vulgar action" (60). Her florid speech is a striking contrast to Stanley's directness: "My clothes are stickin' to me. Do you mind if I make myself comfortable?" (26). Stella's aristocratic background is evident in her grammatically correct English, but she avoids the rhetorical flourishes that are characteristic of her sister.

Even minor characters such as Eunice and Steve have distinct patterns of speech.

There are expressionist touches in *Streetcar* to be sure, such as the blind Mexican woman in scene 9, with her eerie and repetitive chant pointing up Blanche's deepest fear: "Flores. Flores. Flores para los muertos. Flores. Flores" (147). In the scene that follows, in the harrowing moments before the rape, Williams describes the night as "filled with inhuman voices like cries in a jungle" and calls for "shadows and lurid reflections" to move "sinuously as flames along the wall spaces" (159). Blanche's terror is reflected by these grotesque sights and sounds. The play never becomes a subjective distorting lens for Blanche's point of view, however. Williams strongly argued to Kazan that the antagonist, Stanley, should not be played as "a black-dyed villain" (96). As acted by Marlon Brando in the original production, some audiences reportedly were actually rooting for Stanley over Jessica Tandy's Blanche. The very idea of an audience taking sides with one character over another goes to the heart of the structure of *Streetcar*: an agon (contest) or conflict between Blanche and Stanley. Their adversarial relationship is established at their first meeting and escalates through the rising action that culminates in the rape at the end of scene 10. Though both characters carry symbolic weight (Blanche represents female values, the aristocracy, kindness, gentility, civilization, illusion, and so on, while Stanley represents male values, the lower classes, cruelty, brute force, crudeness, truth, and so on), it is their very human actions that drive the play.

The climax of *Salesman* is brought about not by a sustained confrontation with an adversary but rather by a series of events that happen to Willy as his world (and his mind) unravels. These events are depicted in a series of short scenes that chronicle the steps toward his descent. He is unceremoniously and coldly fired, like Mr. Zero in Rice's *The Adding Machine*. In a particularly expressionist touch in this scene, the mechanically reproduced voice of Willy's boss's son precociously reciting the state capitals in alphabetical order takes on a sinister and terrifying quality. Willy then journeys to his next humiliation, to ask his old (and successful) friend Charley for a loan. Then the next stop is the celebratory dinner with his sons at a Manhattan restaurant, where he learns that Biff is not only a failure but a thief as well. His sons walk out of the restaurant, abandoning him. The seismic shocks of these events send Willy's mind reeling into the past, where Biff's discovery of his infidelity is painfully reenacted.

The endings of both plays are emotionally wrenching for audiences, although neither Blanche nor Willy experiences an anagnorisis (recognition) in the Aristotelian sense. Blanche never recovers her sanity after the rape. Willy never sees the truth. Biff confronts his father in the climactic scene: "Pop, I'm nothing! I'm nothing, Pop. Can't you understand that? There's no spite in it anymore. I'm just what I am, that's all." He holds his father, sobbing. Biff, not Willy, has had the recognition, yet it is as if a weight has been lifted from Willy's shoulders. Miller uses the stage direction *"astonished, elevated,"* to describe Willy's next line: "Isn't that—isn't that remarkable? Biff—he likes me!" The stage direction suggests that a major change has occurred. Willy hasn't gained wisdom, however. He is still deluded and full of illusions.

It is impossible not to feel pity for Willy Loman as he plans the suicide that he believes will benefit his son. The little guy has been destroyed by a corrupt system that has used him. But here, as Eric Bentley has observed, the idea of tragedy is at odds with Miller's social drama agenda (84). The salesman is too passive to attain tragic heights, notwithstanding the funeral tributes paid to him in the codalike "Requiem." Blanche, in contrast, has confronted her adversary head-on, and Williams ends his play with action, not speeches. Although her response to her brutal rape is madness rather than recognition, the simple dignity of her final exit on the arm of the doctor as she walks past the poker players speaks volumes more than the most eloquent eulogy.

Works Cited

Bentley, Eric. *In Search of Theater*. New York: Alfred A. Knopf, 1953.

Bigsby, C. W. E. *Modern American Drama: 1945-2000*. Cambridge: Cambridge UP, 2000.

Cardullo, Bert, and Robert Knopf, eds. *Theater of the Avant-Garde 1890-1950: A Critical Anthology*. New Haven, CT: Yale UP, 2001.

Hoeveler, D. L. "*Death of a Salesman* as Psychomachia." *Arthur Miller's "Death of a Salesman."* Ed. Harold Bloom. New York: Chelsea House, 1988.

Miller, Arthur. *Death of a Salesman*. 1949. New York: Penguin Books, 1979.

_____. "On Social Plays." Introduction to *A View from the Bridge*. New York: Viking Press, 1955.

_____. *Timebends: A Life*. New York: Grove Press, 1987.

_____. "Tragedy and the Common Man." *The New York Times* 27 Feb. 1949, sec. 2, pp. 1, 3.

Rich, Frank. "*Death of a Salesman*." *Hot Seat: Theater Criticism for "The New York Times," 1980-1993*. New York: Random House, 1998.

Savran, David. *Communists, Cowboys, and Queers: The Politics of Masculinity in the Work of Arthur Miller and Tennessee Williams*. Minneapolis: U of Minnesota P, 1992.

Williams, Tennessee. *The Selected Letters of Tennessee Williams*. Vol. 2. Ed. Albert J. Devlin. New York: New Directions, 2004.

_____. *A Streetcar Named Desire*. 1947. New York: New Directions, 1980.

A Room That I Thought Was Empty:
The Representation of Repression in
*A Streetcar Named Desire*_____

Neil Heims

> Truth, life, or reality is an organic thing which the poetic imagination can
> represent or suggest, in essence, only through transformation.
>
> —Tennessee Williams,
> "The Author's Production Notes," *The Glass Menagerie* (395)

1

A Streetcar Named Desire is a violent, brutal, and disruptive play
that, at its conclusion, leaves all its characters raw and wounded and, if
properly performed, its audiences unsettled. In it, passion explodes but
is not spent. Whatever the actual issues and themes are that the play approaches—class conflict, resentment, romantic longing, hypocrisy,
mendacity, feminine hysteria, forbidden love, masculine brutality, decadence, homosexuality, or destructive passion—they are not resolved,
only reburied and, consequently, only avoided and put off for another,
indeterminate time.

The volcanic forces smoldering and unleashed in *A Streetcar Named
Desire* suggest that it is a play whose action is a *reaction* to repression,
to suppressed inadmissible material, and that it represents the consequences of repression. It shows the reemergence of that repressed material in dangerously disruptive forms. Repression itself, rather than
the personal, interpersonal, social, cultural, or psychological struggles
the persons of the play encounter, is the subject of *A Streetcar Named
Desire*. The action of the play grows out of repression and represents
that repression as it asserts itself despite all efforts to the contrary. At
the end of the play, although each character has gone through a particular agony and has been turned inside out and has been fully realized,
nothing is settled. Only the equilibrium of disorder is reestablished,

and the repressions that generated the commotion of the play are reinstated and reinforced. Each of the characters has more completely, more hopelessly, realized the identity that was already established at the start of the play and is more inextricably bound to it.

At the end of the stage version of *A Streetcar Named Desire*, after Blanche is removed to a mental hospital for telling the truth, that Stanley has assaulted her sexually, Stella goes on living with Stanley. Stella chooses not to let belief take hold of her. She allows herself to live as if the truth were a lie and a lie, the truth. Eunice conveys the "moral" of the play when she responds to Stella's confession, "I couldn't believe [Blanche's] story and go on living with Stanley," by saying, "Don't ever believe it. Life has to go on. No matter what happens, you've got to keep on going." Life, apparently, can "go on" only if the truth is denied and a communal lie is accepted, if repression is made to trump awareness. In the film version, which Williams wrote with Oscar Saul from an adaptation of the play by Saul (ironically, in order to produce the kind of "moral" ending that would satisfy the censors), Stella leaves Stanley and goes upstairs to Eunice's apartment, holding her newborn baby. The very last shot, however, conveys a grim ambiguity. It shows Stanley bellowing up to her as he did at the end of the poker night in the third scene, after he hit her. The audience cannot know whether or not Stella will respond to his cry now, as she did then; her eyes nearly in a trance, as they were then; drawn by the strength of his sexual magnetism, as she was then. The issue in the film boils down to a conflict between forbidden, immoral desire and moral discipline. The discipline imposed by morality is thus defined as the virtue achieved by repression.

The title, *A Streetcar Named Desire*, indicates that desire is the vehicle that has brought each of the play's persons into the dramatic conflict that the play depicts. Desire rather than love is the focus of the play. The force of thwarted love provides the motor of the play and is at the root of the manifestations of desire presented in the play. Blanche's first love, stifled by Allan Grey's homosexuality, is at the root of the uncontainable desire that haunts the action and finally explodes. In the real world outside the play, homosexuality is the love that is thwarted by the force of society. Within the world of *A Streetcar Named Desire*, homosexuality is the force that smothers the flames of desire burning in Blanche's first experience of love when she discovers Allan's homosexuality.

Both love and desire, in a time of repression, are complex phenomena. Each is dangerous and threatening. Each is a destabilizing force. When love does break forth, after it has endured repression, it emerges deformed by distortions because of its struggle to express itself when it was forbidden. It comes out looking like anything but love, for by repression love is distorted and transformed into other things. No matter what form it takes, under such circumstances love is characterized by passion and violence and can seem to be more like hatred than love. It becomes a destructive rather than a creative force. It brings with it turmoil and suffering. Love in a time of repression is not a generous quality. It is full of misshapen desire, resentment, and need; it is greedy; it is voracious because it has been fed by starvation. It is not selfless and sacrificial but selfish and rapacious. Such love mixes resentment with desire and triumph with satiation. An anatomy of Stanley's relationship with Stella and his attraction/repulsion to Blanche can demonstrate this, just as an examination of Blanche shows that she is always being tormented by desire, whether she is trying to satisfy it or to suppress it.

2

Stanley, as he is portrayed, assertive to the point of volatility, looks anything but constrained by repression, yet his personality and his actions are built on it and are responses to it. Resentment at subordination is the energy that fuels his grace. In his first appearance onstage, Stanley "heaves" a bloody package of raw meat up from the street to Stella standing on a first-floor landing. The stage blocking is emblematic of their class relationship. He is below her; she is above him. But he controls the action: he throws; she catches. The first impression the actress playing Stella must convey to an audience, Williams writes in the stage direction, is that Stella is "of a background obviously quite different from her husband's" (470), that is, she is more refined, more delicate in her sensibility, than Stanley. Stella just manages to catch the bloody package and, despite her "background," laughs as she does with breathless excitement. She has joined his world. Stanley is volatile, virile, assertive, confident, explosive, and violent. Williams describes him as an admirable brute, as an incontrovertible, irresistible force of nature.

> Animal joy in his being is implicit in all his movements and attitudes. Since earliest manhood the center of his life has been pleasure with women, the giving and taking of it, not with weak indulgence, dependently, but with the power and pride of a richly feathered male bird among hens. Branching out from this complete and satisfying center are all the auxiliary channels of his life . . . his heartiness with men, his appreciation of rough humor[;] . . . everything that is his . . . bears his emblem of the gaudy seed-bearer. He sizes women up at a glance. (481)

Blanche says, assessing him, and the audience can see she is accurate—and Stanley overhears it without her knowing it, and it fuels his resentment—"He acts like an animal, has an animal's habits! Eats like one, moves like one, talks like one! there's even something—something sub-human—something . . . ape-like about him" (510). As long as Stella is devoted to him, despite her ability to see the truth of Blanche's assessment, his resentment is mollified by his sense of victory over the manners that Blanche represents, over a standard of behavior that would invalidate him.

Although Stanley is a high-specimen male biologically, socially he comes from the lower, spurned, exploited class and is on the defensive about it. When Blanche calls him a Polack, he controverts her with measured fury: "I am not a Polack. People from Poland are Poles, not Polacks. But what I am is one hundred percent American, born and raised in the greatest country on earth and proud as hell of it, so don't ever call me a Polack" (539). His self-assertion is a rebellion against social subordination and belittling. In his assertion of self, by his very nature, there is always a concomitant assertion of his sexual virility. It is as native to him as the hysterical mist of sexuality that surrounds Blanche, that masquerades as refinement, and that can be sensed in her every gesture and utterance.

At the table a little before Stanley's assertion of his Americanism, when he is unresponsive to Blanche as she tries to joke away her humiliation at Mitch's absence, Blanche notes, "Apparently Mr. Kowalski was not amused." Stella momentarily joins forces with her sister. "Mr. Kowalski is too busy," she says, "making a pig of himself to think of anything else." Then she addresses him directly: "Your face and fingers are disgustingly greasy. Go and wash up and then help me clear the table." This is a class confrontation; Stanley is being diminished through references to his display of seemingly stereotypical lower-class characteristics and behavior inside the context of an interpersonal, domestic power struggle. In response, Stanley proudly asserts a stereotypical lower-class response. He "hurls [his] plate to the floor . . . seizes her arm" and says, "Don't ever talk that way to me! 'Pig-Polack-disgusting-vulgar-greasy!'—them kind of words have been on your tongue and your sister's too much around here! What do you two think you are? A pair of queens? Remember what Huey Long said—'Every man is a King!' And I am the king around here, so don't forget it" (537). Stella is subordinating him by stereotyping him with lower-class vices. But what is particularly offensive to him is that she is telling him what to do, as if she were superior to him and has the right to. Momentarily, she resumes the air of one of his betters, and he, because of the manners of his class, risks being subordinated to her and bent by shame.

His assertion here is the same one he makes throughout the play as he struggles with Blanche for domination. His chief resentment of

Blanche is that, as he sees it, she put on airs, that she tries to seem superior to him by using a flirtatiously teasing sexuality, which is meant to unman him were she to succeed. She redecorates his apartment with lampshades and throw cloths in order to make it more genteel, disdaining the vulgarity she finds in Stanley's world. Blanche boasts to Stella of her condescension at the end of scene 2, after her confrontation with Stanley about the loss of Belle Reve. "I laughed and treated it all as a joke. I called him a little boy and laughed and flirted" (491). Blanche may actually be on the mark, more deeply than she knows or intends. Stanley is like a grown-up "little boy." But his recoil from any suggestion that he is, like the recoil of anyone repressing an unwanted truth about himself—like men afraid of their own homosexuality who beat up homosexuals—must be absolute and assertively violent. His virility is an insistent counterstatement against attempts to deny it. In the end, in scene 10, it can be assured only by being asserted in the most absolute way.

In Stanley, the interplay of the two strains that run through the play, the social and the psychological, are clearly embodied. Class repression and its resulting resentment are at the bottom of his brutish character assertion, his rage against Blanche, and his desire for her. When Stella asks Stanley why he told Mitch about Blanche's past and ruined her chance for a new life with Mitch, he tells her: "When we first met, me and you, you thought I was common. How right you was, baby. I was common as dirt. You showed me the snapshot of the place with columns. I pulled you down off them columns and how you loved it, having them colored lights going! And wasn't we happy together, *wasn't it all okay till she showed here?*" (540-41; emphasis added). Certainly, Stanley's words apply to the sexual electricity he brought Stella, but they are just as much about class manners. Sexual allure itself, in *A Streetcar Named Desire,* is presented as being enhanced by the lack of upper-class constraints that seems to characterize lower-class sensibility. Stanley was excited by the conquest, by the act of leveling he accomplished by exciting Stella. So was she, as she repeatedly tells Blanche. "I was—sort of—thrilled by it," Stella says to Blanche after she tells her how Stanley "smashed all the light bulbs with the heel of my slipper" on their wedding night (505). When Blanche protests that Stella "must have sufficient memory of Belle Reve [their plantation home] to find this place [her two-room apartment with Stanley] and these poker players impossible to live with," Stella explains, "There are things that happen between a man and a woman in the dark—that sort of make everything else seem—unimportant" (509). The lower class is conceived as having a fuller capacity for sexual enjoyment than the aristocracy. Upper-class attitudes are presented as marked by the repression of sexual behavior or the kind of decadence to which Blanche alludes when she speaks of the "epic fornications" (490) that contributed to the loss of Belle Reve. The liberation of sexual excitement, for the upper class, involves the violation of the taboos of constraint implicit in downward mobility. Stanley's sexuality is raw, not decadent.

3

∾ Desire itself, in a time of repression, is a force experienced with conflict and ambivalence. Although desire is a component of love, when love is repressed desire becomes supercharged and overwhelms love, tainting it and even replacing it. In a time of repression, desire is both approached and avoided. Whichever stance one assumes toward desire, whether one expresses or represses desire, whether one attempts to move toward fulfilling desire or away from it, to express desire or to deny it, when repression shapes the dominating cultural ambiance, one is caught in a lie. In a time of repression, one is trapped inside the struggle between expression and suppression. Because the impulses for both are active simultaneously, it is a lie to suppress desire and it is a lie to express it. The conflict is compounded because the desire that can be expressed can be expressed only in a distorted form, symptomatically, mendaciously, in conflict with one's own truer nature, because of the repression that nature has suffered and because of the disguise it must assume if it is to escape the confines of repression. When nature surfaces, it must do so as an act of defiance. If it does not break forth and remains stifled, that failure of expression is also a lie, denying the wish burning at the bottom of one's heart.

This struggle inside the climate of repression between adherence to repression and defiance of it is something that Tennessee Williams himself was writing about overtly at the time he was writing *A Streetcar Named Desire*. In the fall of 1946, Williams was working on two plays. He was calling one "The Poker Night"; the other, "A Chart of Anatomy." "The Poker Night" became *A Streetcar Named Desire*. "A Chart of Anatomy" became *Summer and Smoke*. *Summer and Smoke* is a more schematic, more intellectualized play than *A Streetcar Named Desire*. In *Summer and Smoke*, both the conflict between repression and desire and the consequences of repression when repressed desire is expressed are presented explicitly. The focus of *Summer and Smoke* is the unachieved romance between a repressed preacher's daughter and a wild and thoughtless libertine, a doctor's son. Their failed encounter releases the spiritual, socially conscious component of his eroticism and allows her to express the sexual component of her soul—in both cases, with other partners.

The conflicted commitment to both expression and suppression is not a deliberate and conscious one, for the fruit of repression is the creation of unconsciousness. Repression demands the perverse practice of keeping a secret from oneself, of simultaneously knowing what one does not know and not knowing what one does know. It is within this tangled context, far more than the geographical 1940s New Orleans, a city characterized as "cosmopolitan . . . where there is a relatively warm and easy intermingling of" (469) people of different races from each other, that Tennessee Williams set *A Streetcar Named Desire*. It is a context Williams describes in a stage direction in the middle of the second act of *Cat on a Hot Tin Roof*. He explains, introducing his own authorial "I" into the direction, that the bird that I hope to catch in the net of this play is not the solution of one man's psychological problem. I'm trying to catch the true quality of experience in a group of people, that cloudy, flickering, evanescent—fiercely charged!—interplay of live human beings in the thundercloud of a common crisis. (945)

Crisis is the name given to the moment when the forces of repression break apart and the repressed material breaks forth in a rampage. That breaking process, that rampage, and the results of the rampage constitute the drama of *A Streetcar Named Desire*.

4

Blanche is presented as a victim of repression and as a masterful technician of self-repression in her everyday deceptions. Her very practice of putting on airs is both a symptom and an enactment of repression. Her behavior expresses and quashes her desires. She struggles to keep her fierce appetites in check, but, as with her drinking, she cannot succeed. In the pivotally revealing scene with the newspaper boy, Williams shows the struggle she endures. Stanley describes Blanche accurately, even if unsympathetically, when he tells Stella:

All this squeamishness she puts on! You should just know the line she's been feeding Mitch. He thought she had never been more than kissed by a fellow. But Sister Blanche is no lily. Ha-ha! Some lily she is. . . . She is as famous in Laurel as if she was President of the United States, only she is not respected by any party! (530)

Blanche is not what she seems. The audience has seen that. Stanley's play on the word "party" reinforces the idea that one phenomenon can be hidden behind another.

"I guess it is just that I have old-fashioned ideals," Blanche tells Mitch after she rebuffs his embrace. In the stage direction Williams writes, "She rolls her eyes, knowing he cannot see her face." In response, "Mitch goes to the front door. There is considerable silence between them. Blanche sighs and Mitch coughs self-consciously" (525). Blanche is lying, deliberately pretending to a moral delicacy—"squeamishness," Stanley calls it—that she knows is alien to her. Stanley is right. She is not what she seems. But why this is important is that neither is Williams, and neither is the play. Yet Williams's aesthetic credo rebels against the self-abnegation the times demanded, the lie he was forced to live and, as a dramatist, to tell. In consequence, if he cannot speak the truth, at least he can blast the fact that lying is a fundamental social fact throughout his work.

"Of course it is a pity," Williams wrote in "Person—to—Person," his preface to *Cat on a Hot Tin Roof*,

> that so much of all creative work is so closely related to the personality of the one who does it.
>
> It is sad and embarrassing and unattractive that those emotions that stir him deeply enough to demand expression, and to charge their expression with some measure of light and power, are nearly all rooted, however changed in their surface, in the particular and sometimes peculiar concerns of the artist himself. (875)

"Embarrassing and unattractive"? "The . . . peculiar concerns of the artist himself"? How tantalizing an attempt at a confession of something—"however changed [its] surface"—finally avoided and left to dissolve into abstraction!

Blanche's pretense, forbidding Mitch to embrace her, gives way to her painful and true revelation, to a confession that is well framed, but not abstract. She tells Mitch about Allan Grey. The incident she relates not only reveals a truth about Blanche but also suggests a truth outside the play, a truth that her monologue both reveals and conceals, that gives voice to the hidden source of the play, to something "closely related to the personality of the one who [wrote] it." It touches on "emotions that stir [Williams] deeply enough to demand expression," that his, as Williams wrote in the "Production Notes" to *The Glass Menagerie*, "poetic imagination can represent or suggest, in essence, only through transformation" (395), because they are "embarrassing and unattractive . . . the . . . peculiar concerns of the artist himself."

5

➣ *A Streetcar Named Desire* is a drama about the art of transformation. Blanche is endlessly transforming herself and reality, and by the end of the play, the power of the drama comes from the transformation that has been effected in Stanley and Stella's marriage. Their marriage has been transformed from an expression of something true between them that happens in the dark into a lie they share that must be kept in darkness. The lies presented in the play stand for the lie that Williams must foster in the world outside the play, the reality that he must transform inside the play in order to present "those emotions that stir him deeply enough to demand expression, and to charge their expression with some measure of light and power." Heterosexual suppressions, deceptions, and explosions in the play must stand in place of homosexual ones in the world. The play suggests an unuttered and fundamental sentence by its author: If I am to talk to you and have you listen to me, if I am to make art for you that you can accept, if I am to have any success as a playwright in your theater and as a man in your world, I must lie. ➣

The pervasive and fundamental act of lying is an obsession with Williams, not just in *A Streetcar Named Desire*. It is also at the heart of *Cat on a Hot Tin Roof*, where the cry of "mendacity" is a leitmotif, repeated so often within the text that it hangs independently above the text with urgency and force that transcend the text. As in *A Streetcar Named Desire*, homosexuality is hauntingly present in *Cat on a Hot Tin Roof* by its absence and by its negation. It can be introduced there only if it can be vilified and denied. Brick Pollitt is overtly portrayed as *not* being homosexual. Such sleight of hand will be detected by any in the audience who are adept at seeing in the text a Freudian reaction formation. The homosexuality that disturbs Brick is not his own "tainted" love for his best friend Skipper but Skipper's misbegotten love for him. The possibility of homosexual love on Brick's part is depicted as a revulsion he feels toward even the possibility of a homosexual constituent in his love for his friend. That flip is the lie never explicitly uncovered in the play, but it haunts the play, as Williams indicates it must. In his "Notes for the Designer," Williams imposes this nearly impossible task on the stage designer: Brick and Maggie's bedroom ought to show that it

> hasn't changed much since it was occupied by the original owners of the place, Jack Straw and Peter Ochello, a pair of old bachelors who shared this room all their lives together. . . . the room must evoke some ghosts; it is gently poetically haunted by a relationship that must have involved a tenderness which was uncommon. (880)

And unmentionable! In the film version of the play, released in 1958, the homosexual subtext, as in the film of *A Streetcar Named Desire*, was entirely expunged.

What adds to the power and complexity of repression as a force determining the dynamic of *A Streetcar Named Desire* is that repression operates not only within the play in the psychology of its characters but outside it, too, in the sociology of the environment in which it was written. *A Streetcar Named Desire*, a play written by a homosexual man at a time when homosexuality and homosexuals were vilified and the practice of homosexuality was anathema, offers the possibility of several kinds of readings. Just as the Hebrew Bible can be read either self-referentially or, as Erich Auerbach has done in "Figura," in his study *Scenes from the Drama of European Literature*, as a text that can be read in the context of a subsequent text—events in the Hebrew Bible can be understood to prefigure events beyond it that are recounted in the Christian Scriptures—*A Streetcar Named Desire* can be read, sui generis, as a tragic melodrama, a study of the interpersonal psychological turmoil and tension created by the clash of its dramatis personae, or it can be read as a work signifying something outside itself that cannot be signified by its own particulars and must inhabit others. *A Streetcar Named Desire* can be seen as a work about avoidance and guilty enactment. As in so much of the work of Tennessee Williams, the play itself both expresses and suppresses the theme of homosexuality. It is a work that stands in place of the work that could not be written because of the taboo at the time of its composition, the socially constructed impossibility of presenting the drama of homosexual experience and emotion directly. That does not mean that *A Streetcar Named Desire* is a direct translation from one gender set to another but that the condition that hinders writing a homosexual play and the lie that homosexual people must live in order to live is given expressive dramatic life by this story of repression and lying.

When he wrote of homosexuality in *A Streetcar Named Desire,* Williams wrote as if homosexuality were an attribute of the "other," just as he did some seven years later in *Cat on a Hot Tin Roof,* whereas it was, in fact, his own identity, although a disturbed, unstable identity because he wrote in a time of its repression. But homosexuality and hatred of homosexuality—in the play it is a guilty hatred—are at the center of *A Streetcar Named Desire*, at its vortex, supplying its motive force.

The central event of *A Streetcar Named Desire* has occurred before the play begins, just as in *Cat on a Hot Tin Roof.* In both cases it is an event of guilty and spurned homosexual love and of betrayal of the homosexual by a beloved. Blanche tells of the event to Mitch, and it wins his heart. For him, her confession must seem to be a companion story to the "story connected with [the] inscription" on his cigarette case, the story he told Blanche when he met her, of the "strange, sweet girl" (498) he loved who died of an illness. Blanche tells the story of her betrayal, of her pain, of her agency as the source of pain, and of her remorse. It is the story of a naïve first love, a deceived love, of love on Blanche's part for Allan Grey, "just a boy when I was a very young girl." It was an innocent love on her part, a natural opening of herself to another. But on his, it was a desperate love, entered into in order to disestablish homosexual desire, a strategy bound for failure, and the burden of the failure in their marriage was borne by Blanche. "He came to me for help," she tells Mitch. "I didn't know that. I didn't find out anything till after our marriage when we'd run away and come back and all I knew was I'd failed him in some mysterious way and wasn't able to give the help he needed but couldn't speak of! He was in the quicksands and clutching at me—but I wasn't holding him out, I was slipping in with him." Allan's homosexuality is not explicitly revealed here, although implicitly it is in Blanche's earlier description of him, which suggests it by negation: "There was something different about the boy, a nervousness, a softness and tenderness which wasn't like a man's, *although he wasn't the least bit effeminate looking*"(emphasis added). That denial is an affirmation, the characteristic way repressed matter finds expressive utterance. It is obvious that Blanche was unable to arouse him sexually. For that she assumed the guilt: "I loved him unendurably but without being able to help him or help myself." Her "failure" is the inevitable result of the repression that caused Allan Grey to attempt, to wish, to dissociate himself from homosexual identity and, dependently, to have heterosexuality bestowed upon him by a woman, who *had* to fail at the attempt because of his homosexuality.

Blanche does discover his homosexuality inadvertently and traumatically "by coming suddenly into a room that I thought was empty" and discovering that the room was not empty. It was full of her negation and of humiliation for her and Allan Grey. It was a room peopled by a phenomenon that conferred emptiness upon her. "The boy I had married and an older man who had been his friend for years" were there. No further description is given—not even on Broadway, in 1947, could any be given—but the revelation of homosexuality is cemented by the absence of any further description except, "Afterwards we pretended that nothing had been discovered" as the three of them drove together to the Moon Lake Casino. There, on the dance floor, Blanche told Allan, "I saw! I know! You disgust me." At that, he ran from her, and outside "stuck [a] revolver into his mouth and fired" (527-28). Her disgust is the consequence of the attitude created by the social repression that must infect all members of a repressive society. But the rage that fueled it was the recoil against the emptiness created within her by the implosion caused by her discovery and by the resentment she had to have experienced at having the burden of Allan Grey's sexual unresponsiveness appear to be her fault rather than his disposition. It was a disposition that Stella, in accord with the general consensus of the time, characterizes as "degenerate" when she tries to explain Blanche to Stanley in scene 7 (533).

The scene before Blanche's confession, the one that ends as Mitch brings roses to Blanche at the start of their date, Blanche's encounter with the newspaper boy, is far more meaningful, in retrospect, than it might have seemed originally. It shows Blanche as she is when not dissembling. It shows her in an authentic moment of desire. It shows her struggle against desire even as she acts on it. It hints that her desire is the effect of the trauma of Allan Grey's suicide. The great discrediting secret of her past, although Stanley finds a catalog of past immoralities for her, is her seduction of a seventeen-year-old boy who was one of her pupils. The scene with the newspaper boy must remind the audience not only of that seduction but also, on second viewing or reading, of the frustration of her love for Allan Grey. Blanche lives in the grip of an unfinished situation. A spurned love inside *A Streetcar Named Desire* stands in place of a love that is forbidden in the actual world.

In both cases, whether Blanche's first love or Tennessee Williams's heterosexual tragic melodrama, the core experience reverts to homosexuality. Dramatically Blanche is not Tennessee Williams, but when she says, "Young man! Young, young, young man! Has anyone ever told you that you look like a young Prince out of the Arabian Nights? . . . Come here. I want to kiss you, just once, softly and sweetly on your mouth" (519-20), she is the surrogate speaker of a forbidden longing, a surrogate longing, a homosexual desire transformed into a forbidden heterosexual desire in order to be expressed, and even in this form, it must be quickly suppressed. Stanley's rape of Blanche and her terror of Stanley as he approaches her in scene 10 not only fulfill what Stanley calls the "date" they have "had . . . with each other from the beginning" (555) but also emblematically express the underlying matter of the play schematically represented by the plot and by the actions of each character, the terror produced by the eruption of the repressed.

Work Cited

Williams, Tennessee. *Tennessee Williams: Plays, 1937-1955*. New York: Library of America, 2000.

A Streetcar Named Desire:
A Consideration of Select Criticism_____

Janyce Marson

From its earliest stage performances in Boston, New Haven, and Philadelphia, *A Streetcar Named Desire* was received with great appreciation. This acclaim was confirmed with the play's Broadway debut at the Ethel Barrymore Theatre on December 3, 1947, and with the overwhelming appreciation it received from such prominent drama critics as Brooks Atkinson of *The New York Times*, who declared Tennessee Williams to be "a genuinely poetic playwright whose knowledge of people is honest and thorough and whose sympathy is profoundly human," and Louis Kronenberg, who hailed it as "the most creative new play." Indeed, *A Streetcar Named Desire* was so enthusiastically received that it won the Pulitzer Prize, the Donaldson Award, and the New York Drama Critics' Circle Award. Nevertheless, *Streetcar* was not universally loved by all reviewers. Set in the years immediately following World War II, the play presents the passionate struggle for power between Blanche DuBois and Stanley Kowalski, culminating in Blanche's rape. This power struggle explores multiple complex themes, including the competing social and economic attitudes of the two protagonists. In turn, this class struggle has a direct bearing on the characters' sexuality and conventional expectations concerning gender roles. Additionally, the play raises questions about homosexuality and prostitution. Accordingly, some critics took exception to its shocking material and the various symbolic vehicles through which it expressed its seemingly lurid theme. Mary McCarthy, in a famous review, satirized its tawdry trappings, describing the atmosphere of the play to be composed of "acrimony and umbrage, tears, door-slamming, broken dishes, jeers, cold silences, whispers, raised eyebrows, the determination to take no notice, the whole classic paraphernalia of [which] insult and injury is Tennessee Williams's hope chest" (132).

For the most part, however, *Streetcar* has been an enormous success both on the stage and in Elia Kazan's famous film adaptation in 1951. Among its most enduring critical issues has been the debate centered on the ultimate culpability for the play's tragic conclusion and, indeed, where each character bears some responsibility for the catastrophic events that ensue as well as whether the boundary lines of good and evil are ever clearly demarcated. What distinguishes the debates concerning the inherent ambiguities of *Streetcar*, however, are the historically shifting contexts in which they take place. Those contexts include such issues as the cultural myth of the Old South, the social and economic implications of the class warfare between two characters who contend for dominance over each other, a close reading of the characters' rhetorical patterns, an examination of the symbolism of colors and furnishings in the Kowalski apartment, the persistent question of genre in a play in which both tragic and comic are thoroughly intertwined, and a possible resolution of many conflicting issues in *Streetcar* by the application of various postmodern strategies.

John Gassner's essay "Tennessee Williams: Dramatist of Frustration," published in 1948, is an early critique of Tennessee Williams's treatment of the predicament of southern aristocratic women, which Gassner sees as a quandary in which they are caught in the abyss of a radically different world where the cherished values of social position and economic well-being have been rendered obsolete and can no longer afford them protection. Gassner takes as his focal point the symbolism in *A Streetcar Named Desire* and premises his argument on the belief that the world in which women like Blanche DuBois must struggle to survive is a postlapsarian, naturalistic one in which only the strong can endure. Gassner's essay is an early application of Darwinian theories of natural selection and survival of the fittest—a clash between historical forces in the Old and New South and the tension wrought between Blanche's civilized restraint, the only vestige of aristocratic expression remaining to her, and Stanley's brutal, aggressive, and unbridled response to life's conflicts. Gassner states, "The dramatic action drives directly to its fateful conclusion as plebian and patrician confront each other" (6). Thus, for Gassner, that struggle is best understood as a conflict of social class, where a physically powerful working-class man like Stanley Kowalski is destined to win before he ever encounters Blanche, and the latter is doomed from the start. Within this sociological paradigm, Blanche's final delivery to a state mental institution by Stanley, with her sister Stella's tacit approval, would seem to be a logical outcome, given that the Kowalskis' priority is the preservation of their marriage. Gassner sees Stella as allowing herself to be "declassed . . . by an earthy marriage to Stanley Kowalski and saved herself" (7). To emphasize Blanche's attenuated, outmoded, and even abstracted status, Gassner makes an interesting analogy between her and Pablo Picasso's painting *Demoiselles d'Avignon*, where the five women depicted appear utterly disconnected from one another. It is also interesting to note that Avignon is the name of a street in Barcelona that was known for its brothel.

Anne Fleche elaborates on the issue of abstraction in *Streetcar* in her discussion of the ways in which Williams subverts our realistic understanding of the characters and their setting in post-World War II New Orleans and, instead, presents us with abstract character types that lack true individuality according to the relatively new language of human evolution. According to Fleche, the inherent ambiguity in *Streetcar*, where both Blanche and Stanley are simply acting out their emotional functions, results from the fact that Williams intended the play to be a representation of the nature of desire itself—that which always seeks fulfillment and an end to its own compulsion—and the violent manner in which it is communicated. In a word, Fleche discusses *Streetcar* as an allegory of desire, a commentary on the way in which it masks its self-destructive agenda in a rhetoric of realism. "The metalanguage of desire seems to preclude development, to deny progress. . . . The play is full in fact of realism's developmental language of evolution, 'degeneration,' eugenics. Before deciding that Stanley is merely an 'ape,' Blanche sees him as an asset" (324). Another critical point in Fleche's essay on the way in which Williams seeks to blur the distinction between reality and illusion is the manipulation of space in *Streetcar.* Fleche argues persuasively that the reality of space is deceptive, for the characters of Elysian Fields all suffer from a predominance of confinement and a severe lack of privacy, so much so that there is a confusion between the interior of the Kowalski flat and the various peripheral events and circumstances on the street below. Within this two-room apartment there is simply no place for Blanche or Stella to hide from the vulgar card games and crude commentary of Stanley and his friends. This lack of privacy is thus a symptom of the true lack of boundaries within *Streetcar,* despite all its illusion of a separation of interior demarcations and an exterior world, which challenges the very notion of a territorial struggle for the domestic turf of the Kowalski household. Most important for Fleche, however, is the fact that the blurred distinction between interior and exterior denotes the loss of the characters' true inner being into their respective roles in the emotional allegory of desire.

Beginning with a discussion of Williams's earlier characters derived from two one-act plays and blended to form Blanche DuBois, Benjamin Nelson takes up the question of Williams's sympathies in what he characterizes as a "deceptively complex query." The first one-act play, *The Lady of Larkspur Lotion,* concerns a former southern belle living in a rooming house while advancing the illusion that she is waiting for funds from her rubber plantation in Brazil; in *Portrait of a Madonna,* an old spinster is about to be transferred to an asylum. According to Nelson, *A Streetcar Named Desire* can be understood as either "the disintegration of a woman or, if you like, of a society," the key concept being either the breakdown of an individual or the destruction of a community. Nelson begins his examination of Williams's sympathies with the introduction of a rough-and-ready brute, Stanley Kowalski, a man crude in habits who nevertheless manifests "animal shrewdness and vitality." When Blanche enters the Kowalski household, she opines that he may have a place within the DuBois family, a belated observation, as Stanley has already married into the family and set the standards for his part in it. Stanley and Stella's relationship is a simple one, based entirely on a satisfying sexual union as they await the birth of their first child. According to Nelson, Blanche's response is filled simultaneously with abiding interest and revulsion, though she herself has been given over to sexual excess following the suicide of her homosexual husband, Allan. Nelson's assessment of the dramatic conflict takes on a decidedly social critique of the problem. Based on his reading of John Gassner, Nelson writes that "Blanche [is] the intruder into the crude but normal 'precincts of the uninhibited, uncomfortably heavy proletariat'—the Kowalskis" (135).

Nelson further makes the case that Blanche is ambivalent in her feelings for Stanley—namely, her physical attraction on one hand and her outright disgust and abhorrence of his crude manners and uncouthness on the other. Added to the complexity of Blanche's predicament is the fact that her sister has turned her back on their aristocratic upbringing and allowed herself to fall in with Stanley Kowalski's world of violent responses to life and like-minded friends and associates. Nelson states: "Her attraction is the lure of the flesh, but her repulsion is more complex. It is a repulsion with sexuality which is almost animalistic, but also with the knowledge that this animality was bringing pleasure to her sister while she was watching their family and home crumble into decay" (135). As a result of Stanley's overhearing of Blanche's assassination of his character to Stella, Nelson maintains, Stanley has no choice but to fight Blanche on her own terms, which is to uncover her colored past and expose her own unbridled sexual excesses. Because each of them has played a role in precipitating a crisis in the Kowalski household, Nelson believes, both Blanche and Stanley share responsibility for the rape. "In the final scene Blanche is led from the house to an asylum, lost forever in the illusory world in which she sought shelter from a vital and overpowering reality with which she could not cope. . . . Stanley is victorious, and deservedly so. Although he is brutal and coarse, he calls a spade a spade" (136). Nelson maintains that Stanley Kowalski represents the "new American, rough, tough, but alive with the sense of his own being and power," in opposition and clear superiority to any obsolete ideology of a privileged aristocracy.

With respect to the question of the play's genre, Leonard Berkman makes the case that Blanche DuBois achieves true tragic stature. Berkman begins with the premise that *A Streetcar Named Desire* exemplifies an important aspect of what is considered to be traditional tragedy, namely, "the terms according to which 'victory' may be considered within the heroine's grasp, the struggle toward victory, and the pivotal moment in which the struggle turns to defeat" (249). In making his argument for Blanche as a tragic heroine, Berkman is also quick to state that he is working against those critics of modern American drama writing after the late 1940s who focused on the antihero, the "common man," a character who enters the stage as one already defeated, with the consequence that the representation of a tragic downfall is no longer possible. For Berkman, the subject matter of Williams's play is anything but a portrait of the common man. As part of his effort to gainsay prior critical attempts to read Blanche as a member of the community of common men, Berkman discredits the interpretation of her tragic nature as the representation of a coarse, selfish, and promiscuous woman who tenaciously clings to illusions of gentility when in fact she is anything but ordinary. In making his point, Berkman responds to John Mason Brown's searing 1963 commentary in which Brown condemned Blanche for "her pathetic pretensions of gentility even when she is known as a prostitute" (250). For Berkman, the historical context of *A Streetcar Named Desire* is crucial. In a post-World War II world where education and culture were proven no longer to be an assurance of one's humanity, Berkman attributes Blanche's exceptional character, which makes her vulnerable to a tragic downfall, to her belief in intimate relationships as the ultimate achievement toward which individuals should direct their lives. Equally as important for Berkman are the flawed defenses of Blanche's character on the basis that she represents the sensitive, cultured artist who is destined to be misunderstood. Further, based on this premise, he takes issue with critiques that augment her symbolic function as a representation of civilization itself threatened by Stanley's savageness. Having set the parameters of his argument, Berkman recognizes an inherent ambiguity within *Streetcar* as to Tennessee Williams's sympathies toward the passionate life versus the more refined and necessarily restrained way of being. With this tension in mind, Berkman believes that the resolution of this question resides in an understanding that Blanche's status does indeed change during the course of the drama; her relentless desire and extraordinary efforts in the face of humiliating obstacles to establish intimacy in her life, a "classically noble" cause, are evidence of her eminently dignified nature and tragic stature within *Streetcar*. Among those gallant efforts to find intimacy Berkman includes Blanche's marriage to Allan Grey, and he argues that her subsequent excesses and affairs with strangers were in fact born of her failed marriage. Finally, Berkman states that Blanche's futile efforts to come clean with Mitch are a brave attempt to face the truth about her past in the hope of finally securing a relationship based on honesty. It is Berkman's conclusion that Blanche's downfall is the result of her rejected but valiant endeavors to realize truth and intimacy only to be cast into the very image of a whore that she so desperately sought to escape.

With a different take on the subject of nobility, Thomas E. Porter argues that *Streetcar* is a cultural critique of the death of an ideal, namely, the virtue and nobility of the Old South, hopelessly eradicated as a result of the Civil War. Furthermore, as Porter points out, Williams was greatly invested in this mystique given the fact that he grew up in Mississippi, the grandson of Thomas Lanier, a southern poet who likewise "celebrated the glories of the New South in the spirit of the Old" (155). Using the focal point of Blanche's predicament in *A Streetcar Named Desire*, Porter analyzes the characters within the play as types who variously relate to this myth of the Old South. In the case of Blanche, one sees a misguided clinging to this alluring but deceptive myth. In the characters of Mitch and Stella, one can see an attenuated version of these southern ideals, and in the most radical and extreme departure from any notion of gentility one encounters the character of Stanley Kowalski. The essential elements of the complex myth of the Old South, as Porter presents them, are a graciousness permeating every aspect of life based on an inviolable code of personal honor and a tradition that places great importance on family and inheritance. Further elucidating this idyllic life, Porter discusses details of the "plantation myth," with its pristine world of white-columned houses set on vast acres of lawn and garden, with slaves residing on the periphery in cotton fields, along with notions of "chivalric virtues and patrician vices" and slaves seen as "devoted serfs, contented with their lot" (157). It is a myth with strong adherence to time in its reverence of the past and the importance of space in its agrarian setting. Moreover, with respect to Blanche's predicament, the plantation myth mandates a woman's refinement and delicacy. The central conflict of the play, as outlined by Porter, begins when Blanche, as representative of the plantation way of life in Belle Reve (literally, "beautiful dream"), intrudes on the Kowalski residence in an old section of New Orleans, a city both urbane and rooted in the old southern tradition. Given the parameters of propriety and nobility that constitute the myth, Stanley and Blanche become types representing the clash between an outworn ideal to which Blanche fatally adheres, "exhibit[ing] the idiosyncrasies of the Southern heroine in profusion, adding to the schizoid impression by her frantic attempts," and the shockingly real and violent world to which Stanley belongs. Porter notes: "There is no schizoid tendency in Stanley's personality; he knows his place in the world and holds it confidently. . . . He questions Blanche about the loss of country place because he shares a right in his wife's property and doesn't like being swindled" (166). Furthermore, as a couple, Stanley and Stella are the embodiment of a small society living in the present moment as opposed to Blanche's fantasy world. Mitch represents a self-conscious and inept version of the southern gentleman who ultimately does not understand the code by which Blanche lives. Though he has elements of the romantic in his character, such as a watch inscribed with a quote from the Victorian poet Elizabeth Barrett Browning, he nevertheless belongs to Stanley's world and succumbs to its way of thinking. In straddling these two opposing perspectives, both Stella and Mitch underscore the ambiguity of *A Streetcar Named Desire*. Ultimately, within this mythic context, Porter maintains, Blanche bears some measure of responsibility for her rape, for she is the one who initially violates Stanley's turf and threatens his sovereignty:

> Blanche invades Stanley's domain armed with a traditional sensibility and culture. She attempts to win Stella's support and half-succeeds; . . . Stanley is ruffled by her superiority and reconnoiters till he discovers the chink in her armor. . . . Blanche herself is partially responsible for the triumph of force and material resources over sensibility and ideals. (169)

According to Porter, a reversal of the myth occurs in which the Old South becomes the invader.

Building on this notion of a southern ideal, W. Kenneth Holditch considers the dichotomy between naturalism and romanticism. Beginning with the premise that transcendence is impossible in *A Streetcar Named Desire*, Holditch discusses the ways in which Blanche DuBois and Stanley Kowalski embody two competing perspectives, namely, the romantic vision of Blanche's ideals of a genteel and cultured world versus the indomitable force of Stanley's self-confident sexuality and unshakable belief in his ability to prevail. Naturalism in *A Streetcar Named Desire* is represented by Blanche and Stanley and is a means for defining the central conflict between them, a fight to control the Kowalski household wherein Stella, who plays a mediating role, becomes the bargaining chip. For Holditch, Blanche DuBois is the hopeless romantic; she enters the stage as an all-but-obsolete remnant of an aristocratic southern family, desperately clinging to an ideal of courtly gentlemen, refined sensibilities, and an appreciation for art and poetry. Holditch notes, "Already damaged by the loss of Belle Reve and the harsh realities of disease and death, Blanche's Romanticism is reduced in some moments to nothing more than sentimentality" (155). As for defining the essence of Stanley Kowalski, on the other hand, Holditch applies Arthur Schopenhauer's definition of naturalism as the primacy of sexuality to identify the driving force behind his personality, a force representative of the naturalistic perspective, where survival of the fittest is the rule. "His ideals are limited to the fleshly, his vision centered in his own body, specifically in the sexual organs. Stage directions portray him as the breeder in Naturalistic terms that exemplify the driving will Schopenhauer identifies as the abiding motivation behind human action" (157). As Holditch also points out, literary naturalism draws from a variety of traditions to include scientific discovery as well as new political, sociological, and psychological attitudes. Stanley is firmly rooted in the material world and, far from ascribing validity to class distinctions, sees himself as a full participant in "the leveling process of modern 'Democracy,'" a man determined to maintain control over his household and his world. Holditch's point is that biological determinism, along with a firm adherence to the phenomenal world, is the key to understanding Stanley's power. Blanche DuBois is simply no match for him. Her unrealistic dream of refashioning the world has been a part of her tragic history since long before she ever arrived in New Orleans. Within Holditch's paradigm of romanticism versus naturalism, Stella and Mitch are pivotal figures who straddle the two perspectives and, in so doing, remain weak and indecisive, ultimately yielding to Stanley's influence and control. In the final analysis, Holditch maintains that Blanche's ultimate insanity is the direct result of a clash between these two competing perspectives: "The final triumph of the Naturalistic view of life is acted out in no uncertain terms in the rape. This scene is a capsule version of the movement in the play from the Ideal to the Naturalistic view of human existence" (163).

Writing in opposition to those critics who have read Blanche as a hopelessly deluded and tragic woman on whom Stanley Kowalski preys, Bert Cardullo takes the position that Blanche and Stanley are equally responsible for their own downfalls, and, consequently, both emerge as tragic victims. Cardullo states that although Blanche's rape by Stanley may be the final deed that consigns her to an institutionalized existence, she is in fact an agent of her own destruction, defining her predicament as a struggle from within herself that long precedes her arrival in New Orleans—namely, a struggle to achieve intimacy in her life. Indeed, Cardullo maintains that it is Blanche's inability to cope with her husband's homosexuality—"her rejection of Allan Grey on the dance floor of the Moon Lake Casino many years before Stanley's rape . . . thus comes to appear the ironic physical incarnation of a defeat whose seeds she herself ultimately cultivated with 'intimacies with strangers'"—that ultimately seals her fate ("Drama" 138). According to Cardullo, Blanche's greatest regret is not the discovery of her husband's sexual proclivities but rather her inability to show him compassion, which in consequence causes a life of unmitigated guilt; further, all her subsequent attempts at forming close relationships are utterly doomed, even her attempts to bond with Stella. "When she tells Stella that she is all but destitute, a 'veiled plea for rescue from a life bereft of warmth and affection' Stella responds 'with little more than an offer of five dollars and a Bromo'" ("Drama" 141). The real tragedy in *Streetcar* emanates from Blanche's futile attempts to establish closeness with others.

As for Stanley, Cardullo finds him not so much malicious as he is blind to Blanche's suffering and, equally as important, overwhelmed by her education and verbal skills. Cardullo renders the struggle between Stanley and Stella as a battle of incommensurates within the medium of language. This is evidenced in Stanley's inability to confront his sister-in-law's searing condemnation of his undignified character and brutish way of being. Cardullo argues that Stanley adopts a nonconfrontational role because, though angered by her derogatory remarks, he realizes that he is no match for Blanche's rhetoric. By her very nature, Blanche DuBois introduces an intellectual understanding of the world that is both inaccessible and completely alien to Stanley's way of being. "Blanche brings an element of complexity to his life here that he fails to comprehend" and, accordingly, he must use the situation as an opportunity to test Stella's allegiance to him and is convinced only when she throws herself at him. "In a word, she chooses to head back with her brute" and poignantly demonstrates an intimacy that is utterly lacking in Blanche's life. Ironically, however, for all of Blanche's sensitivity and love of poetry, she too suffers from an inability to understand or feel compassionate toward Stanley. Cardullo maintains that although Stanley succeeds in having Blanche committed to an asylum, where she will be forever denied the intimacy she has so desperately sought, his denial of the rape is a far more profound and horrible act than any of the lies Blanche ever concocted. As a result, Stanley does not emerge victorious. He has destroyed a trust he can never regain, for his relationship with Stella has been irrevocably damaged. In conclusion, Cardullo finds *A Streetcar Named Desire* to be a modern version of classical tragedy, specifically a Christian one: "Unlike Greek tragedy, which I would call the tragedy of self, of man, Christian tragedy, as epitomized in *Streetcar*, is the tragedy of life, of men. At once burdened with the notion of original sin and tempted with the idea of salvation in the hereafter, [he] . . . resolves to insulate himself as much as possible against the arbitrariness, the 'cruelty' of life" ("Drama" 151).

In his discussion of the genre of *A Streetcar Named Desire*, John M. Roderick provides a very interesting and thought-provoking analysis of the play as a "brilliant tragicomedy," identifying inherent tensions that he believes other critics have ignored. Roderick maintains that within this complex genre heartbreaking events are constantly mitigated by the introduction of comic elements that create a complexity of meaning that requires a dual reading of the play and that results in two vastly divergent conclusions. "We begin with the traditional elements of a sacred arena suddenly profane. . . . Part of this ambivalence lies in the possibility that the play lends itself to a reading on two levels, one social, the other psychological" (117), and leads to two sharply contrasted interpretations of the conflict between Stanley and Blanche.

A Consideration of Select Criticism

From a sociological point of view, Blanche DuBois represents a tragic remnant of an all but extinct southern aristocracy with all the refined sensibilities and love of art and literature that this class holds dear. Her interpretation of Stanley Kowalski is that he is fundamentally a "survivor of the Stone Age! Bearing the raw meat home from the kill in the jungle!"—a judgment that reveals her profound prejudice toward lower-class working people who lack her education and presumed good breeding. For his part, Stanley represents the hostile working-class perspective bent on destroying those very same aristocratic ideals—so much so that his abusive behavior toward Blanche displays antagonism and is more than just a violent reaction to his sister-in-law. Stanley's reaction becomes a struggle against the social class to which Blanche once belonged. Within the context of a sociological framework, Blanche is the superior of the two. From a psychological perspective, however, Stanley has the upper hand and appears to be the normal one. He is in a marriage that is based on a vibrant sexual relationship, a fact that, as Roderick points out, is supported by the parallel marriage of Stanley and Stella's upstairs neighbors, Steve and Eunice, and Mitch's statement to Blanche that despite their violent interaction, Stanley and Stella are crazy about each other. Furthermore, it is Stanley's home life that has been so abruptly and insensitively intruded upon by his sister-in-law with the threat that she intends to take Stella away from him. If the achievement of intimacy is the test, Blanche is seen as deeply unhappy and utterly incapable of attaining a close and loving relationship with anyone, as her entire history amply demonstrates. From a marriage that ends tragically in the suicide of her homosexual husband to her highly inappropriate escapades with young boys, which in turn get her thrown out of a teaching position, Blanche carries around a lot of profoundly unhappy and frustrated baggage. Roderick maintains that, when one looks at the Blanche-Stanley conflict from a psychological angle, Blanche bears responsibility for her rape, as she is the one guilty of irreverence, having intruded on the Kowalskis' sacred, if vulgar, marriage: "Psychologically speaking, then, Blanche represents the profanation of Stanley's sacred, if crude, marriage. But we must cope with both the social and the psychological levels simultaneously. Thus the ambiguous duality in our appraisal of Stanley and Blanche is encouraged by Williams" (119). This ambiguity resides in the humorous instances that belie the dramatically charged interaction between Blanche and Stanley, such as Stanley's citation of the Napoleonic code and his intention to consult with a litany of professional appraisers as to the value of Blanche's trunk. However, Roderick does not mention Blanche's humorous moments, such as spraying Stanley with cologne and constantly steaming up his bathroom with her long and disruptive hot baths. While the sociological and psychological readings provide very different understandings of the two protagonists, Roderick seems to suggest that it is the humorous that somehow allows for these two divergent readings and for life to go on in spite of all that has gone terribly wrong in *A Streetcar Named Desire*.

Verna Foster adopts a similar interpretation of the tragicomic elements in *A Streetcar Named Desire* and sees these two facets as working symbiotically to enhance the tragic elements by preventing them from lapsing into melodrama. In making her argument, Foster maintains that this symbiosis is essential to modern drama, a historical distinction that Williams made in a 1974 interview: "One can't write a tragedy today without putting humor into it. There has to be humor in it now; it's so hard for people to take tragedy seriously because people are so wary now" (quoted in Foster 227). What this distinction essentially says is that tragedy no longer serves the purpose once served by classical tragedy, which, according to Aristotle, was a catharsis of the emotions. Instead, Williams's version of tragedy would prove a subtle and unsettling experience better suited to a mid- to late-twentieth-century audience. This intricate and disturbing intertwining of the comic and the tragic is exemplified first and foremost between Blanche and Stanley, each extremely capable of eliciting both humorous and profoundly heartbreaking responses from the audience, with Williams careful always to balance the two extremes of emotion. Nevertheless, Foster points out, the comic aspects of these two characters are distinct, a difference that she reads as the classic conflict between the soul and the body, between Blanche and Stanley, respectively: "Blanche's comedy is intellectual and playful, consisting of flirtation, conscious role-playing, and irony directed at others and also at herself, emphasizing at once her resilience and her vulnerability. Stanley's humor, by contrast, is always self-aggrandizing; it consists of physical horseplay . . . or literal-minded sarcasm that can be as cruel as it is funny" (232).

Beyond their individual virtuosity in displaying a sense of humor within the context of a frightening domestic conflict that threatens to end in disaster, the ultimate duality is *Streetcar*'s exploration of the oppositional dynamics between death and desire. Ultimately, Foster maintains, the most shocking aspect of the play is that life does go on for the Kowalskis because Stella realizes that she cannot allow herself to believe the truth that Stanley in fact raped Blanche. This appalling reality in which all are losers, according to Foster, is underscored by the entrance of the Kowalski baby at the end of the play: "Thus the baby reminds us of Blanche's essential innocence and vulnerability and that his birth coincided with her destruction, and Stanley's" (235).

In regard to the play's symbolism, Henry I. Schvey provides a very thoughtful consideration of the relevance of pictorial elements in *A Streetcar Named Desire*—namely, Williams's reference to the impressionist painting *The Night Café* (1888), by Vincent van Gogh, in the third scene, as well as the significance of color symbolism and the implicit iconology of Renaissance painting. As to the significance of *The Night Café*, Schvey reminds us that the original title of the play was "The Poker Night," which was an allusion to a particular van Gogh painting of a billiard room at night, described in scene 3, a print of which adorns the Kowalski kitchen. With its garish primary colors, it underscores the gaudy and violent atmosphere of the poker games over which Stanley presides. "The kitchen now suggests that sort of lurid nocturnal brilliance, the raw colors of childhood's spectrum. . . . The parlor players . . . wear colored shirts . . . they are men at the peak of their physical manhood, as coarse and direct as the primary colors" (71). Most important, color in *Streetcar* is indicative of emotional states and moods as well as physical setting. "Specifically, the canvas is marked by the contrasts of the blood red walls and yellow floor with a dark green, coffin-shaped billiard table set diagonally in the middle, casting an ominous shadow," a foreboding further enhanced by "the figure of the landlord in white coat who faces the viewer from behind the table" (72). As to Schvey's second point regarding the importance of color, he maintains that the central conflict is manifested through the various painterly descriptions assigned to the characters. While Blanche, whose name means "white," professes to Stanley her prefer-ence for artists who use "strong bold colors," it is Stanley, who bears a "red-stained package from a butcher" and alternately wears a "green and scarlet silk bowling shirt" and gaudy pajamas, who is indeed the incarnation of the tawdry and implicitly threatening effects of the van Gogh painting.

Schvey further maintains that Blanche's character, as a tragic hero-ine who forfeits her sensuality at the end of the play in exchange for a "new innocence," suggests a "spiritual rebirth." She is represented in a way analogous to the Virgin Mary in Renaissance art—from her rhine-stone tiara and brilliant silver slippers, much like the image of "Mary as Queen of Heaven," to Williams's ironic reference to her as a "'lily,' a flower suggestive of death (and picked up later in the old Mexican woman's cry, 'Flores para los muertos') but also traditionally symbol-izing the purity of the virgin amid the sins of this world" (75). Most sig-nificant for Schvey, however, is the religious imagery of the final scene, reflecting Blanche's transcendence from the depths of hell to the spiritual realm.

Focusing on the victimization of women, the feminist critics San-dra M. Gilbert and Susan Gubar have interpreted the essential conflict in *A Streetcar Named Desire* as a dramatization of the abuse to which women are subjected. These authors assail Tennessee Williams for becoming an apologist for Stanley Kowalski, who uses sex as the means to dominate all women, a character "who represents in his brutishness the phallic origin of the male species." At the same time, they admire Blanche DuBois for her sensitivity and creative thinking and view her as an inspired artist, qualities that place her far beyond the intellectual abilities of all the other characters. They also find Blanche's estimation that Stanley and Stella's marriage is a doomed union between two diametrically opposed characters, with the brutish Stanley having pulled Stella down to his "apelike" way of relating to the world, to be entirely correct: "In many ways the drama proves that she is right, for the drunken, sweaty, poker-playing Stanley beats his wife, and the submissive Stella seems sexually enthralled by his violence" (51). They further criticize Williams for his very negative portrayal of Blanche as culpable for her past indiscretions with young men and, worst of all, for implying that her rape by Stanley is punishment for her history of sexual misconduct.

Writing in response to ideological critics who identify the central conflict in *A Streetcar Named Desire* as a gender-based struggle or a battle indicative of social malaise in "a materialistic, misogynous American society" Bert Cardullo sees Stanley Kowalski and Blanche DuBois as "mutual victims of desire," each of whom is guilty of emotional violence toward others and, consequently, both of whom are destined to suffer the same fate—namely, one of unrequited desire. Cardullo begins with the premise that Stanley does not occupy a symbolic role of a "phallic brute" intent on subjugating women and that Blanche does in fact insinuate herself into his home and marriage. Cardullo views Blanche as a woman who is desperately trying to make amends for her past sexual indiscretions so that she may finally have an intimate relationship with Mitch based on trust. Providing a detailed and balanced analysis of all the characters in *Streetcar* vis-à-vis the imagery of birth, death, and rebirth, Cardullo concludes that everyone must forfeit something in the end. While Blanche loves her hot baths, symbolic of a wish to cleanse and purify herself, and hopes to celebrate her birthday with her sensitive suitor, Mitch, whose proposal would represent a rebirth to a better life, Stanley dashes her hopes for happiness when he exposes her past. Stanley, on the other hand, is hardly the victor, though he succeeds in banishing Blanche from his domicile. In fact, in raping Blanche and lying to Stella, Stanley in effect loses his power over Stella, who, in turn, will now invest all her love in their baby, as evidenced by the fact that Stella does not speak to him once in the final scene. Stanley's past way of being finally catches up with him, as Blanche's past life does with her. For Cardullo, the desire felt by Stanley and Blanche ends in a "living death" for each of them, while the rebirth in *A Streetcar Named Desire* is the Kowalski baby, who remains unnamed ("Birth").

Reframing the many questions surrounding the inherent ambiguities of *A Streetcar Named Desire*, Anca Vlasopolos provides a brilliant analysis of the play as an allegory of reading and, in so doing, offers a perspective that responds to decades of critical debate concerning Williams's attitude toward the generic and ethical issues raised in the play. The main premise of Vlasopolos's argument is that *A Streetcar Named Desire* is a modern "crisis" play, the origins of which she traces back to Elizabethan times with Shakespeare's so-called problem plays, and as such must be understood far differently from a classical drama such as *Oedipus Rex*, in which the supreme authority of the oracle is readily identifiable and unquestioned. Gone, too, is the cathartic purging of emotion in classical tragedy, so that the modern audience is now left anxious and disquieted. For *Streetcar*, there is no absolute or easily identifiable authority but rather a struggle between the two protagonists, Blanche DuBois and Stanley Kowalski, to establish dominance over each other and, ultimately, control over how events, both past and future, will be interpreted. According to Vlasopolos, the real struggle is between sanity and reason, and the supreme judge of the agon between Blanche and Stanley is actually the modern discipline of psychiatry, "the scientific judgment of the soundness of the soul. Yet unlike the gods and their decrees, the final arbiter does not overtly envelop or determine the plot, so that the weight of authority oscillates throughout the play from Blanche to Stanley, giving it the seeming incoherence or generic indeterminacy that has troubled critics and audiences" (325).

The competition over whose version of events takes precedence takes place through a complex network that includes legal documents, photographs, inscriptions, and personal impressions and animosities, as well as gossip from acquaintances and strangers, as Blanche, a woman of aristocratic breeding and literary sophistication, cajoles, flirts, and otherwise shrewdly argues with her crude working-class brother-in-law, an incompetent reader who speaks plainly and is motivated only by a desire to take back what he believes is rightfully his. Though the balance of power vacillates for a while, Vlasopolos maintains that Blanche is doomed from the start for several reasons. She is first and foremost a displaced woman, having been driven from Belle Reve and ultimately out of her hometown of Laurel owing to her promiscuous behavior. As Vlasopolos points out, however, more poignantly and far more subtly, Blanche is powerless, for as a woman she is relegated to a "gender-determined exclusion from the larger historical discourse" and Stanley, though a highly incompetent "reader," gains ultimate male control over how to read Blanche's "insanity" and the tragic ending that he presents her as having brought upon herself. Indeed, a clue to this critical shift of power in favor of Stanley resides in a tiny detail, Blanche's name, which in French means white and, by extension, makes her a metaphoric blank page on which Stanley can triumph in "writing" his version of the story and having Blanche removed from his home to an institution. Vlasopolos notes: "Unlike generically pure tragedy, *A Streetcar Named Desire* leaves us unpurged of the emotions it elicits. We resist being sucked in by Blanche's stories, for that way madness lies; while Williams makes us see and hear like Blanche, and perhaps feel like her, the authority of history is on Stanley's side" (337-38).

Works Cited

Berkman, Leonard. "The Tragic Downfall of Blanche Du Bois." *Modern Drama* 10.3 (1967): 249-57.

Cardullo, Bert. "Birth and Death in *A Streetcar Named Desire.*" *Confronting Tennessee Williams's "A Streetcar Named Desire": Essays in Critical Pluralism.* Ed. Philip C. Kolin. Westport, CT: Greenwood Press, 1993. 167-80.

_____. "Drama of Intimacy and Tragedy of Incomprehension." From *Tennessee Williams: A Tribute.* Ed. Jac Tharpe. Jackson: UP of Mississippi, 1977. 137-53.

Fleche, Anne. "The Space of Madness and Desire: Tennessee Williams and *Streetcar.*" *Modern Drama* 38.4 (1995): 324-35.

Foster, Verna. "Desire, Death, and Laughter: Tragicomic Dramaturgy in *A Streetcar Named Desire.*" *New Readings in American Drama: Something's Happening Here.* Ed. Norma Jenckes. New York: Peter Lang, 2002. 227-37.

Gassner, John. "Tennessee Williams: Dramatist of Frustration." *College English* 10.1 (1948): 1-7.

Gilbert, Sandra M., and Susan Gubar. "The Battle of the Sexes: The Men's Case." *No Man's Land: The Place of the Woman Writer in the Twentieth Century.* Vol. 1. New Haven, CT: Yale UP, 1988. 2-62.

Holditch, W. Kenneth. "The Broken World: Romanticism, Realism, Naturalism in *A Streetcar Named Desire.*" *Confronting Tennessee Williams's "A Streetcar Named Desire": Essays in Critical Pluralism.* Ed. Philip C. Kolin. Westport, CT: Greenwood Press, 1993. 147-66.

McCarthy, Mary. *Sights and Spectacles: 1937-1956.* New York: Farrar, Straus and Cudahy, 1956.

Nelson, Benjamin. "You Didn't Know Blanche as a Girl." *Tennessee Williams: The Man and His Work.* New York: Obolensky, 1961. 130-54.

Porter, Thomas E. "The Passing of the Old South: *A Streetcar Named Desire.*" *Myth and Modern American Drama.* Detroit: Wayne State UP, 1969. 153-76.

Roderick, John M. "From 'Tarantula Arms' to 'Della Robbia Blue': The Tennessee Williams Tragicomic Transit Authority." *Tennessee Williams: A Tribute.* Ed. Jac Tharpe. Jackson: UP of Mississippi, 1977. 116-25.

Schvey, Henry I. "Madonna at the Poker Night: Pictorial Elements in Tennessee Williams's *A Streetcar Named Desire.*" *From Cooper to Philip Roth: Essays on American Literature.* Ed. J. Bakker and D. R. M. Wilkinson. Amsterdam: Rodopi, 1980. 71-77.

Vlasopolos, Anca. "Authorizing History: Victimization in 'A Streetcar Named Desire.'" *Theatre Journal* 38.3 (1986): 322-38.

CRITICAL
READINGS

Desire, Death, and Laughter:
Tragicomic Dramaturgy in
A Streetcar Named Desire[1]

Verna Foster

Tennessee Williams, like Ibsen, Chekhov, and O'Casey before him, understood that in modern drama tragic experience can be expressed only through tragicomedy.[2] In an interview in 1974 he remarked, "One can't write a tragedy today without putting humor into it. There has to be humor in it now; it's so hard for people to take tragedy seriously because people are so wary now" (Devlin 273). While working on *A Streetcar Named Desire* in 1945, he commented in a letter to his agent, Audrey Wood, that he was "writing it with as much lyrical and comedy relief as possible while preserving the essentially tragic atmosphere" (Qtd. in Burks 21). The comedy in *Streetcar*, however, does not simply provide relief from the play's tragic strain; rather the tragic and the comic function symbiotically, the comic modifies, and by subverting, also protects what is tragic from becoming either melodramatic or laughable and, indeed, renders the tragic more bitter. Lyle Leverich reports in his biography of the dramatist that while watching his own plays in the theatre, Williams would often choose moments of pathos or suffering to laugh out loud with his "mad cackle," which he has said was "only a substitute for weeping."[3] If a "mad cackle" is the equivalent of "weeping," then, as Shaw remarked of Ibsen in *The Wild Duck*, Williams presents tragicomedy as "a much deeper and grimmer entertainment" than tragedy (32).

Although many critics, especially in the earlier years of the play's reception, have read *A Streetcar Named Desire* as a tragedy, such a reading not only raises problems about Blanche as a tragic protagonist, but also fails to account for the appeal that Stanley has for audiences, and thus does not adequately comprehend how Williams's complex dramaturgy creates a peculiarly modern form of tragic experience that opens like an "abyss" out of comedy[4] (Dürrenmatt 255). Unlike Arthur

Miller, who contributed to the (problematic) definition of his own *Death of a Salesman* as a tragedy, Williams himself has commented in various interviews on both tragic and comic elements in *Streetcar*. In this essay, then, I propose to examine how Williams's subtle handling of the relations between weeping and cackling create *A Streetcar Named Desire* as tragicomedy, a genre that offers its audience a less cathartic, more ambiguous and disturbing kind of theatrical experience than tragedy might, but also an experience better suited to the needs and tastes of audiences in mid-to-late twentieth-century America. *Streetcar*'s tragicomic genre, I would suggest, is one reason for the play's continuing vitality and contemporaneity in the theatre. The tragicomic opposition in *A Streetcar Named Desire* inheres most obviously in the conflict between Blanche and Stanley. Just as Blanche represents the soul, culture, and death (the moth drawn to the candle) and Stanley (the *"gaudy seed-bearer"* [29]) the body, the primitive, and life, so Blanche seems to embody the play's tragedy and Stanley its comedy. However, the tragic and the comic are related in a much more integral and complicated way than this rather diagrammatic account of the play suggests. Both Blanche and Stanley are tragicomic figures, and *Streetcar* is richly ambiguous: it presents a sensitive, tormented woman cast out from her final refuge, deprived of her last hope of happiness, and brutally destroyed by her crude brother-in-law and/or a down-to-earth working man defending his home and his masculinity from a neurotic, snobbish intruder who would destroy both and indeed almost succeeds. Williams has said that "the meaning of the play" is that Blanche, "potentially a superior person," is broken by the "falsities" of society and also that "the meaning of the play" is that Stanley "does go on" with Stella at the end (Devlin 81, 275). But it might equally be true to say that Stanley *has* to "go on," though his sexuality and his family life are forever tarnished, and that Blanche in some sense escapes, if only into madness, on the arm of her last kind stranger, the Doctor. Throughout the play Williams carefully balances the audience's sympathies between Blanche and Stanley by his orchestration of tragic and comic effects, producing finally not the catharsis of tragedy but instead the richly stimulating discomfort that is characteristic of the endings of tragicomedies.

Blanche is at the center of *Streetcar*'s tragic action and also the focal point for much of its comedy. She is tragic in her attempt to expiate her guilt over her young husband's death and to find consolation in "intimacies with strangers" (118), and in her self-destructive sexual game-playing with Stanley that leads him finally to rape her. I do not wish to suggest that anything Blanche does excuses Stanley for the crime of rape, but rather that her own complicity in bringing it about produces the tragic inevitability of her downfall ("We've had this date with each other from the beginning!" [130]) and makes Blanche a tragic figure rather than merely a victim.

Despite her tragic trajectory, however, Blanche is in many ways a comic character. Underscoring in various interviews the comedy of *Streetcar*, Williams has focused particularly on Blanche, describing her as "funny" and as having a "comic side, her little vanities, and her little white lies"; as "a scream"; and as "really rather bright and witty" (Devlin 277, 285, 316). If we ignore the comic perspective created both by Williams's attitude to Blanche and by Blanche's ironic detachment from her own behavior, as a tragic persona Blanche is too febrile and too self-indulgent to evoke the kind of emotional identification that an audience typically feels with the sufferings of a tragic protagonist. But Williams's comedy cuts into and allows the audience to laugh at Blanche's fantasies, her vanity, her selfishness, her hypocrisy about her drinking, and even her aggressive sexuality. By presenting the weaknesses that contribute to her downfall in a comic light, Williams creates in the audience a degree of critical detachment from Blanche but also protects her from the audience's disapprobation by making her vanity and her role-playing endearing to us though annoying to Stanley. By also giving her an intelligent and even comic apprehension of her own tragic situation, Williams ensures that Blanche has the capacity to engage the audience's sympathetic understanding. Paradoxically, then, it is as a comic rather than as a tragic character that Blanche wins the audience's sympathy for her tragic situation.

One of the chief ways in which Williams creates almost simultaneous engagement with and detachment from Blanche is through her theatricality. As C. W. E. Bigsby has pointed out, Blanche "is self-consciously her own playwright, costume designer, lighting engineer, scenic designer and performer"; she enacts "southern belle, sensitive virgin, sensuous temptress, martyred daughter, wronged wife" (4). Since Blanche in some sense is all of these roles, she quite appropriately elicits the audience's sympathy for herself in each character. But the theatricality of her behavior also serves to block complete identification and create the critical distance needed for a comic response to the performance as well as a tragic response to the persona.

Today we tend to associate the blocking or partial blocking of empathy with Brecht. Brecht certainly has taught us to understand and appreciate the theatrical uses of detachment, and his own *Verfremdungseffekte* has contributed to the repertoire of distancing devices available in late twentieth-century theatre. But the manipulation of dramatic engagement and detachment to create complicated audience responses long precedes Brecht's work. It is a defining characteristic of both Renaissance and modern tragicomedy. Both Shakespeare and Beaumont and Fletcher in their tragicomedies often use a dramatic style that is at once moving and absurd: Leontes's expressions of jealousy in *The Winter's Tale*, for example, or Arbaces's internal conflict over committing, supposedly, incest in *A King and No King*. And, similarly, in a modern tragicomedy, *The Wild Duck*, Ibsen creates in Hjalmar Ekdal a comic character who sees himself as tragic. The audience is moved by the genuinely tragic nature of Hjalmar's plight, the death of his daughter, not because of his self-regarding, pseudo-tragic posturing, which is indeed comically alienating, but because his absurdity throughout the play has rendered him endearing and thus sympathetic.[5]

As a comic character Blanche is more complex than Hjalmar. She understands herself, as Hjalmar does not understand himself, and thus solicits as well as elicits laughter. We are wryly amused when she is being "bright and witty," in some of her turns of phrase ("epic fornications" [43]), for example, and in the way she plays up to and with Mitch. "I guess it is just that I have old-fashioned ideals!" she tells Mitch, rolling her eyes to express the absurdity of any such sexual reticence on her part. Sometimes, seeing Blanche through Stella's eyes, we laugh in a good-natured way at her foibles. After she grandly orders Stella not to clean up after Stanley, Stella asks, "Then who's going to do it? Are you?" Blanche replies in comic shock, "I? I!" (66). The punctuation says it all.

Most often the audience both laughs at and pities Blanche's behavior. Her attempts to hide her drinking, for example, become a running joke, a comically obvious form of role-playing to save appearances. Blanche gushes to Stella in the first scene, "I know you must have some liquor on the place! Where could it be, I wonder? Oh, I spy, I spy" (19), even though she has already had a drink and carefully washed her glass. Later she tells Mitch, "I'm not accustomed to having more than one drink" (54). When we consider, however, that Blanche drinks to forget her past and to make living in Stanley's apartment bearable; that she hides her drinking because she needs to maintain a ladylike image if she is to persuade Mitch, whom she sees as her last hope of salvation, to marry her, then the behavior we have laughed at becomes pitiable. Pirandello's definition of "humor" (essentially tragicomedy) is helpful here. We move from the *perception of the opposite* (that Blanche's behavior is the opposite of what she pretends to be), which produces laughter, to the *feeling of the opposite* (recognizing the reasons for Blanche's behavior), which creates sympathy (Pirandello 113); our laughter at Blanche and our pity for her are thus inextricably bound together, producing a quintessentially tragicomic response. By scene nine when Mitch knows the truth (at least Stanley's truth) about her, Blanche's pretense of abstemiousness has become more painful than funny: "Here's something. Southern Comfort! What is that, I wonder?" (115). The joke is the same, but the audience no longer laughs.

Another comic motif that turns tragic is Blanche's insistence on be-having like a southern lady in an environment ignorant of and even hostile to any such elegant manners. As she walks through the room where the men are playing poker in the play's last scene, Blanche says, "Please don't get up. I'm only passing through" (138). "Please don't get up" is an exact repetition of what she gaily says to the poker players in scene three when Stella and she return home before the game is over (48). On the earlier occasion Stanley's comeback emphasizes the comic inappropriateness of Blanche's expectation of gracious manners in his home: "Nobody's going to get up, so don't be worried" (48). Blanche's repetition of her earlier line underscores how she has been unwilling and unable to change her behavior to fit her new circum-stances. Her inability to change, however, is not only an example of Bergsonian comic rigidity but also expresses a tragic commitment to values and traditions—art, poetry, and music (72), "beauty of the mind and richness of the spirit and tenderness of the heart" (126)—that are not relevant in Stanley's world but are finer than anything that might replace them. Blanche's repetition of "Please don't get up" (this time most of the men do stand) superimposes on the audience's memory of the earlier comic exchange between herself and Stanley a sense of sad-ness and loss, reinforced by her self-deprecating addition "I'm only passing through." This tragicomic use of repetition with variation is typically Chekhovian.[6]

The most overtly comic elements in *Streetcar* are the exchanges be-tween Blanche and Stanley, such as the one I have just discussed, that underscore the oppositions between them and often take on the force of repartee. When Stanley asks Blanche how much longer she is going to be in the bathroom, she tells him, "Possess your soul in patience!"; Stanley quickly responds, "It's not my soul, it's my kidneys I'm wor-ried about" (102). This exchange, little more than vulgar verbal humor in itself, here represents the classic conflict between soul and body, the sublime and the grotesque, whose union, Victor Hugo suggested, pro-duces the modern genre of tragicomedy (Hugo 357-61). Stanley transforms Blanche's fine phrase and her spiritual, therapeutic use of the bathroom for cleansing that is symbolically regenerative (giving her "a brand new outlook on life" [105]) into a physical need to use the bathroom for purposes of evacuation. The spiritual sublime becomes the physical grotesque.

Since the sparring couple is a staple of romantic comedy, the relationship between Blanche and Stanley provokes both ready laughter and uneasy anticipation of their (quasi-incestuous) coupling. Their diverse comic styles, however, appropriate to the personality, attainments, and way of life represented by each, emphasize the unlikelihood of any rapprochement between them. Blanche's comedy is intellectual and playful, consisting in flirtation, conscious role-playing, and irony directed at others and also at herself, emphasizing at once her resilience and her vulnerability. Stanley's humor, by contrast, is always self-aggrandizing; it consists in physical horseplay (smacking Stella on the thigh to assert his ownership of her [48]), crude jokes dealing with bodily functions that draw attention to his own body, or literal-minded sarcasm that can be as cruel as it is funny. Stanley's aggressive humor can, of course, be interpreted as a mark of his own vulnerability.

Early audiences sympathized with Stanley because they identified with a working man defending his home from an invader who despises him and everything he stands for and because of the charm and sensitivity that Marlon Brando brought to the part (Clurman 72-80; Spector). They were prepared to laugh with him at Blanche's expense, as Stanley repeatedly takes her down a peg or two. He refuses to accommodate her fine airs or to flirt with her or to allow her to gain any sexual advantage over him; he reduces her fantasies to sober facts; and he sees through all of her pretenses, often in a wry, humorous way: "Liquor goes fast in hot weather" (30). As the play progresses Stanley's humor at Blanche's expense becomes more cruel. When Blanche corrects Stanley, saying that her millionaire is from Dallas, not Miami, Stanley undercuts her fantasy with the retort "Well, just so he's from somewhere!" (124). Their repartee pungently expresses the opposition between Blanche's fantasy world and Stanley's world of facts. Sometimes Williams develops this tragicomic opposition throughout a whole scene, creating a counterpoint between reality and fantasy, death and life. In scene seven Stanley plans to give Blanche a one-way ticket out of town, while offstage Blanche, happy for once in anticipation of seeing Mitch, sings "Paper Moon," a song about the make-believe nature of love and happiness. In scene eleven Blanche, depending on the kindness of strangers, leaves for a kind of death in the asylum, while the community of men play a game of poker with its implications of raw male sexuality: "This game is seven-card stud" (142).

The most important tragicomic opposition in the play is that between desire and death. Desire, says Blanche, is the opposite of death (120). Rather than constructing any such simple dichotomy between desire and death in *Streetcar*, however, Williams renders desire tragicomic and makes desire and death identical as well as opposites. Stanley, the "*gaudy seed-bearer*" (29), who smashed the light bulbs on his wedding night, who is forever taking off his shirt, and who plans to wave his "brilliant pyjama coat . . . like a flag" when he hears that his son is born (125), possesses a comic satyr-like sexuality that is life-giving when he impregnates Stella, but death-giving when he rapes Blanche. Blanche's sexuality seems to her an escape from death—from "the bloodstained pillow-slips" (119) of her dying relatives—but actually leads her to it. After a sexual encounter with a young male student, Blanche is sent away by her school principal, Mr. Graves. Arriving in New Orleans, she takes a streetcar named Desire, transfers to Cemeteries, and arrives at Elysian Fields. Both psychologically and symbolically, Blanche's sexual experiences lead her on a journey to death.[7]

According to Lyle Leverich, Williams "once said that desire is rooted in a longing for companionship, a release from the loneliness that haunts every individual" (347). So it is with Blanche. As Blanche describes her sexual promiscuity to the uncomprehending Mitch in scene nine, Williams powerfully elicits the audience's sympathy for the terrible loneliness and the need to forget the death of her husband and the grotesque, drawn-out deaths of her relations that drove Blanche into self-destructive "intimacies with strangers." Blanche's condition, to which her guilt for the death of her husband and her own desperate need have brought her, exemplifies a tragic boundary of the human spirit, worked out in psychosexual terms. However the need that drives Blanche is not to be explained simply in such terms. It is rather a more existential loneliness and a more metaphysical need that impel her and other Williams characters into self-destructive behavior. As Bigsby remarks, "The irony which governs the lives of his protagonists, whose needs are so patently at odds with their situation, is less a social fact than a metaphysical reality" (39). Bigsby finds in Williams's work a strong affinity with the "absurd."

Indeed, while the need that drives Blanche's sexual behavior retains its tragic and metaphysical force, Williams often presents the particular manifestations of her sexuality as comic and even mildly grotesque. The comedy of sex is most obvious in the scenes (three and six) in which Blanche plays with Mitch. The comedy of the two scenes arises out of the interplay between a knowing Blanche, who can flatter Mitch into believing in her "old-fashioned ideals" (91), and a fumbling Mitch, concerned about his jacket, his sweat, and his weight, who is easily dazzled by Blanche's charms. Some of Blanche's lines seem to convey a sophomoric wink at the audience, as when, knowing that Mitch cannot understand French, she asks him, "Voulez-vous coucher avec moi ce soir?" (88). In these scenes we laugh with Blanche. But in the scenes in which she tries unsuccessfully to play similar sexual games with Stanley, we are obliged to view her more objectively. Stanley induces the audience, if not quite to laugh at Blanche's expense, yet to become uncomfortably critical of her behavior. When Blanche sprays Stanley with her perfume, for example, he responds, "If I didn't know that you was my wife's sister I'd get ideas about you!" (41).[8]

Williams evokes an even more complex response to Blanche's behavior with the Young Man, who calls to collect money for *The Eve-*

ning Star (scene five). This tense scene, a reenactment of Blanche's tragic attraction to boys that cost her her teaching job, exists at the border of the terrible and the farcical. Williams uses expressionist techniques both to convey the drama Blanche imagines occurring and to comment on it. The visual and aural imagery of the scene is intensely sexual: it is dusk and *"a little glimmer of lightning"* plays about the building (82); blues music is heard in the background; Blanche asks the young man to light her cigarette. Though literally only a shy, polite newspaper boy who is comically eager to leave, the unnamed Young Man symbolically takes on the sinister role of Blanche's nemesis. In the list of characters the Young Man is referred to as a Young Collector, reminding us perhaps that everything, even the evening star (as Blanche jokes), must eventually be paid for. Blanche's overt desire for the Young Man threatens to disrupt any future she might have with Mitch; she only just manages to control herself and let the boy go with one kiss.

Despite the scene's disturbing quality, there is, nonetheless, an element of comedy in Blanche's self-consciously predatory use of *double entendres*: "You make my mouth water" (84), referring both to the young man and his cherry soda. Blanche herself is able to adopt a comic stance towards her own sexuality, and it is this self-awareness that gives a tragic dignity to her sexual obsessions. She mocks even the horror of her life at the Flamingo and Mitch's disgust with her promiscuity by satirically calling the hotel where she brought her "victims" the "Tarantula Arms" (118), an allusion that is lost on Mitch. This scene (nine) is quintessentially tragicomic. Williams makes Mitch's sexual obtuseness, at which we have previously laughed, destroy any hope Blanche might have for a secure future when, unable to see her as anything other than a whore, Mitch rejects her as unfit to be his wife. Blanche is finally destroyed by both Mitch's sexual diffidence and Stanley's sexual predatoriness, both of which Williams initially presents as comic.

The play's last scene, depicting the consequences of Stanley's rape of Blanche, counterpoints life and death in an even more disturbing tragicomic mix.[9] Blanche's mental breakdown is not, of course, a literal death, but Williams evokes the idea of death as at once absurd, terrifying, and in Blanche's imagination at least a prelude to resurrection. Blanche imagines dying at sea from "eating an unwashed grape" (136). Her fantasy of being "buried at sea sewn up in a clean white sack and dropped overboard—at noon—in the blaze of summer—and into an ocean as blue as . . . my first lover's eyes!" (136), spoken against the sound of the cathedral chimes, suggests purification, peace, and resurrection: "That unwashed grape has transported her soul to heaven" (136). This echo in Blanche's fantasy of one of the defining features of Renaissance tragicomedy—the resurrection motif—is given a certain objective warrant by the sound of the cathedral chimes, but it is also countered by the appearance of the Doctor and especially the Matron— "*a peculiarly sinister figure*" (139)—who have come to take Blanche to the asylum and whom Williams presents expressionistically as death figures.[10]

The play's contrary ending, depicting the life that "has got to go on" (133), in Eunice's words, is at best problematic, at worst another kind of death in life. *Streetcar* allows its audience to experience neither tragic catharsis from Blanche's destruction nor comic satisfaction that Stanley "does go on" with Stella. In fact, the continuation of their life together is the most appalling thing about the play's ending and in that sense more truly moral than the ending (in which Stella says that she will never return to Stanley) imposed by the censors on the 1951 film version. Stella implicitly knows that Blanche was telling the truth about Stanley's raping her, even though she also knows that in order to go on living with Stanley, she must not believe it. At the end we see her crying "*luxurious[ly]*" (142) with Stanley's hand in her blouse, a prelude to sex. But now more than ever sex seems to be a narcotic.[11] The ending of *Streetcar* is as horrifying, as disturbingly tragicomic, for Stanley and Stella as it is for Blanche. Though Blanche has "lost" and Stanley has "won" whatever game they were playing, the outcome for each remains ambiguous. Blanche may have found a terrible release in fantasy; Stanley's relationship with Stella is forever tarnished.[12] For the audience, even Stella's baby, who should be a sign of new life and hope (like the children who are reunited with and reunite their parents in Shakespeare's late tragicomedies), is symbolically linked through his blue blanket with Blanche, whose final outfit is "the blue of the robe in the old Madonna pictures" (135).[13] Thus the baby reminds us of Blanche's essential innocence and vulnerability and that his birth coincided with her destruction, and Stanley's.

In *Streetcar* Williams entertains such conventional elements of comedy as marriage, birth, and reunion but gives them all a tragic twist. The wished-for marriage (between Blanche and Mitch) is abortive, the birth occasions rape, and the reunion (of Stanley and Stella) remains horrifyingly ambiguous. Through these distortions of comic conventions Williams creates the moral and aesthetic discomfort that is a defining characteristic of tragicomedy.

Apart from obviating the problems in writing tragedy in the modern age, tragicomedy provided Williams with the most effective way to explore the darker regions of human sexuality since tragicomedy allows for the expression of both the painful and the absurd in sexual experience as well as the creation of a peculiar relationship between sex (carnal, life-giving, and thus comic) and death (tragic). Desire may be the opposite of death, just as comedy is the opposite of tragedy, but in *A Streetcar Named Desire* tragicomedy fuses an emotionally charged and psychologically acute symbiosis between them.

From *American Drama* 9, no. 1 (Fall 1999): 51-68. Copyright © 1999 by the University of Cincinnati. Reprinted by permission.

Notes

1. A shorter version of this essay was given at MLA in Toronto in December, 1997.
2. Williams's acknowledged master was Chekhov (Devlin 114). He was also impressed by the "quick interchange of comedy and tragedy" in O'Casey's *Juno and the Paycock* (Leverich 344).
3. On Williams's laughter see Leverich 112, 202, 240, 562.
4. Adler discusses the early critical reception of *Streetcar* as tragedy (47-50). See also the essays by Harwood and Cardullo ("Drama of Intimacy and Tragedy of Incomprehension"). Roderick discusses the play as tragicomedy but focuses more on the juxtaposition than on the integration of tragic and comic elements.
5. See Foster, "Ibsen's Tragicomedy: *The Wild Duck*."
6. See Foster, "The Dramaturgy of Mood in *Twelfth Night* and *The Cherry Orchard*."
7. For a discussion of the play's symbolism see Quirino.
8. For a good discussion of the sexual relationship between Blanche and Stanley, especially Blanche's sexual game-playing, see Davis (60-102).
9. Cardullo points to the importance throughout *Streetcar* of images of "birth and death, of rebirth and death-in-life" ("Birth and Death in *A Streetcar Named Desire*").
10. Schvey sees the end of the play as "an expression of spiritual purification through suffering" (109); Adler comments, "Blanche leaves the stage a violated Madonna, blessed by whatever saving grace insanity/illusion can provide" (46); and Schlueter points out that the John Erman film of *Streetcar* (1984), starring Ann-Margret and Treat Williams, ends with a view of the cathedral and the sound of its chimes, suggesting a "sacramental context for Blanche's wish for purification" (80). Leverich comments that Williams "used the passage from crucifixion to resurrection as a constant theme in his work" (582).
11. Williams describes Stella as exhibiting an "*almost narcotized tranquility*" (62) after a night of sex, following violence, with Stanley.
12. Bigsby comments, "Even Stanley now has to live a life hollowed out, attacked at its core" (46).
13. On color symbolism in *Streetcar* see Schvey. Cardullo provides a good discussion of the baby ("Drama of Intimacy and Tragedy of Incomprehension," 153, n.5).

Works Cited

Adler, Thomas P. *A Streetcar Named Desire: The Moth and the Lantern*. Boston: Twayne Publishers, 1990.
Bigsby, C. W. E. *Modern American Drama, 1945-1990*. Cambridge: Cambridge UP, 1992.
Burks, Deborah G. "Treatment Is Everything: The Creation and Casting of Blanche and Stanley in Tennessee Williams' 'Streetcar'." *Library Chronicle* 41 (1987): 17-39.
Cardullo, Bert. "Birth and Death in *A Streetcar Named Desire*." Kolin 167-80.

_____. "Drama of Intimacy and Tragedy of Incomprehension: *A Streetcar Named Desire* Reconsidered." Tharpe 137-53.

Clurman, Harold. *Lies Like Truth*. New York: Grove P, Inc., 1958.

Davis, Walter A. *Psychoanalysis, Modern American Drama, and the Audience.* Madison: U of Wisconsin P, 1994.

Devlin, Albert J. *Conversations with Tennessee Williams*. Jackson: UP of Mississippi, 1986.

Dürrenmatt, Friedrich. "Problems of the Theater." *Plays and Essays*. Ed. Volkmar Sander. New York: Continuum, 1982. 231-62.

Foster, Verna A. "The Dramaturgy of Mood in *Twelfth Night* and *The Cherry Orchard.*" *MLQ* 48 (June 1987): 162-85.

_____. "Ibsen's Tragicomedy: *The Wild Duck.*" *Modern Drama* 38 (Fall 1995): 287-97.

Harwood, Britton J. "Tragedy as Habit: *A Streetcar Named Desire.*" Tharpe 104-115.

Hugo, Victor. Preface to *Cromwell* (1827). *European Theories of the Drama*. Ed. Barrett H. Clark, rev. Henry Popkin. New York: Crown Publishers, 1965. 357-70.

Kolin, Philip C., ed. *Confronting Tennessee Williams's "A Streetcar Named Desire": Essays in Critical Pluralism.* Westport, CT: Greenwood P, 1993.

Leverich, Lyle. *Tom: The Unknown Tennessee Williams*. New York: Crown Publishers, 1995.

Pirandello, Luigi. *On Humor*. Introd. and trans. Antonio Illiano and Daniel P. Testa. Chapel Hill: U of North Carolina P, 1960.

Quirino, Leonard. "The Cards Indicate a Voyage on *A Streetcar Named Desire.*" Tharpe 77-96.

Roderick, John M. "From 'Tarantula Arms' to 'Della Robbia Blue': The Tennessee Williams Tragicomic Transit Authority." Tharpe 116-25.

Schlueter, June. "'We've had this date with each other from the beginning': Reading toward Closure in *A Streetcar Named Desire.*" Kolin 71-81.

Schvey, Henry I. "Madonna at the Poker Night: Pictorial Elements in Tennessee Williams's *A Streetcar Named Desire.*" *From Cooper to Philip Roth: Essays on American Literature*, edited by J. Bakker and D. R. M. Wilkinson (1980). Rpt. in *Tennessee Williams's A Streetcar Named Desire*. Ed. Harold Bloom. New York: Chelsea House Publishers, 1988. 103-109.

Shaw, Bernard. "Tolstoy: Tragedian or Comedian?" *The London Mercury* IV (1921): 31-34.

Spector, Susan. "Alternative Visions of Blanche DuBois: Uta Hagen and Jessica Tandy in *A Streetcar Named Desire.*" *Modern Drama* 32 (1989): 545-60.

Tharpe, Jac, ed. *Tennessee Williams: A Tribute*. Jackson: UP of Mississippi, 1977.

Williams, Tennessee. *A Streetcar Named Desire*. New York: New American Library, 1947.

Tragedy as Habit:
*A Streetcar Named Desire*_____

Britton J. Harwood

As the theater of Chekhov, Beckett, Pirandello, Ionesco, or Brecht may not, Tennessee Williams' *A Streetcar Named Desire* troubles us with the question of genre. Going no further than the language of the play, we find Williams' stage direction calling for Blanche to assume "a tragic radiance" (I, 406). Yet critical opinion is nearly unanimous that, if Williams intended his play to be judged in the terms of tragedy, it fails.[1] No one, on the other hand, has held that the play is one that makes the question of kind irrelevant. I mean to develop here the answer that *Streetcar* is intended, and ought, to be understood as a sort of *double* of tragedy, the "lurid reflection" of it (to borrow one of Williams' favorite directions in the play) rather than the thing itself—the inevitable continuation of a tragic action already past.[2] As a dramatic action in its own right, *Streetcar* recalls the tragic by redoing it in an ironic register.

The endings of many, if not all, great tragedies are deeply ambiguous. While this is not the place to develop that notion in detail, we can point to Lear, who realizes he is "a very foolish fond old man" only to convince himself at the very end that Cordelia still breathes; or Hamlet, who concludes that "no man knows aught of what he leaves," and yet enjoins Horatio to stay alive for a while to tell the correct version of Hamlet's "story." That is, notwithstanding the protagonist's discovery and the suffering that may attend it, he cannot stop saying or doing the very thing which, one way or another, is the very condition for his guilt.

When Blanche leaves the Elysian Fields, she allows the doctor "to lead her as if she were blind" (p. 418). That might recall the blinded Oedipus, ordered by Creon to go inside where he could not pollute the light of the sun. Yet Blanche enters the play as one who must already "avoid a strong light" (p. 245), her eyes bearing a "blind look" (p. 250). In scene nine, near hysteria, she concedes to Mitch that she has "had many intimacies with strangers." At her first entrance, however, she is already "faintly hysterical," protests too much her blamelessness for the loss of Belle Reve, is terribly fearful, sickens with the memory of her husband's death, and, at the opening of scene two, is in the first of the many hot baths meant to cleanse her from the "filthy tub" (p. 386) of Laurel. Even before Stanley asks her about Shaw (scene five), Blanche frankly admits to Stella that "brutal desire" has "brought me here" (p. 321). I am pointing out not that the action in *Streetcar* is static, but that its ending has certain things in common with its beginning. While not tragic, the action of *Streetcar* is unintelligible except as an analogy to tragedy, and its uniqueness lies in its taking its protagonist, already burdened with perception and guilt,[3] through an experience which has the structure but not the content of tragedy. Like other protagonists at the ends of plays, Blanche at the beginning of this one is unable *not* to recapitulate the stages of her crime. To describe the peculiar distortion which *Streetcar* is intended to work upon the mythos of tragedy, one must risk speaking of tragedy itself.

In tragedy, a hero is aware that he is impinged upon, his existence threatened from without by the blind sweep of an Other. This sense of impingement is signified at the outset—by the lameness which gives Oedipus his name, by Ahab's missing leg, by the "vicious mole" (*Hamlet*). This is to say that the hero experiences the Wholly Other in the boundaries which it sets. In *The Idea of the Holy*, Rudolf Otto writes that "The difference between the 'feeling of dependence' of Schleiermacher and that which finds typical utterance in the words of Abraham . . . might be expressed as that between the consciousness of *createdness* and the consciousness of *creaturehood*. In the one case you have the creature as the work of the divine creative act; in the other, impotence and general nothingness as against overpowering might. . . . [With *creaturehood*] we come upon the ideas, first, of the annihilation of self, and then, as its complement, of the transcendent as the sole and entire reality" (pp. 20 ff.). The source of this annihilation, the nature of this sole and entire reality, is often layered as deep in the poem as it is in the mind of the hero. Nearly eight hundred lines of *Oedipus Rex* have elapsed before Oedipus discloses the "desperate horrors" prophesied for him while he was still in Corinth. Most of *Absalom, Absalom!* is over before we learn that the adolescent Thomas Sutpen came to a sense of himself simultaneously with being turned away from a front door and run off the road. We are three hundred pages into *Tender Is the Night* before we learn of a moment when Dick Diver "realized that he was the last hope of a decaying clan." And it is the fifth act of *Hamlet* before we confront, with Hamlet, the man who has been making graves only since the day Hamlet was born. The hero tries to get out from under what threatens to digest meaning to its own absurdity, in the way that "your worm is your only emperor for diet." To be, which means to be conscious, is what he wants ("conception is a blessing," says Hamlet), and the hero's purpose, as a tragedy begins, is to secure his being by securing his consciousness, by translating flesh into word; by projecting and reifying an idea. So the hero not only moves to a place he imagines to be safe—Thebes, Sutpen's Hundred, Dick Diver's Tarmes, "the pales and forts" of Wittenberg, perhaps—but knows that he enjoys it because he acts in consistency with his idea, because he acts on what we may call his ethic. For Agamemnon and Orestes, this means to be just, for Sutpen to be white, for the protagonist of Ibsen's *Master Builder* to make homes, for Dick Diver "to be brave and wise." Hamlet can be a man provided he can be reasonable.

The action of a tragedy is the hero's purposing to be good and then discovering he has always been bad, that his reward for describing an ethic is to find himself guilty in precisely those terms. Agamemnon and Orestes behave compulsively and therefore unjustly, Oedipus finds he does not know himself, Solness burns his own home, Quentin finds himself possessed by the blackness that Sutpen tried to shut out, Dick Diver *inadvertently* cures Nicole by indulging himself with Rosemary. Thus the radical crime, the choice of human existence rather than "impotence and general nothingness," is discovered and understood as the hero's violation of his own ethic. The radical crime becomes understood with a precision that the crime itself—articulating an ethic as a haven for consciousness and therefore as a means for individual existence—has made possible. By trying to circumscribe such a haven, the hero initiates a process which leads to the discovery of criminality within the magic circle of his own consciousness. "I could be bounded in a nutshell and count myself a king of infinite space, were it not that I have bad dreams" (*Hamlet*). Self-knowledge is a crime against the Other; it is the Promethean light, the illusion of individual existence shining like the light and gold of Heorot. Self-knowledge being criminal, it is ironically punished with anagnorisis, self-discovery. At the end, the hero's self-loathing internalizes the Other, which he thought he had fled.[4] The annihilation which is our understanding of the Wholly Other becomes intelligible as guilt. This is the action of a tragedy.

It is part of the specialness of *Streetcar* that the protagonist's confrontation with the nature of the Other,[5] a confrontation which is logically prior to the hero's decision to be, is chronologically first as well. Blanche's insistence that she will wear "nice clothes" (p. 257), her bathing to feel "like a brand new human being" (p. 276), to get hold of herself and make "a new life" (p. 313), occur no earlier in the play than her expressed awareness of the Other. Her nervous joke about "the ghoul-haunted woodland of Weir" (p. 252)—only the railroad tracks—anticipates the locomotives that will roar by, making her crouch and cringe, just before she tells Mitch about her cruelty to Allan or just before she is raped. What she must "keep hold" (p. 250) of herself against is annihilation: "Margaret, that dreadful way! So big with it, it couldn't be put in a coffin! But had to be burned like rubbish! . . . the struggle for breath and bleeding" (pp. 261-62). The Wholly Other is the source of "Death—I used to sit here and she used to sit over there and death was as close as you are" (pp. 388-89).

The Other known by our impotence is (as Otto writes) both dreadful and fascinating. "These two qualities, the daunting and the fascinating, now combine in a strange harmony of contrasts. . . . The daemonic-divine object may appear to the mind an object of horror and dread, but at the same time it is no less something that allures with a potent charm, and the creature, who trembles before it, utterly cowed and cast down, has always at the same time the impulse to turn to it, nay even to make it somehow his own" (p. 31). Stanley's "drive" (p. 293) is, of course, exactly this "strange harmony of contrasts." First of all, Blanche feels Stanley as "Violence!" (p. 308). "Somebody growls—some creature snatches at something—the fight is on!" (p. 323). The streetcar leading to Cemeteries leads as well to the "red-stained package from a butcher's" (p. 244),[6] in which the bloodstained pillowcases of Belle Reve (p. 388) represent themselves. Stanley smashes things (p. 312), and at each noise, as he bangs around the flat, "Blanche winces slightly" (p. 328). She recognizes him as an "executioner" (p. 351) and his home as "a trap" (p. 409).

Blanche is nevertheless fascinated by Stanley. When she is alone she picks up his photo (p. 263), and, in the second scene, she flirts with him. If the terrified body, the shaking hand, is something to keep hold of, so is, from the protagonist's point of view, the impulse to make the Other somehow one's own: "A man like that is someone to go out with—once—twice—three times when the devil is in you. But live with?" (p. 321). In fact, since dread is the complement of fascination, not "to bed with him" (p. 319) is not to survive. The "date" which Stanley and Blanche have had from the beginning is a showdown because it is not a tryst.

It is tempting simply to accept Blanche's own account of her promiscuity. Desire being the opposite of death, she reacted to the decay of Belle Reve by going to the arms of young soldiers, much as Mrs. Maartens, in Aldous Huxley's *The Genius and the Goddess*, went to Rivers: "It's the line of a woman who . . . suddenly finds herself standing on the brink of the abyss and invaded, body and mind, by the horrible black emptiness confronting her. . . . She had to reestablish her contacts with life—with life at its simplest, life in its most unequivocal manifestations, as physical companionship, as the experience of animal warmth. . . . It was a matter of self-preservation" (p. 119). The soldiers sprawling "like daisies" on the lawn are in their own way "Flores para los muertos" (p. 389). Yet Blanche, who, in common with other tragic protagonists, intends to resist the intuitive or compulsive response, can be only vague to Mitch about her motives: "After the death of Allan—intimacies with strangers was all I seemed able to fill my empty heart with. . . . I think it was panic." The meaning for her of her own sexuality, however, once she has known the blinding Apollonian light (p. 354), derives from, rather than displaces, as we shall see shortly, the meaning of desire in that original Dionysian oneness, voiced in the blue piano and drums, where orgiastic joy and original pain flow endlessly into each other and reverse.[7] The basic character of the sexual for Blanche, then, is a "potent charm" inextricable from repulsive brutality, continuing to threaten her in New Orleans as it had defeated her illusion that Allan was "almost too fine to be human" (p. 364). Blanche's forebears strike at her both with their "epic fornications" and with the horror of their dying.

But Stanley is the Other with a difference. He is vile, not uncanny; sporadic and impromptu, not relentless. He is not only the antagonist, but a member of the chorus, moved in the first place, perhaps, because on the poker night he is getting only a cold supper; he is vain, childishly petulant, ready to lie to cover a mistake, proud to be typical. By arriving at the Elysian Fields in so compulsive a state as to perceive in its "commonness" the annihilation and filth she has known in Laurel both without and within, Blanche raises Stanley to consciousness and to vindictiveness, because she makes him ashamed. Blanche desperately wishes to be away from Stanley, as the tragic protagonist flees the Other. But her flight would have merely the *form* of tragedy, for Stanley is not a tragic phenomenon. Only the tragedy that, for Blanche, is already over could account for her dread in the presence of no more than the leader of the chorus, the captain of the bowling team.

The tragic protagonist, whose life is the Apollonian illusion of individuality,[8] makes consciousness of himself as an individual[9] contingent upon his being conscious of innocence of a certain kind—innocence, more exactly, upon his own terms. If Blanche were to discover something at the crisis of the action, clearly it would not be the knowledge of her own unchastity. Although she works to create for Mitch the illusion that she is a beleaguered virgin, she does not believe her own artifice. That is at least one sense in which she "never lied" in her heart (p. 387). When she tells Mitch she cannot let him do more than kiss her because she has "old-fashioned ideals" "she rolls her eyes, knowing he cannot see her face" (p. 348).[10] Only after the rape and her breakdown does she imagine that a trifle like an unwashed grape might be enough to transport "her soul to heaven" or that her body might bear scrutiny in the full light of "noon—in the blaze of summer" (p. 410). Otherwise, she uses hot water to give herself the physical sensation of innocence and is fully aware of her thirst for the innocence she lacks. When the newsboy tells her he drank a "Cherry" soda, she says: "You make my mouth water. . . . Come here. I want to kiss you, just once, softly and sweetly on your mouth! [She does so.] Now run along, now, quickly! It would be nice to keep you, but I've got to be good—and keep my hands off children" (pp. 338-39). The same thirst—guilt, that is—undoubtedly drew her to the seventeen-year-old boy in Laurel and thus brought her to New Orleans, where she must work so much the harder at her factitious virginity: "little breathless cries and peals of laughter are heard as if a child were frolicking in the tub" (p. 362).

Where the mythos of tragedy leads us to look for the protagonist to articulate the value that is critical for him, we find Blanche affirming a range of values, but with a banality that gives us again, as Williams intends, the structural feature evacuated of the tragic phenomenon. "Sorrow makes for sincerity, I think," she says (p. 298). While she declares she cannot stand "a vulgar action" (p. 300), the triteness of her "favorite sonnet" and of her "attempt to instill . . . reverence for Hawthorne and Whitman and Poe!"—together with her genteelness ("I brought some nice clothes to meet all your lovely friends in," "The Little Boys' Room is busy right now")—has a profound vulgarity of its own.

Although Blanche is genuinely in flight, the security sought against instinct by human self-consciousness—the security imaged for Nietz-sche in the high stage, above the orchestra and the dreaming chorus—is represented in *Streetcar* as something already lost. Blanche blesses the "Seven Sisters," the Pleiades, cozily going home "all in a bunch" (p. 342). But the stars, for whom no collections need be taken up, are out of the reach of this "poor relation"; and her own sister, "Stella for star," chooses for her the ironic security of an asylum. The lofty white columns have already been "lost," and Blanche's only crown is rhine-stones, "next door to glass"—assimilated, in fact, to the "Corones" for the dead (p. 388). Neither real security nor the possibility of innocence on which it depends is available to her from the beginning of the play; and therefore, despite the genuineness of her flight, the haven she de-scribes clinks like a counterfeit: "my sister—there has been *some* prog-ress . . . ! Such things as art—as poetry and music—such kinds of new light have come into the world since then! In some kinds of people some tenderer feelings have had some little beginning! . . . In this dark march toward whatever it is we're approaching. . . . *Don't—don't hang back with the brutes!*" (p. 323). What Blanche knows is that she must get away: hence the words she believes in are "progress," "march," "don't hang back!" The aim she posits, "such things as art—as poetry and music," is characteristic of the inevitably Apollonian tragic pro-tagonist; but it is an aim she does not believe in. It is expressed in the clichés of the high school English class she draws upon in "improvis-ing feverishly" to Mitch: "Physical beauty is passing. A transitory pos-session. But beauty of the mind and richness of the spirit and tender-ness of the heart—and I have all of those things—aren't taken away, but grow! Increase with the years!" (p. 396). It should have been no surprise when these speeches, spoken by Jessica Tandy, sounded "phony."[11] They serve well enough to isolate Blanche from the choral "commonness" (p. 351) of the French Quarter,[12] although they are doubtless to be associated with her "saccharine popular ballad" (p. 359)—another sample from her "heart-shaped box."

One reason she can be such a propagandist for these values at the same time she drinks heavily and takes "hydro-therapy" is that they are not the ethic she has violated, nor, in a more important way, is chastity. Obviously, she could not relieve her sense of guilt by talking all summer about the terms of it. The ethic which has been peculiarly hers, which she violated, and which, at points when she is in extremity in *Streetcar*, she obliquely reveals comes clearest where, among the eleven scenes of the play, one would expect the crisis—the sixth scene, when Blanche, drinking, on edge since Stanley mentioned Shaw, tells Mitch about her loneliness, and before that how she had fallen in love with Allan, who had come to her for help. "He was in the quicksands and clutching at me—but I wasn't holding him out, I was slipping in with him! I didn't know that. I didn't know anything except I loved him unendurably but without being able to help him or help myself. Then I found out" (p. 354). She recounts Allan's suicide, then "sways and covers her face." "It was because—," she says, "on the dance floor—unable to stop myself—I'd suddenly said—'I saw! I know! You disgust me. . . .' And then the searchlight which had been turned on the world was turned off again and never for one moment since has there been any light that's stronger than this—kitchen—candle . . ." (p. 355). Here her confession of responsibility for Allan's death is collocated exactly with the dim light in which, throughout the play, she hides herself. The years that now line her face, which is to say the cycles of guilt and flight which filled them, followed directly from her saying "I saw! I know! You disgust me." In self-loathing, she turns the sixteen-year-old girl that she was into the Tarantula, the female version of the older man in bed with Allan, repeating the act that disgusts her, then tries to escape by starting again with virginal boys.[13] Because it was she who extinguished the "blinding light," she feels every "naked bulb," now, as a merciless accusation. She tries to hide, not just her years and how she spent them, but what caused her to spend them that way. Not the deaths at Belle Reve extinguish the light, but the criminal knowledge which is death internalized.

Loyalty—standing by someone who needs help—is Blanche's

ethic. She speaks authentically of it in the matter of Belle Reve: "you are the one that abandoned Belle Reve, not I! I stayed and fought for it, bled for it, almost died for it!" (p. 260). Although Blanche fears the consequences if her Laurel reputation gets to New Orleans, the notion of being unchaste—present, for instance, in her expressed wish to get her hands on the newsboy or to sleep with Mitch—does not make her anxious in itself, for it is not the idea on which her existence depends. By contrast, she is "uneasy" (p. 259) and defensive about the loss of Belle Reve, for that trenches on the question of loyalty. She defends herself here at length because she can defend herself. Margaret and the others sometimes said "Don't let me go," and she did not reject them even if she could not stop them. She not only "Saw! Saw! Saw!" (p. 262) but "stayed." Nevertheless, this loyalty in a situation, however unpretty, where she could control herself can never remove from her experience her disloyalty to someone else who was "clutching" (p. 354) at her, whom she also "saw!"—and to whom she said "You disgust me."[14]

Blanche refers (obliquely again) to loyalty in telling Stanley that "when a thing is important I tell the truth" (p. 281). She has, in fact, had to make her way with lies ever since she told the truth to Allan, who did disgust her, after all. But truth, in addition to being a correspondence with the "facts," means fidelity, of course, as in "true blue" (which by no accident, I think, is the color Blanche cares most about). Where her talk of high culture wilts before the animal vitality of the Quarter, the ethic vital for her can be little better than aped: "Mitch is a buddy of mine," Stanley tells Stella. "We were in the same outfit together—Two-forty-first Engineers. We work in the same plant and now on the same bowling team. You think I could face him if—" (p. 365). Stanley calls "conscience" the "deliberate cruelty" with which he avenges an insult. "Deliberate cruelty," a frenzied Blanche will tell him later, "is not forgivable. It is the one unforgivable thing in my opinion and it is the one thing of which I have never, never been guilty" (p. 397). And this is true enough. Where there is deliberation in the rape ("Come to think of it—"), Blanche blurts out the three sentences to Allan ("unable to stop myself"). Allan, essentially a stranger who had depended upon her kindness, she betrayed with an undeliberated cruelty. Only the choice of an ethic is deliberate, however, not the violation of it. Perhaps there is no tragic protagonist whose crime is not compulsive, obscured. It is obscure because, often if not always, it precedes the ethical articulation which will bring it to light. The actual crime (as opposed to the discovery of it) happens before the protagonist posits the terms of it; likewise, conscious intention is clearly not, especially in Blanche's case, a precondition for guilt.

I have been showing, then, that the values explicitly and strenuously defended by Blanche in *Streetcar* ("poetry and music," "richness of the spirit and tenderness of the heart") are meant by Williams to be bogus, the "reflections," however, of the ethic in an antecedent tragic action. They stand to this metonymically, as effect to cause; for the ethic was, as in tragedy it always is, violated. The lies she must tell recapitulate the lie she was not loyal enough to live.

The structural feature of the discovery occurs where we would look for it, but the tragic content is again distorted, for Blanche makes the discovery to Mitch rather than experiences a "recognition" herself. Nor does it result in guilty anguish. To the contrary, Blanche, who is steadily punished from the beginning of the play for urging her imitation illusions, is embraced by Mitch and relaxes "in long, grateful sobs" (p. 356).

The fact of guilt is thus delayed, only to be transformed also. Blanche had reacted to Allan's death self-destructively, internalizing each new death, in effect, by taking another victim into the Tarantula Arms. Each feverish rehearsal of "softness and tenderness" (p. 354) in *Streetcar* glances at the ethic which was to have secured individual existence against dissipation of the "beautiful dream"; it points as well to the betrayal, which was to set death up within the circle of her own consciousness as guilt, expiated in *Streetcar* rather than diminished. That is, following scene six, where ironically the discovery is Mitch's, there is no accession of guilt, because that has been present, of course, since the beginning of the play. After the crisis—again ironically—guilt is displaced into external threats (the bus ticket back to Laurel, Mitch's accusations, Stanley's destruction of her hopes as not "a goddam thing but imagination!" and finally the rape). These punish her for having to "tell what *ought* to be truth" (p. 385), a necessity which results, as we have seen, from her disloyalty. "I hurt him the way that you [therefore!] would like to hurt me . . ." (p. 282). The mobilization of this vengeance is the plot of *Streetcar*. This overdetermines and distorts the reflection of the tragic action: the rape, which consummates the punishment, is also the distorted image of the tragic protagonist's accession of guilt. Raped by a man whom she once described as mad (p. 313), she internalizes, in the final scene, his madness. Thus, in this "doubling" of the tragic, she is more hysterical at the end than at the beginning but not more guilty.

Keats's nightingale ode, it is often suggested, begins where the urn ode ends, when a certain intensity of visual experience is no longer possible. The nightingale ode reproduces the ascent to "heaven's bourne" rather than realizes it, and the reproduction is unsatisfactory: "Adieu! the fancy cannot cheat so well/ As she is fam'd to do, deceiving elf." That unsatisfactoriness is, in part, the subject of the poem. This does not make the poem inferior to the urn ode. Only different. *A Streetcar Named Desire* begins where a tragedy has already ended. Its own action transposes the elements of tragedy into ironies, at the expense of the woman whose punishment takes her through a version of the tragic in which no real purpose or perception is possible. That in part is the subject of *Streetcar*, not tragic itself, but referring to tragedy, and generically unintelligible except through that reference.

From *Tennessee Williams: A Tribute*. Jac Tharpe, ed. 104-115. Copyright © 1977 by University Press of Mississippi. Reprinted by permission.

Notes

1. See, e.g., Signi Falk, "The Profitable World of Tennessee Williams," *Modern Drama* 1 (1958), 175; R. E. Jones, "Tennessee Williams' Early Heroines," *Modern Drama* 2 (1959), 218-19; Nancy M. Tischler, *Tennessee Williams: Rebellious Puritan* (New York: Citadel Press, 1961), pp. 273-74; J. N. Riddel, "*A Streetcar Named Desire—* Nietzsche Descending," *Modern Drama* 5 (1963), 423; John Gassner, "*A Streetcar Named Desire*: A Study in Ambiguity," in *Modern Drama: Essays in Criticism*, ed. Travis Bogard and W. I. Oliver (New York: Oxford University Press, 1965), pp. 375-77; and J. T. von Szeliski, "Tennessee Williams and the Tragedy of Sensitivity," in *Twentieth Century Interpretations of A Streetcar Named Desire*, ed. J. Y. Miller (Englewood Cliffs, N.J.: Prentice-Hall, 1971), pp. 65, 67.

2. Cf. E. F. Callahan, "Tennessee Williams' Two Worlds," *North Dakota Quarterly* 25 (1967), 62.

3. Cf. Roger Asselineau, "Tennessee Williams ou la nostalgie de la pureté," *Etudes Anglaises* 10 (1957), 440-41.

4. It would be possible to provide either a psychoanalytic description of this, in terms of the instinctual defusion consequent upon the child's introjection of the parent (cf. Freud's *The Ego and the Id*), or a phenomenological one, in terms of the movement from defilement to guilt (cf. Paul Ricoeur's *The Symbolism of Evil*); but there is no need to go into that here. No satisfactory psychoanalytic criticism of *Streetcar* exists, although Philip Weissman has a study of Blanche ("Psychological Characters in Current Drama: A Study of a Trio of Heroines," *American Imago* 17 [1960], 276-84).

5. Cf. Alvin Kernan's remark that Williams is convinced "there is a 'real' world outside and inside each of us which is actively hostile to any belief in the goodness of man . . .": "Truth and Dramatic Mode in the Modern Theater: Chekhov, Pirandello, and Williams," *Modern Drama* 1 (1958), 111.

6. Cf. Stanley's "licking his lips" (p. 323).

7. See Friedrich Nietzsche, *The Birth of Tragedy*, trans. F. Golffing (Garden City, N.Y.: Doubleday, Anchor, 1956), pp. 38-39.

8. See ibid., p. 56 and passim.

9. Cf. Gassner, p. 376; and Esther Merle Jackson, *The Broken World of Tennessee Williams* (Madison: University of Wisconsin Press, 1966), p. 299 (where she quotes Elia Kazan's comment on Blanche's "compulsion to be *special*").

10. "Blanche has no illusion about her illusions": Benjamin Nelson, *Tennessee Williams: The Man and His Work* (New York: Obolensky, 1961), p. 143.

11. See Harold Clurman, *Lies Like Truth* (New York: Macmillan, 1958), p. 79.

12. Cf. the stage direction at the beginning of scene four: "There is a confusion of street cries like a choral chant."

13. Cf. John J. Mood, "The Structure of *A Streetcar Named Desire*," *Ball State University Forum* 14: 3 (1973), 9; and R. B. Heilman, "Tennessee Williams: Approaches to Tragedy," *Southern Review* (n.s.) 1 (1965), 772.

14. Cf. the way in which Lord Jim's deliberately coming to Doramin to be shot does not substitute, in Marlow's eyes, for his having deserted the *Patna* when his imagination overwhelmed him.

"Stanley Made Love to Her!—By Force!"
Blanche and the Evolution of a Rape_____

John S. Bak

> Arise and fly
> The reeling Faun, the sensual feast;
> Move upward, working out the beast,
> and let the ape and tiger die.
> —Alfred Lord Tennyson, *In Memoriam*, CXVII.25-28

Despite its successful run on Broadway, *A Streetcar Named Desire* was not immediately optioned, as most profitable Broadway plays were, by any of the Hollywood studios.[1] Hollywood had never before attempted a film of such an adult nature and failed to see how *Streetcar* could be "retooled into a family movie," packaged, that is, for a mass audience.[2] As R. Barton Palmer explains,

> With its revelation and dramatization of sexual misconduct, its delineation of a horrifying descent into madness, its portrayal of women driven and even controlled by desire, the play, in fact, offered themes that could not be accommodated to any Hollywood schema.[3]

When *Streetcar* was finally optioned by Warner Brothers, Williams was thus not entirely surprised by the demand for scriptural changes that were to become, as Nancy Tischler describes, "the crux of the conflict involving numerous individuals and organizations, from the producers, directors, and advisers to the Hays office and the Roman Catholic Church."[4] Whereas the theatre venue—where *Streetcar* proved its staying power—had already contained the seeds of its own "censorship" through the high cost and limited availability of tickets, the cinema, which was more democratic by nature, had to rely on less economic forces to police its moral character. The Production Code of the Motion Picture Association of America (MPAA), then headed by Joseph Breen, exercised that force by demanding that Williams and Kazan expurgate from the film version "the homosexuality of Blanche's late husband, her evidently aggressive sexual appetite, and Stanley's violent rape of his wife's sister."[5]

This history of *Streetcar*'s censorship has been well documented, with Tischler, Palmer, and Phillips among others describing in various ways how Williams and Kazan effectuated Breen's demands in altering the play for the screen, particularly the rape scene. As their research has shown, Williams, all too familiar with the economics of Hollywood morality (he had, after all, been recently "sold" there by his agent Audrey Wood for $250 a week in April 1943), was ready to accept some of the necessary changes to the script and therefore did little to derail efforts to remove references to homosexuality (these could be reinserted anyway through a queerly encoded language of private allusions and metaphors) or to keep Stanley from being punished for his act by the film's end, which he is when Stella apparently leaves him.[6] Williams refused, however, to budge on the rape. In his letter to Breen, for example, Williams explained his reasons for maintaining the integrity of the climactic rape scene, which, if excised, would decenter *Streetcar* not only dramatically but, more importantly, *thematically*: "The rape of Blanche by Stanley is a pivotal, integral truth in the play, without which the play loses its meaning. . . ."[7] To soften it under censorship laws, then, would be to diminish, if not lose entirely, *Streetcar*'s and Williams's souls, for as Palmer posits, "the rape was the plot's central event"—remove it and "the story, and the characters whose development it traced, would no longer make any coherent sense."[8]

None of these critics, however, has convincingly treated the reasons why Williams felt the rape was so essential to the film in the first place. There were, to be sure, potentially dozens of ways Williams and Kazan could have had Stanley exact his vengeance on Blanche in the film, dozens of ways they could have articulated Blanche's tragic suffering at the hands of her executioner. Given that Williams had fought less over removing references to Allan Grey's homosexuality, and with it much of the evidence of Blanche's guilt, it would appear that he was less concerned with getting across to his film audience why Blanche was in New Orleans than he was with what had forced her to leave. So what was it about the rape that Williams felt could not be compromised?[9]

The answer, I believe, lies more in Blanche than it does in Stanley, and more in Williams's esoteric understanding of the word "rape" than in his audience's collectivist definition of it. We (readers, viewers, and critics alike) have perhaps focused too much on Stanley and the reasons behind his actions than we have on Blanche and why Williams felt her rape was inescapable.[10] One of the reasons behind this truth lies in our having been visually influenced by performance, particularly Brando's in Kazan's interpretation of the play as it moved from the ephemeral stage to eternal celluloid. As Gene Phillips posits, "When he finally assaults her in the play's climax . . . , it is the action of a desperate man equipped with more brawn than brains to cope with a calculating creature who declared war on him when she first stepped across his threshold."[11] Once the rape was acted out on stage or on screen by a real Stanley, it forever left the realm of the symbolic, which is what Williams had envisioned from the start, and irrevocably entered the mimetic. In other words, as Stanley passes from Williams's literary tool to the audience's dramatic antihero/antagonist, we are forced into either decriminalizing the rape (as Kazan had effectively done) or acknowledging its tragic consequences (which Harold Clurman, director of the road version of the play, had enacted) because we are naturally incapable or unwilling to recognize or accept any of the private, metaphysical intentions Williams might have attached to the heinous act.

There exists, then, a continental divide between Williams's epistemology and our positivist/phenomenological readings of the rape, and to transcend the mimetic we would be obliged to read it in a way entirely unorthodox (if not simply dangerous) to social order and convention: as an act of symbolic liberation of a trapped spirit (represented by

Williams's ubiquitous bird imagery) locked within the confines of a sexual body (his cat or tiger, in perpetual war with the bird). It is precisely this reading of Blanche's rape that I wish to undertake here. To understand fully the polemics of the rape in the film, however, necessitates our returning first to the manuscripts themselves, whose story testifies to the struggle Williams had first in understanding who Blanche was—the sexual predator or the spiritual victim—and then, once having found her, determining what consequences that dialectic would generate in her (madness) and on those around her (social warfare). The complex evolution of *Streetcar* would prove the rape to be more a working through of one person's metaphysical debate than a climactic end to a dramatic *pas de deux*—less victim/aggressor and more warrior/facilitator, which is wholly the reason why Williams allowed no substitution when the play was adapted to the screen. This essay, then, examines *how* Williams arrived at the rape as the sole means of providing dramatic closure to his morality play, though, once chosen, moved the play irreparably from the symbolic toward the mimetic; a future essay will attempt to explain *why* Williams chose rape and how the play's potential message became distorted once the signifier left the page and found itself first on the stage and then on the screen.[12]

"Looking for Mrs. Goodbar": Blanche in the Early Manuscripts

When Williams began drafting scenarios that would eventually become *Streetcar*, there is little doubt that he was concerned with Blanche's thematic development before her dramatic one, for in his *Memoirs* Williams writes,

Almost directly after *Menagerie* went into rehearsals I started upon a play whose first title was *Blanche's Chair in the Moon*. But I did only a single scene for it that winter of 1944-45 in Chicago. In that scene Blanche was in some steaming hot Southern town, sitting alone in a chair with the moonlight coming through a window on her, waiting for a beau who didn't show up. I stopped working on it because I became mysteriously depressed and debilitated and you know how hard it is to work in that condition.[13]

That was not, research has since proven, Williams's first version of *Streetcar* or of Blanche. Several critics have in fact traced the evolution of *Streetcar* and Blanche from the one-act plays in the 1945 collection *27 Wagons Full of Cotton*—which were written as early as 1941— three or four years prior to Williams's recollection—through to the manuscript drafts of *Streetcar*, which Williams had begun as early as 1944.[14] While Vivienne Dickson argues that *Streetcar* developed through the manuscripts—with changes in locale, character name, and nationalities—from a romance to a tragedy,[15] Deborah Burks posits that Williams created Blanche first but that the play did not find its strength until Williams had heard Brando read for the role, discovering for the first time a humanism in Stanley that would counter his antago- nistic bestiality.[16] Despite their individual conclusions, both studies suggest that, while factually inaccurate concerning dates in his *Mem- oirs*, Williams was precise in his assessment of *Streetcar*'s conception: Blanche drew the focus of his attention first, and Stanley second, with Williams inverting the story of Genesis in having his Adam created only to seduce Eve. Being more holistic in their approach to explaining the genesis of *Streetcar*, however, neither of these studies attempts to trace how Blanche was conceived or why Williams labored so inten- sively toward her inevitable rape, two ideas essential to comprehend- ing the play's final moments.

Williams was often, more consciously than not, a revisionist con- cerning facts about his own past, which (like many of his characters) he viewed in equal balance between pleasure and pain. Yet, while the facts may have changed, the truth behind them invariably remained. So even if his *Memoirs* do not recount the first version of *Streetcar*, he re- membered it as such probably because it contained the essential truth behind *Streetcar*'s meaning for him, or at least the initial message it purported to carry, as evidenced by the early manuscripts. There are five extant manuscripts of the early drafts of *Streetcar*, dating from the (ca.) 1944 "Scenario for a film" entitled "A Street-car Named Desire" (presumably written after Williams left M-G-M) to before the fall of 1946 with a draft called "The Primary Colors."[17] In each of these five drafts, including the fragment "Electric Avenue" and "Go, Said the Bird!," the locus of change for Williams is not just that of Blanche, with Stanley developing simply from "a good-natured 'pretty-boy' to the potentially explosive 'strong silent type,'"[18] but more specifically her gradual progression from an anachronistic southern belle, whose gentility is accosted by the virile landscape of modernity, to a *femme fatale* whose sexual appetite is at once gilded with spiritual affectations and at other times sublimated by a puritanical superego.

In the three-page draft "A Street-car Named Desire," for example, Caroline Krause, a twenty-five-year-old junior high school teacher in New Orleans who suffers from an inferiority complex, is given advice from a doctor to go "away somewhere" and "get married."[19] Marriage, he tells her, will stop her "insomnia—palpitations—acute and unreasonable self-consciousness—feeling panic—nerves. . . . All without any physiological basis" [2]. Learning that the school has lost five eligible bachelorette teachers already "to matrimony" [2], Caroline becomes so depressed that by the end of the school year she does leave to "go away somewhere" [3] but not for reasons of matrimony. A stock character in the Williams canon (we find her equivalent in Miss Jenny Starling of a later Williams screenplay, *All Gaul Is Divided*, and in Dorothea Gallaway from *A Lovely Sunday for Creve Coeur*), Caroline is distraught most by the fact that the marriage question itself is the cause of all of her problems:

But there isn't anybody, there hasn't been. I don't see how there could be. I'm not attractive enough. And even if I were pretty—I'm dull—and stupid! I can't talk to people! I don't know how to laugh. [3]

Lacking self-confidence and charisma, Caroline is more like Alma Winemiller than Blanche here, especially given that her nervousness and southern gentility signal the beginnings of a mental breakdown. Sexual desire is, of course, present here, though only alluded to in the title of the scenario, as well as in the novel Caroline reads while riding the streetcar: *Forever Amber*, Kathleen Winsor's scandalous 1944 novel about sixteen-year-old Amber St. Clare's sexual prowess in seducing and sleeping her way to becoming Charles II's mistress.[20] However, innocent romance is not yet sexual desire and Caroline only resembles Blanche in her occupation and in its relationship to her virulent fear of spinsterhood.

Similarly, in another early draft, "Electric Avenue" (whose composition is also ca. 1944, around the time of *The Glass Menagerie*'s short run in Chicago from December 1944 to March 1945), Blanche, Stella Landowski's sister, simply "has suffered."[21] Because the three pages constitute the "LAST SCENE" of this playlet, we are not sure as to what has caused her suffering. All that Williams makes clear is that Eddie Zawadski, ignoring his best friend's Stanley's demand that he abandon Blanche, has come to end Blanche's suffering by taking her as his wife, making this one the only draft to end happily: "You need somebody. I need somebody, too" [3]. Eddie eases her mental unrest by accepting whatever dastardly deed she is guilty of. "In spite of– <all>—? {—even with—?}" [3], she says and goes to the window and tells Eddie that she is looking for "God's face in the moon!" [3] to thank Him for Eddie's forgiveness: "I didn't know there was—going to be so much—pity . . ." [3]. What would eventually develop full-blown into Blanche's flesh/spirit dialectic, however, is only inchoate here, despite our never knowing what prompts it. The implication, both in the electricity of the title and in Blanche's demureness in revealing all that prompts Stanley from having his best friend stoop to accepting Blanche as his wife, is simply sexual indiscretion; but Williams makes Blanche here appear to be nothing more than a fallen woman who is given, as this draft's epigraph from *Prometheus Bound* by "Aeschuyles" [*sic*] prepares us for, "*blind hope* . . ." [3].

After establishing Blanche's fear of spinsterhood in these first two drafts, Williams begins experimenting more fully with her potent sexuality. "Go, Said the Bird!" written in December 1945, has Blanche Shannon and George (Mitch) discuss, among other things, her superiority complex, her tenuously hidden strip-tease behind the open portieres, her gay lover, and her affair with the high school student. Yet the locus of Blanche and George's conversation is on sex: how Blanche was once promiscuous at Blue Mountain High School but is now frigid toward George: "You're lily white? . . . So is mud!"[22] Despite her coyness, Blanche's sexuality is latent, as George denotes in his description of her undressing in full view before him:

When I met you the night of the poker party and you took off your shirt with the portieres open and turned around and smiled at me with the light on you—

I thought, My God—This woman is a tiger! . . . The tiger was a sweet young English teacher, visiting her sister for her summer vacation. Butter wouldn't melt in that sweet mouth of hers. [2]

In this fragment, Blanche acquires the nature of the tiger she will embody in *Streetcar*—vibrant sexuality. She is not ashamed of her past encounters and tells George, "what people do with their bodies is not really what makes good or bad people of them!" [3] She will not give in to George's sexual desires, though, until he asks her to marry him, which he won't now because "laid end to end" Blanche's lovers would "stretch all the way from here to Frenchman's Bayou!" [5].[23] To further connect her sexuality with the cat, Williams writes in the closing scene just before the curtain descends: "(. . . ON A FENCE NEARBY A CAT SCREECHES. BLANCHE LEANS SUDDENLY FORWARD AND IMITATES THE SCREECH)" [6].

Although no real reference to the bird exists in the fragment that makes up "Go, Said the Bird!" there is one in its title, where the reference to the bird indirectly suggests Blanche's spiritual side, one which

Williams would repeatedly use throughout his canon, especially in *Streetcar*. Moreover, Williams often used epigraphs, as he did colorful and informative titles, to provide clues to decoding his cryptic plays, just as he does here.[24] Therefore, the title and epigraph to this draft, "Go, said the bird, go, go, go, said the bird! Human/ kind cannot bear very much reality" (a misquote of T. S. Eliot's "Burnt Norton" that was later dropped and then found its way instead into *Ten Blocks on the Camino Real* and *Camino Real*), further recall the spiritual fight Blanche encounters with her sexually feline side evidenced in the script, with the indirect reference to reality here denoting that such a struggle often implies a rupture between the rational and irrational mind.[25]

Within these first three drafts, Williams apparently shifted his view of Blanche away from the spiritually distraught teacher and more towards the sexually vibrant siren. And yet the dialectic is always somehow present, with Williams simply inverting the spiritual/sexual subtext through the titles of his drafts. If, for instance, spiritual piety is Caroline's lot in life in the film scenario "A Street-car Named Desire," Williams informs us that a burning sexuality inevitably lurks unconsciously behind that identity, just as the licentious Blanche Shannon in "Go, Said the Bird!" belies a liminal purity. Within each of these fragments, however, that duality is inscribed solely in reference to Blanche. The various characters who incarnate Stanley Kowalski either support or judge Blanche's many avatars, but do little beyond providing advancement in the plot. Williams was closer to writing a medieval morality play here than he was a twentieth-century tragedy, with little to no dramatic conflict vehicling the philosophic import, as it does in *Streetcar*. Nor is there any significant sexual or spiritual struggle between the Stanley and the Blanche in the fourth, untitled draft, though for the first time Stanley's character begins to signify a sexual presence in the story.

Set in Chicago, this three-page manuscript (the third page has only "Rosa:" at the top) begins exploring more recognizably the conflict of

Streetcar, especially the love triangle and the marriage question, though the most significant changes are found only in the character names (Lucio, Rosa, and Bianca for Stanley, Stella, and Blanche, respectively) and nationalities.[26] Lucio (the "light" that will eventually attract/burn Blanche the moth), Rosa, and their visiting relation Bianca, Rosa's "older unmarried sister" [1] from Baton Rouge, are Italian, and Williams makes much of this fact in his stage setting, the first of its kind here to make any significant literary contribution to the story. The scene is described as a claustrophobic two-room "south side flat of an Italian American menage in Chicago" with a "Latin-Catholic richness of color contained in such items as a painting of the Virgin, prayer candles in crimson glasses, a silk kimona [*sic*] sprinkled with red poppies hanging on the chair . . ." [1]. In addition to the symbolic setting, we are finally given insight into Lucio's (Stanley's) character, who halfway through the fragment becomes Ralph (which, Johns notes, suggests that Williams was already working through the conflict of nationalities). Despite his "weakly good-looking" appearance and "playful tenderness" amounting to "effeminacy if he were not Italian" [1], he wears a sexually-signified "silk bowling shirt with the name of his firm's team, The Busy Beavers, applied in scarlet" [1]—a prurient detail Williams no doubt adds to foreshadow Bianca's past. Bianca, however, again an "old maid school teacher" [2] who cannot secure herself a husband, resembles Blanche only in what she is and not really in who she is. Though the characters are still nothing more than tools to work out plot and locale, and Blanche's inner dialectic is suggested only in Bianca's failing beauty and desire to be married,[27] the stage signification of sexual tension between Blanche and Stanley is explicit and begins preparing for their conflict. In each of the subsequent drafts, in fact, Williams moves closer and closer to exploiting their mutual sexuality, with Blanche's spirituality all but getting pushed aside.

Williams quickly abandons the locale and characterization of Lucio, Rosa, and Bianca in his fifth draft, now set in Atlanta and comprising thirty-two pages of similar character traits and interaction between

Stella and Ralph and between Blanche and Howdy/Mitch. Though the first two fragments of this draft reflect a nonsequential revision process (using Mitch in one and Howdy in the other) and have some variance in plot, the third fragment of this draft is cohesive and entitled "The Primary Colors." Blanche's surname is now Collins, like Lucretia Collins in *Portrait of a Madonna* (*Streetcar*'s closest one-act predecessor), and although there are several noteworthy changes in the series of these early drafts that are important to *Streetcar*, the one of significance here is Blanche's clearly established sexuality and direct promiscuity toward Ralph (Stanley). Though Blanche falls prey to Stanley in *Streetcar*, Ralph here is the victim of Blanche's overt sexual aggression.

Still an "old maid school-teacher," Blanche is preparing for a date with Mitch. Though not entirely Blanche's ideal suitor, Mitch at least "isn't <Irish> {common!} like Ralph.[28] She sees her sexuality fading, however, and realizes that this will be her last attempt at marriage, an institution which she feels will at once secure her reputation and preserve her innocence (that is, sexual intercourse is sanctioned through marriage and thus eliminates any sense of religious guilt). And yet, at the end of this first fragment, after Stella and Ralph (whose antagonism toward Blanche in *Streetcar* is here mere cajolery) have left for the evening, Blanche sits patiently for Mitch to arrive, waiting to tell him that she will marry him (though she is still hesitant about her decision). As Blanche goes to the window to sit in her chair,

(RIGHT OUTSIDE AN ALLEY-CAT RAISES A LONG NOCTURNAL HOWL.)
(BLANCHE LEANS SLOWLY FORWARD, HER WHOLE FIGURE TAUT LIKE A CAT ABOUT TO SPRING. THEN SHE TWISTS HER MOUTH DOWN AND IMITATES THE CRY OF THE CAT.)
(LONG AND HIDEOUSLY!) [24; cf. 13]

This stage direction, and Ralph's earlier jibe that Blanche leaves the apartment smelling like a "cat-house" [24] after she primps for her date, clearly signifies her latent feline sexuality, though Williams returns to the Blanche of before—the prudish spinster afraid of sexual commitment. Sex, the flesh, is for her only a means to ensnaring a husband, which is now indirectly a way for her to preserve her delicate spirit. But her artistic refinement and haughtiness only further ostracize her from a potential mate.

This sexuality becomes more pronounced when, in the second fragment of this fifth draft, Williams continues the scene with Blanche and her suitor (now called Howdy) after Stella and Ralph have left. Blanche's nervousness is again poignant here as she tells Howdy, "I'm out of my mind" [28], though her mental capacity is far more stable here than it will be in *Streetcar*. After some uncomfortable laughter about his new job on the "precision bench of the spare parts department" [25]—a position Blanche feels is beneath her desire for social status—they start into the Southern Comfort, "a *lick-cur*" [27], as Howdy says, which gets them drunk. Released from her inhibitions through the effects of alcohol, Blanche winds up in bed with Howdy, and the scene ends with Stella and Ralph discovering them in the apartment. What Williams was searching for here, it seems, is the balance between Blanche's sexuality and femininity: she is not as coarse as Howdy but realizes that at twenty-seven (and this is her birthday), her chances at marriage are diminishing. While she learns that sexuality need not be conditional, we are still left wondering how her desire for social status will accommodate Howdy's blue-collar status.

Blanche's sexuality, couched in her mimicry of the cat before Mitch's/Howdy's arrival, becomes less obtuse in the third fragment of the fifth draft (the only fragment that contains the title "The Primary Colors," where in his stage directions themselves Williams refers clearly to Blanche's sexual overtures to Ralph Stanley, as he is now called). "Pale, refined and delicate," though "charged with with [*sic*] plenty of that blue juice which is the doves of Aphrodite's or anyone's car!" [2], Blanche is slowly integrating her flesh and spirit. As she had done in the previous fragment, Blanche takes a bath to cleanse away her fleshly corruption; afterwards, she demands white clothing and a white handkerchief [5], the purity of which also identifies her as the moth/soul of *Streetcar*. Moreover, Williams begins fleshing out Ralph here, having him rebuff Stella's sexual advances and behave uxoriously toward Blanche. The antagonism that will electrify Blanche and Stanley's sexual attraction is not yet apparent, however; instead, Williams chooses to symbolize that eventual encounter, albeit now mutual, through the signification of colors, hence the fragment's title.

For example, after her bath and before the scene blacks out, Blanche enters wearing a "BRILLIANT SCARLET SILK KIMONA [*sic*]," while Ralph has on his "VIVID GREEN SILK BOWLING SHIRT" [6]. After some playful banter, Blanche says to Ralph, commenting upon the nature of the color of their clothing, "We're like a stop-light, aren't we? Red and green!" [12]. Just prior to this sexual play, however, Williams establishes the innocence of their attraction. With Stella preparing for a night out with Eunice and Blanche wanting into the bathroom to retrieve her "finger-nail scissors" (the tiger claws that the matron nurse in the final lines of *Streetcar* says need trimming), we next hear about Blanche's love for both Stella and Ralph and that she will be leaving them soon since Mitch has asked her to marry him (though she is still uncertain in accepting the offer since his job, still "on the replacement bench—in the spare parts department" [10], lacks the prestige she desires in life: "I don't want to slip in the world. I want to improve myself" [11]). Only once Stella leaves does Blanche utter her comment about their clothing. The effect here is of Williams working through the unconsciousness of Blanche and Ralph's attraction to show that nothing was premeditated (an important development toward the rape). In another version of the scene, Williams writes,

> *Blanche:* "What a charming costume. . . . Green! And Red!
> Like a stop-light!"
> *Ralph:* "What's red?"
> *Blanche:* "My—Kimona [*sic*]."

Ralph:	"Like a stop-light?"
Blanche:	"Yes!"
Ralph:	"Or a go signal?"
	(Pause) [32]

Blanche answers him silently as she lets him come up "VERY CLOSE TO HER, EXTENDING THE CIGARETTE" [33]. In this version, Williams attributes for the very first time to Ralph a hint of culpability in his attraction to Blanche, while continually maintaining Blanche's invitation to his advances. Moreover, we begin to see the dichotomy of Blanche sincerely emerging, where her talk of purity and higher aspirations seems in earnest despite her dominant sexuality.

In these early five drafts, then, Blanche's sexual nature is clearly established, as is the cat imagery that will eventually accompany it in the final play. Again, near the end of third version of the draft, after Stella leaves her alone for the evening with Ralph and tells them to have fun, Blanche says, "Oh, I am sure to have some fun—that's all I'm sure of" [13]. As Blanche retreats to the window,

(AN ALLEY CAT, JUST OUTSIDE, RAISES A LONG NOCTURNAL HOWL.
(BLANCHE TWISTS HER MOUTH DOWN AND IMITATE'S [*sic*] THE CAT'S CRY, LONG AND HIDEOUSLY. [13]

As for her spiritual side, Williams continually insists on her artistic nature, her repeated baths, and her need for things white and unsoiled. Though late in entering the storyline in these early drafts, however, Blanche's sexuality now far outweighs her spirituality. In the subsequent drafts, those coming from the penultimate version of *Streetcar*— "The Poker Night"—Williams would look to refining her spiritual side so as to make its dialectical relationship with her instinctive sexuality more pronounced. Yet Williams would be troubled by this dialectic: knowing now who Blanche was, and understanding Ralph's/Stanley's role within her dialectical struggle, Williams did not yet know how that dialectic would be worked out through their mutual attraction.

Prometheus *Un*bound:
Stanley and the Development of the Rape

By late 1945, then, though not in the fashion that it would become, the cat and the bird imagery accompanies Blanche's budding southern dialectic[29] (as Stanley's ape imagery would his primitiveness), which transforms this story from the Shakespearean romance of Bianca and Lucio in the slums of Chicago to the metaphysical battle between flesh and spirit in the sultry Vieux Carré of "The Primary Colors." Had Williams intended *Streetcar* from the start to end in Blanche's final submission to the one man who breaks her, then the rape could understandably be interpreted as the polemic that some critics have branded it. But the ending did not come easily for Williams, despite his experimentation with it elsewhere as a viable dramatic possibility.

In fact, in the now-famous letter to his literary agent Audrey Wood, dated 23 March 1945—more than two years prior to completing *Streetcar*—Williams's proposal of three possible endings reflects his continued uncertainty:

One, Blanche simply leaves—with no destination.

Two, goes mad.

Three, throws herself in front of a train in the freight-yards, the roar of which has been an ominous under-tone throughout the play.[30]

This letter suggests Williams's conscious effort to resolve Blanche's dilemma, one that he had explored fully in the drafts of the past year or so as well as in the one-act plays from *27 Wagons Full of Cotton and Other Plays*; and just as he had found it difficult to resolve the dialectic there, Williams would struggle to find that resolution in the drafts of *Streetcar* for the next two years. Only by strengthening Stanley's sexuality and instilling fear in Blanche of her own potency did Williams recognize that the rape was the only dramatic solution to the thematic dilemma he had confronted in Blanche.

Williams had explored his first proposed ending in "The Primary Colors," then again in a few early fragments of Williams's next draft, "The Poker Night" (what Johns calls the "morning after" scenes), where Williams experiments with the result of this attraction. Whereas before it was Blanche who was the aggressor, here it is finally Stanley, though Blanche's disinterest in fighting him is evidenced through her lackluster attempt to keep him at bay and in her eventual (and even passionate) response to his advances. In one three-page sketch, for instance, after having had a sexual encounter that is closer to sexplay than rape, Ralph says, "I can't see you and me and Stella all in two rooms together after last night."[31] Blanche agrees and decides to leave so as not to create unnecessary tension between the two of them. Then, Ralph congratulates Blanche on putting up a good "fight <that any man could be proud of>," and Blanche responds, "A trapped human being will always put up a fight" [2]. What sounds like rape, though, soon blurs into seduction, for Blanche brings to the surface her unconscious desire for Ralph to take her sexually:

Blanche: "Yes?—What about last night [*sic*]"

Ralph: "In fifteen years of experience—"

Blanche: "I stand alone?"

Ralph: "Like nothing—a man—could dream of—"

Blanche: "Ha! Since we're exchanging bouquets, let me add this one. Everything's been a preparation for you in <what else> what I've gone through, also! I am really surprised the walls are still standing. There was one moment when I thought we were lying out-doors halfway between this crazy old world and the moon! (THEY BOTH ALUGH [*sic*] A LITTLE.) I guess that was the moment when I—scratched you. . . ." [3][32]

Even in this repeated attempt at the first ending, albeit more fully realized than the innuendo which closes "The Primary Colors," the rape is still less an act of Ralph's sexual violation and more their liminally-desired mutual attraction, with Blanche being only predictably coy to his sexual advances.

Williams must have soon recognized that this recipe for desire was more melodramatic than tragic, and needed to submerge Blanche's desire more so as to make her not only theatrically believable for an audience but also morally acceptable. Thus, in another two-page fragment from scene ten of "The Poker Night," Blanche now expresses her disgust for Ralph, though her words, then her actions, belie her conscious desires. Ralph, equally irate with and sexually charged by Blanche's elitist reproaches, begins advancing toward her threateningly, saying, "<Didn't you know that?> We've had a date with each other from the beginning! . . . Didn't you know that!"[33] Ralph's "(EYES AND TEET<C>H CATCH THE GLARE" while Blanche "RETREATS TOWARD THE WINDOW)":

(SUDDENLY SHE THROWS HER FISTS UP IN THE AIR AND SHAKES THEM CRAZILY WITH A SHRILL, TORMENTED OUTCRY). . . . Yes, yes, yes, yes, yes! [2]

As Johns points out, Blanche in this scene, as in several others, is "evidently aroused to erotic heights by aggression and violence": "Ralph overcomes Blanche with physical force, but she responds passionately after a fierce struggle against him."[34] As with the last fragment discussed above, there is some driving force bringing Blanche and Ralph together, and that destiny is not entirely unwanted or undesired by either, but since Williams moves it out of the plot and into the realm of the symbolic or at least the subconscious, he begins opening the play up to higher levels of artistry.

That destiny, which perhaps also begins hiding Williams's stronger social message in the play, is realized only once in all of the extant manuscripts. On the verso of two title pages entitled "The Passion of a Moth"—exhibiting once more Williams's insistence that Blanche carry a fragile, spiritual nature along side her sexual one—are various attempts at displaying Blanche's phantasm of being the Madonna of the Modernist Christ, one who successfully integrates the clash of opposing worlds (hers and Stanley's) and dialectical conflicts (flesh and spirit certainly, but also past and present, time and timelessness, etc.). In this fragment, Blanche accepts Stanley's gift of a bus ticket for her birthday, as well as "a couple of ten-spots on the dresser."[35] It is the morning after their love-making, and Blanche is preparing to leave, though she has "no plans whatsoever!" [verso 1]. After delivering her "unwashed grape" monologue (in holograph, thus Williams's first draft of her speech, though here it is delivered romantically to Stanley whereas in the play it will be spoken to Eunice and Stella at the end to signal her madness), Blanche pontificates on what her life might bring her. Though Stanley has left the room without her knowing it, Blanche continues to tell him:

(Suddenly laughing) You know what I've just thought of? This unholy union of ours may not have been fruitless. I may bear you a son. That strikes me as being in the realm of probability. (Laughs) I'll bear you a son. I'll creep in some lightless corner or drop in a ditch somewhere and bear you a child that will be more beast than human.—Because our collision, that awful crashing together, could not result in anything more than a beast or less than an angel. And this, this angelic monster coming to be, will rise out of smoke and confusion to clear it away. He will clear it all away. He will clear it all, all away. All the confusion, all the brutality, all the sorrow, [sic] will be washed off and we will be shining again!—What shall we call him? We'll call him Le Fils de Soleil—the Sun's child! [. . .]
    And I, the anonymous drab who was his mother—will be lost in the crowd about the—colisseum! [sic] Ha-ha!—Proudly smiling with tears on her ravaged face. . . . [. . .] But now I've got to get packed—and be going—somewhere. . . . [verso 2]

As this is the end of the fragment, with the curtain falling just after a final stage direction describes the forces of modernism in the form of the locomotive outside the window, it reveals in shocking clarity how Williams saw Blanche and Stanley's sexual encounter not in mimetic terms but rather in symbolic ones, not as theatrical movement but rather as divine (or at least determinist) intervention.

This ending, like each of the attempted endings prior to it, suggests that Williams labored to resolve Blanche's dialectic through an act of the flesh, though it was her spirit that preoccupied him the most. Yet rape was simply not within the realm of possibilities Williams imagined his play would likely end; Blanche desired, first consciously then not, her and Stanley's encounter too much for it to prove licentious. He would begin experimenting more with Blanche's unconscious desire, brought to the surface only after Stanley awakens it through his conscious lust for her. In another four-page fragment of "The Poker Night," for example, written on the verso of the typescript for the 1943 story "The Angel in the Alcove," Blanche describes precisely what Johns says of all of these early drafts, that is, what "started as rape ended in satiety"[36]:

> Remember you took me, [*sic*] It wasn't I that took you. So if you got somewhat more than you bargained for, Mr. Kowalski—If you hadn't suspected a lady could be so <awful> {violent}—(could give such a wild performance when aroused)—try to remember the way it started, not I but you, putting dynamite under the tea-<pot> {kettle}.[37]

The reason why the rape had not yet become what it would be in *Streetcar* is that Blanche, simply put, is still the stronger of the two sexually, and therefore could not be "broken" by Ralph's/Stanley's first passive then active advances. Williams's difficulties in "The Poker Night" would continue until the moment he recognized that his answer to ending Blanche's dialectic lay in a sexually stronger Ralph/Stanley and a more frightened Blanche.

The third option stated in Williams's letter to Audrey Wood, in which Blanche throws herself in front of a passing train, is never realized in writing. Williams must simply have known early on that Blanche's inner-strength was life-affirming and not life-terminating, which is partly why she is helpless in resolving her dialectic by herself. In the second ending, though, Williams would find his solution and would work arduously to achieve it. In a world of illusion, one Blanche tried to make New Orleans into with her candles, paper lanterns, and liquor, one where all Stanley Kowalskis become Shep Huntleighs, creatures like Blanche DuBois can flourish. And the perfect illusion is one that only the mind can create for itself. Blanche, incompatible with either world, must coexist in both. But since she cannot deny Stanley's reality (which holds that wildcat in her, that *animus* of her spirit, in chains), she cannot wholly accept Shep's illusion either (despite all that it promises for her). If she could permanently cleave in her mind these contradictory worlds, leaving her wholly the bird, the *anima* forever freed from the harsh realities of the Kowalski world (for she never could exist solely as the wildcat, not in her time anyway, nor would her guilt allow for it), then she could live forever in stasis, which for her is not an undesirable existence. All that was left for Williams to decide was what, thematically and dramatically speaking, would finally push an already demented women further into madness—the rape.

Not until he began envisioning Stanley's raw sexuality, then, did Williams see what sex could do with respect to Blanche, how Stanley's character could function beyond being her dramatic foil. Once he discovered this, Williams began weaving Stanley's sexuality into the fabric of his dramatic tapestry. Therefore, in subsequent attempts to find the right balance between them, Williams increased Ralph's liability in the rape and further removed Blanche's conscious duplicity. Their attraction is still there, but Blanche is now more frightened by him than before. In one late sketch of "The Poker Night," for example, after she and Ralph had their torrid encounter, Blanche comments about the scratches she has left on his back, to which Stanley responds,

"Scratches all over like a tyger [*sic*] clawed me!"[38] It is at first ambiguous as to whether these marks were due to her passion or her repulsion. In another fragmented dialogue on the verso of this same sketch, it is now Stanley who declares sole responsibility for the result of their desire:

> You know, I admire you, Blanche. You got into a tight corner and you fought like a wild-cat to get back into the open. I was a son of a bitch to stand in your way. Protecting Mitch? Hell, I didn't care about Mitch. I wanted you for myself is the truth of the matter. Did you know that?[39]

Similarly, in a late version of scene eleven, which Williams crossed out and then left directions, either to himself or to a typist, to insert an emended page of new dialogue, Eunice and Stella are talking about Blanche's claim that "Stanley made love to her!—[. . .] . . . by force!"[40] In that inserted page, Williams added that Stella does not want to believe Blanche's story, but she cannot deny that his "pyjamas [*sic*] are torn to shreds and his shoulders and back are covered with scratches as if a wild-cat had clawed him" (121). Whereas Williams had in these last fragments unquestionably strengthened Stanley's role in the rape, there was still missing something in Blanche to counter Stanley's aggression: to remove her sexuality entirely and make Stanley the dominant aggressor and her the helpless victim would be to undo all of the complexities Williams had been building up in her character. In other words, to replace Blanche's sexuality with Stanley's would be to simplify her nature and to privilege melodrama over tragedy.

Williams had found his missing element, curiously enough, again in Blanche's spirituality. Whereas Williams had first envisioned Blanche as a nervous, man-hungry spinster whose genteel sensibilities aspired toward the spiritual, and then only gradually developed her strident sexuality (shaping her into a *femme fatale*) all the while increasing Stanley's, Williams could no longer make Blanche truthfully repel the encounter with her nemesis for purity's sake alone: she simply desired

Ralph/Stanley too much to be repulsed by his advances. Yet if the answer to the play's resolution lay precisely in Blanche's fear of sexuality all the while proselytizing it (but, as we have just seen, dramatizing that fear solely through its relationship to Stanley's strength would diminish the play's tragic overtones), then making Blanche afraid of her own sexual nature to the point of desiring its elimination would satisfy the needs Williams had in both establishing her tragic stature and justifying Stanley's role in finally bringing that stature about. By the time he began refining "The Poker Night," then, Williams exploited Stanley's newfound purpose and turned Blanche's fear symbolically inward and dramatically outward: whereas before she had openly celebrated her sexuality, she is now frightened by it and looks for ways in which to counter, control, and finally extirpate it.

In a late fragment of "The Poker Night," for example, the same one that finally depicts Ralph as the "GAUDY SEED-BEARER" who "SIZES WOMEN UP AT A GLANCE, WITH SEXUAL CLASSIFICATIONS,"[41] Blanche is now frightened by the screeching cat, as she would be in *Streetcar*, rather than imitating it, as she had done before. In another thirteen-page scene, a cat screeches outside; frightened, Blanche asks Stella what the cry was. Though Stella assures Blanche that it was "just—cats," Blanche shows disdain toward them: "(with distaste) Cats!"[42] So averse now to the sexual force that controls her and is shaping her into the animal that she identifies Stanley as, Blanche gradually descends into madness. With this final twist in her character, Williams justified Blanche's paradoxical repulsion toward and complicity in Stanley's rape: since she is the "tiger," she cannot deny her desire towards his bestial kind, but as she now detests the fact that modernist man/woman is forever slouching toward Caliban rather than rising toward Belle Reve, she can equally feel repulsed by desire itself.[43] Stanley appears, then, as her welcomed executioner, making her both victim and victimizer in her manipulation of Stanley into raping her, that is, in killing the sexuality in her that has hindered her aspirations of purity.

Williams understood the dialectic he was developing in Blanche, for even in one of the last drafts of scene five of *Streetcar* (ca. 25 August 1947), he wanted to make clear how Blanche should be read. Here, in a stage direction following Stanley's discovery of Blanche's sordid past in Laurel (which would eventually be cut from the final version), Williams explains the balance in her character that he was seeking:

> This scene is a point of balance between the play's two sections, Blanche's coming and the events leading up to her violent departure. The important values are the ones that characterise [*sic*] Blanche: Its function is to give her dimension as a character and to suggest the *intense inner life* which makes her a person of greater magnitude than she appears to have [*sic*] on the surface.[44]

So conscious was he of Blanche's struggle between flesh and spirit, past and present, and desire and death (Stanley's job was at one time a mortuary goods salesman) that Williams devoted the majority of his attention to developing her character.

Thus when Blanche and Stanley have their infamous confrontation near the end of *Streetcar*—considering all that Williams attempted, discarded, then refined in the drafts—we begin to see that it is less the case of Blanche fighting Stanley, and more the manifestation of her sexual energy, threatened with extinction, struggling for its survival all the while her spiritual nature is looking skyward.[45] With respect to this interpretation, Blanche in this final version of the rape sounds more like the bestial tiger that Stanley calls her, slowly backed into a corner, than a woman fighting to remain dignified in an incredibly demeaning situation. When Stanley says to her, "Come to think of it—maybe you wouldn't be bad to—interfere with," Blanche shouts, "Stay back! Don't you come toward me another step or . . . [an] awful thing will happen!" (1.401). That "awful thing" becomes the cat in her lashing out with its symbolic claws—the jagged edges of the broken bottle. Curiously, Blanche, now armed, does not say that she is dangerous but that, as the raised hair and pinned-back ears of a cat alert to, she is "in danger!" (1.401). It is fitting here that Stanley should say moments before raping her, "Tiger—tiger! Drop the bottle-top! Drop it! We've had this date with each other from the beginning!" (1.402), for he is addressing Blanche the cat, whom he is about to kill and whom the doctor's nurse must eventually declaw with her scissors.[46]

Conclusion

The rape that brings *Streetcar* to its climax, then, was certainly not an afterthought, nor did Williams envision it as a way to portray Blanche's innocent victimization at the hands of a nefarious individual or an indifferent society. Stanley does destroy Blanche in many ways when he rapes her, but *Streetcar*'s controversial rape scene is more the thematic confluence of Blanche's inability to sequester her own sexual attraction toward Stanley than it is the dramatic climax of their visceral attraction. Since she fails to cope with her dialectical dilemma alone, Blanche must end it; since she lacks the inner strength to end it in denial and Mitch fails to provide her with that strength, Blanche turns to Stanley, whom she has known all along to be her executioner. The rape in the play frees as it demeans, extirpating for her all the desires of the flesh so that her needs of the spirit can be actualized. Therefore, while the rape functions dramatically as a horrifying act of violence (the point upon which most critics have focused), Williams presents it thematically as the neutralizer to Blanche's personal struggle brought on by the debilitating effects of her southern dialectic.

To be sure, by the time he completed the abundant sketches that constitute "The Poker Night," Williams had refined Blanche's dialectic and Ralph's role in ending it. Having traveled a long way from the "weakly good-looking" and "playful tenderness and vivacity which would amount to effeminacy" of Lucio to the Ralph of "The Poker Night" who possesses "TRAITS OF AN INDIVIDUAL TOTALLY ANTIPATHETIC,"[47] or the psychologically fragile and socially inept

Caroline Krause to the metaphysically divided Blanche, Williams succeeded in constructing a play that delicately balances social with psychological readings. From Lucio/Ralph came Stanley, the ignorant savage of the animal kingdom who kills out of instinct. We can hate him no more than we can the fox for breaking into the hen house. From Caroline/Bianca came Blanche, the sexually divided neurotic of the spiritual kingdom whose loss of her cat-like nature is celebrated in the release of her bird-like spirit.[48]

In his 1963 essay "T. Williams's View of T. Bankhead" for *The New York Times*, Williams all but declares this when he writes, "I don't suppose anyone reads 'Streetcar' anymore, but if they did, they would discover that Blanche is a delicate tigress with her back to the wall."[49] That "wall"—the rape—necessitates its direct association with the sexual nature she possesses that put her there. Remove the "wall," and we remove not only the sense of *how* she got there but also the *why* of its necessary transgression. In closing his letter to Joseph Breen in a final attempt to convince the censors not to cut the rape scene from Kazan's film adaptation of *Streetcar*, Williams wrote,

> But now we are fighting for what we think is the heart of the play, and when we have our backs to the wall—if we are forced into that position—none of us is going to throw in the towel! We will use every legitimate means that any of us has at his or her disposal to protect the things in this film which we think cannot be sacrificed, since we feel that it contains some very important truths about the world we live in.[50]

Being backed into a corner is an essential part of life; having the strength to fight one's way out, no matter what the reason, is not just a sign of strength but also of resolve, be it one's metaphysical trauma or one's commitment to delivering the truth. The rape in *Streetcar*, however we understand it for ourselves in our world, was for Williams Blanche's truth.

From *The Journal of American Drama and Theatre* 16, no. 1 (Winter 2004): 69-97. Copyright ©
2004 by Martin E. Segal Theatre Center. Reprinted by permission.

Notes

1. A shorter version of this article first appeared in a collection of essays prepared for French students taking the *CAPES* and *Agrégation* exam.

2. Gene D. Phillips, *The Films of Tennessee Williams* (Philadelphia: Art Alliance, 1980), 81. See also his "Blanche's Phantom Husband: Homosexuality on Stage and Screen," *Louisiana Literature* 14, no. 2 (Fall 1997): 36-47.

3. R. Barton Palmer, "Hollywood in Crisis: Tennessee Williams and the Evolution of the Adult Film," *The Cambridge Companion to Tennessee Williams*, ed. Matthew C. Roudané (Cambridge: Cambridge University Press, 1997), 214.

4. Nancy Tischler, "'Tiger—Tiger!': Blanche's Rape on Screen," *Magical Muse: Millennial Essays on Tennessee Williams*, ed. Ralph F. Voss (Tuscaloosa and London: University of Alabama Press, 2002), 52. Tischler devotes her entire essay to precisely the problems of the rape scene on film, comparing it first to its "conjugal rape scene" (54) predecessor in the 1939 film *Gone with the Wind*, then providing more detailed information about the behind the scenes maneuvering to bypass the Hays office and the Production Code censors, including an analysis of playwright Lillian Hellman's requisitioned revisions of the film's script.

5. Palmer, in Roudané, 215.

6. Stella leaves Stanley at the end of the 1951 film version, fleeing to Eunice's flat as she had done the night of the poker party. Yet in *Streetcar*'s 1994 director's cut Kazan restored the Production Code's expurgated footage of the original ending, which intimates that Stella's flight might again be short-lived.

7. Qtd. in Phillips, 82.

8. Palmer, in Roudané, 218.

9. Nearly half a century's academic criticism on *Streetcar* has repeatedly asked this question, which often led to two other perennial questions: with whom, then, are we to sympathize at the end, and, because this question is so difficult to answer, is the resultant ambiguity an artistic failure on Williams's part? The majority of scholarship on *Streetcar* addresses one question, the other, or both. Simply put, *Streetcar* criticism had become bifurcated between those who saw *Streetcar* as a social play about the struggle between Blanche and Stanley, and those who saw it as a psychological play about Blanche's sole contention with herself. In terms of the social reading of the play, critics have felt that the rape was a metaphor of the North's ravenous assault on Southern agrarianism during Reconstruction, Stanley, an obvious mouthpiece of the New South, destroying the Old South's false pretensions and literally fertilizing it with a new breed of carpetbagger mercantilism. For those reading *Streetcar* psychologically, the rape was the destructive culmination of all realistic social forces against the nonrepresentational imagination of one of Williams's famed fugitive kind.

10. What, for instance, motivates him, since an objective correlative for his sexual

impropriety was never established earlier in the play, and since (and more importantly) his wife was simultaneously giving birth to their child, of which he felt earnestly proud?

11. Though he does not wish to "justify Stanley's rape of his sister-in-law" but rather "to explain it" (73), Phillips in a significant way echoes what essentially Kazan himself had initiated more than half a century earlier.

12. This essay, entitled "*A Streetcar Named* Dies Irae: Williams and the Semiotics of Rape," is nearing completion.

13. Tennessee Williams, *Memoirs* (Garden City: Doubleday, 1975), 86.

14. Lyle Leverich suggests that even by November 1939, when Williams was completing *Battle of Angels*, he already had *Streetcar* or, more accurately, Blanche, in mind: "have an idea for a new long play—*rather*, a character for a new long play—in New Orleans—Irene—." See his *Tom: The Unknown Tennessee Williams* (London: Hodder & Stoughton, 1995), 332.

15. Vivienne Dickson, "*A Streetcar Named Desire*: Its Development through the Manuscripts," *Tennessee Williams: A Tribute*, ed. Jac Tharpe (Jackson: University Press of Mississippi, 1977), 154-71.

16. Deborah G. Burks, "'Treatment Is Everything': The Creation and Casting of Blanche and Stanley in Tennessee Williams' '*Streetcar*,'" *Library Chronicle of the University of Texas at Austin* 41 (1987) : 16-39.

17. Concerning all dates surrounding the composition of *Streetcar*, I refer to Sarah Boyd Johns's excellent 1980 dissertation, "Williams' Journey to *Streetcar*: An Analysis of Pre-Production Manuscripts of *A Streetcar Named Desire*," Ph.D. diss., University of South Carolina, 1980. Though a bit different from Burks's stemma of and commentary on the drafts, Johns competently traces the development of the pre-production drafts of *Streetcar* not to suggest Blanche's literary ancestry but to provide a chronology to and theory behind the play's construction. I also spent time at the Harry Ransom Humanities Research Center at the University of Texas at Austin studying the manuscripts and thus cite here from the manuscripts themselves, respecting all of Williams's spelling and grammatical conventions, as well as his dramatic use of punctuation (particularly ellipses and dashes). Any of Williams's deletions or emendations made in the text, either in type or in holograph, are surrounded by < > or { }, respectively. Any editorial changes I include are enclosed in square brackets.

18. Johns, 16. Stella and Mitch (called Howdy and George at various times) remain relatively consistent throughout these early drafts, acting only as foils to Blanche as she journeys through her psychological maelstrom. Only in the penultimate draft, "The Poker Night," is Stanley's character developed and his relationship with Blanche precariously balanced, suggesting from the start that Williams was concerned first and foremost with Blanche and her dialectic long before he began grappling with Stanley's character.

19. Unpublished typed manuscript fragment, "A Street-car Named Desire (Scenario for a film)," n.d., pp. 2, 3, Harry Ransom Humanities Research Center (hereafter HRHRC), University of Texas at Austin, Texas. Further page references to this draft are cited parenthetically in the text. Page numbers given within square brackets indicate that no page number appears on the manuscript page.

20. *Forever Amber* was so popular in America that, despite (or because of) being banned in Boston for its raciness, it was the best-selling novel of the 1940s. Blanche reads this, along with Mitchell's *Gone with the Wind*, in a very late fragment of scene five in *Streetcar*. See unpublished typed manuscript fragment, "[A streetcar named desire: Scene V]," n.d., pp. 1, HRHRC, University of Texas at Austin, Texas. At other times, Blanche tells Stella she wants a man "who has read a couple of books, not just <only the Mother Goose book and> Forever Amber." See unpublished typed manuscript fragment, "[A streetcar named desire: Scene]," n.d., pp. 1, HRHRC, University of Texas at Austin, Texas; cf. unpublished typed manuscript, "A streetcar named desire (A play)," Tccms, with A inserts [2 pp.], T inserts [15 pp.], and A emendations on 15 pp., n.d., pp. 62, HRHRC, University of Texas at Austin, Texas.

21. Unpublished typed manuscript fragment, "[A streetcar named desire] Electric avenue: last scene," n.d., pp. 3, HRHRC, University of Texas at Austin, Texas. Further page references to this draft are cited parenthetically in the text.

22. Unpublished typed manuscript fragment, "[A streetcar named desire: Scene IX]," n.d., pp. 2, HRHRC, University of Texas at Austin, Texas. Further page references to this draft are cited parenthetically in the text.

23. In an even later version of "The Poker Night," Williams uses this reference again, though altered, to show not only how prodigious were Blanche's lovers, but also how proud she is of her sexual exploits. For when Mitch says that Stanley told him that if he laid "every mother's son" she seduced from "feet to forehead, they'd stretch all the way from here to Lake Pontchartrain," in other words "about three miles." Blanche, now drunk, laughs and replies, "No, further! . . . Further than that. His estimate is too modest. The men who've enjoyed me, the strangers to whom I gave pleasure, would pave a glittering highway from here to—Mobile!" See unpublished typed manuscript, "A streetcar named desire (A play)," Tccms, with A inserts [2 pp.], T inserts [15 pp.], and A emendations on 15 pp., n.d., pp. 109, HRHRC, University of Texas at Austin, Texas.

24. As Delma E. Presley and Hari Singh write, "The epigraphs to Tennessee Williams' plays provide insights usually ignored in critical discussions of his works" and are "helpful clues for the interpreter of each play" (2). Since epigraphs to Williams's plays always suggest the work's major theme, the theme of the final version of *Streetcar* has allusions to Hart Crane's poem "The Broken Tower." As this is the case here, early epigraphs to *Streetcar* allow us to trace Williams's reworking of his theme, displaying for us that his sympathies in *Streetcar* obviously lay from the start with Blanche and her spiritual nature. See Delma E. Presley and Hari Singh, "Epigraphs to the Plays of Tennessee Williams," *Notes on Mississippi Writers* 3 (Spring 1970): 2-12.

25. Unpublished typed manuscript fragment, "[A streetcar named desire] Go, said the bird! (A play)," T title page, pp. 1, HRHRC, University of Texas at Austin, Texas. Johns believes this separately filed title page is meant to accompany the six-page fragment entitled "Scene IX" discussed above, presumably because both cite the character name "Blanche Shannon," one not found elsewhere in any of the other manuscripts.

26. Unpublished typed manuscript fragment, "[Streetcar named desire (early form)]," n.d., HRHRC, University of Texas at Austin, Texas. Further page references to this draft are cited parenthetically in the text. Johns also dates this fourth draft from

around December 1944 to March 1945, during the Chicago run of *The Glass Menagerie*.

27. For a brief analysis of how the characters here compare with Shakespeare's Bianca in *The Taming of the Shrew* and Lucio in *Measure for Measure*, see Joan Wylie Hall's "'Gaudy Seed-Bearers': Shakespeare, Pater, and *A Streetcar Named Desire*," *Notes on Contemporary Literature* 20, no. 4 (September 1990): 9-11.

28. Unpublished typed manuscript fragment, "[A streetcar named desire] The primary colors (A play)," n.d., pp. 22, HRHRC, University of Texas at Austin, Texas. Further page references to this draft are cited parenthetically in the text.

29. Although the "southern dialectic" is my neologism, its traditions date back to the Fugitives from Vanderbilt and are encountered in nearly every significant southern hero/heroine of the writers of the Southern Renaissance. Drawing from what southern historian W. J. Cash called the "Cavalier thesis" in his *The Mind of the South* (1941; reprint, New York: Knopf, 1970), the southern dialectic adds a southern twist to the Platonic search for Truth through duologue and Hegel's essentialist science of synthesis. This dichotomous nature of the South had a lasting impact on how Williams viewed the world around him, for, as he wrote of himself in 1947, "there was a combination of Puritan and Cavalier strains in my blood which may be accountable for the conflicting impulses I often represent in the people I write about." See his *Where I Live: Selected Essays*, ed. Bob Woods and Christine R. Day (New York: New Directions, 1978), 58.

30. Tennessee Williams to Audrey Wood, 23 March 1945, HRHRC, University of Texas at Austin, Texas.

31. Unpublished typed manuscript fragment, "[A streetcar named desire: Scene]," n.d., HRHRC, University of Texas at Austin, Texas. Further page references to this draft are cited parenthetically in the text.

32. This long speech by Blanche is marked between brackets in ink with the word "cut" handwritten in the right margin. On the verso of page one is handwritten the following dialogue:

—What is the matter with my back?
—Scratches!
—Scratches all over like [*sic*] tyger [*sic*] clawed me!
—[illegible]
—Now, I just want to get dressed and get out of here.
—That's an old story, my dear. [verso 1]

33. Unpublished typed manuscript fragment, "[A streetcar named desire: Scene X]," n.d., HRHRC, University of Texas at Austin, Texas. Further page references to this draft are cited parenthetically in the text.

34. Johns, 102-03.

35. Unpublished typed manuscript fragment, "[A streetcar named desire] The passion of a moth (A play in ten scenes)," n.d., verso p. 1, HRHRC, University of Texas at Austin, Texas. Further page references to this draft are cited parenthetically in the text. The trouble in reading and citing from this fragment is that Williams reused typing paper liberally, even if there was something already written on one side, which might

have nothing to do with what he was at present writing. That is the case here. Williams experimented frequently with various versions of the same scene, and all of this was done on the verso of a title page of previous draft. HRHRC catalogued both the title pages and the fragments as it deemed them independently relevant to discerning *Streetcar*'s evolution.

36. Johns, 17.

37. Qtd. in Johns, 108.

38. Qtd. in ibid., 105.

39. Unpublished typed manuscript fragment, "[A streetcar named desire: Scene X]," n.d., p. 2, HRHRC, University of Texas at Austin, Texas. Further page references to this draft are cited parenthetically in the text.

40. Unpublished typed manuscript, "A streetcar named desire (A play)," Tccms (132 pp.) with A inserts (2 pp.), T inserts (15 pp.) and A emendations on 15 pp., n.d., pp. 120-21, HRHRC, University of Texas at Austin, Texas. Further page references to this draft are cited parenthetically in the text.

41. Unpublished typed manuscript fragment, "[A streetcar named desire]," composite Tms/inc (57 pp.) with A emendations on 22 pp., n.d., HRHRC, University of Texas at Austin, Texas. Citing page numbers from this composite series poses immense problems as the scenes and pages are mixed together without much order.

42. Ibid.

43. Benjamin Nelson writes, for example, "If Blanche is a moth woman in the tradition of Laura Wingfield and Matilda Rockley, she is also a tiger" (143). Nelson, though, is referring to Blanche's "fierce desire . . . for life" and not to any dual nature in her character (143). See his *Tennessee Williams: The Man and His Work* (New York: Obolensky, 1961). In an interview later with Joanne Stang in 1965, Williams commented specifically on Blanche's feline nature: "Blanche was much stronger than Kowalski. When he started to assault her, he said, 'Tiger—Tiger!' She *was* a tiger, she had much more strength than he, and *she surrendered it to him out of desire.* These fragile people—they're always spiritually stronger, sometimes physically stronger, too." See *Conversations with Tennessee Williams*, ed. Albert J. Devlin (Jackson: University Press of Mississippi, 1986), 110-11 (emphasis added).

44. Unpublished manuscript fragment, "[A streetcar named desire]," Tms/mimeo, 136 pp., n.d., p. 64, HRHRC, University of Texas at Austin, Texas (emphasis added).

45. Cat and bird imagery, to be sure, fills *Streetcar*. In the first scene, for instance, Williams immediately establishes his cat imagery. While Blanche is introducing herself to Eunice, "a cat screeches"; Blanche "catches her breath with a startled gesture" (1.250). Williams then introduces his bird imagery: Stanley enters "with the power and pride of a richly feathered male bird among the hens" (1.265). Williams finishes this first scene with the cat again, having Blanche spring up at the screech of a cat, yelling "What's that?" with Stanley responding, "Cats" (1.267). By placing the bird imagery between these two cat references, Williams successfully achieves the necessary tension that foreshadows the tightening of Blanche's relationship with Stanley and with herself. Later, when Blanche is not frightened by the cat, she becomes the cat, for during her later attempted seduction of Mitch, he calls her a "wild cat!" (1.383). And when Blanche is not the cat, she is the bird, "spending the summer on the wing, making fly-

ing visits here and there" (1.325). When Stanley finds Blanche's fake summer furs, for example, he says to Stella, "Look at these feathers and furs that she come here to preen herself in!" (1.274). This line explicitly foreshadows the rape when Stanley says to Blanche moments before he attacks her, "What've you got on those fine feathers for?" (1.392). These are the same feathers that make Blanche the hen of Steve's joke during the poker party, as "light as a feather" to Mitch (1.347), and "flighty" to Stella (1.364). Even Steve's "joke" serves to portend the confrontation Blanche later has with the "male bird" Stanley: Stanley says to her and Stella, "You hens cut out that conversation in there!" (1.294). When Stanley calls Blanche the "canary bird" (1.359) for the first time, he does so to mock her bathroom airs, but his comment also describes her entrapment. He says to her again, "Hey, canary bird! Toots! Get OUT of the BATHROOM!" (1.367), as if to strengthen her avian identification. Finally, Blanche's spirit is a caged bird desperately seeking its freedom. Williams supports both confrontations when he combines the cat and bird images, which war unequivocally in Blanche, in scene seven: having uncovered Blanche's two diametrically opposed lives in Laurel and in New Orleans, Stanley says to Stella, "now the cat's out of the bag! . . . Some canary bird, huh" (1.358-59). Tennessee Williams, *The Theatre of Tennessee Williams*, 8 vols. (New York: New Directions, 1971-92). Further page references to the play are cited parenthetically in the text.

46. In Williams's frequent borrowing throughout the manuscripts of William Blake's spelling of "Tyger," lost in the final version of the play, we should recognize the Romantic implications of man's duality as Blake explored in *Songs of Innocence and Experience*. Given that Blake's two poems "The Lamb" (with the lamb suggesting the innocence of a child, like Stella to Blanche whom she calls "Precious lamb" [1.251] or the paperboy whom she calls "honey lamb" [1.339]) and the "Tyger" reflect the contrastive struggle between or "symmetry" of "Innocence" and "Experience," Stanley's calling Blanche a "Tiger" here only complements her own lamb-like nature. When Stanley insists that she did not pull "any wool over this boy's eyes" (1.398), we also get that complexity now intermingling the boy/lamb with man/wolf duality (Shep/ Sheep Huntleigh/Hunter) that Williams exploits throughout the play.

47. Unpublished typed manuscript fragment, "[A streetcar named desire]," composite Tms/inc (57 pp.) with A emendations on 22 pp., n.d. See note 41 regarding problematic pagination.

48. It is not coincidence that until very late in the revision process, Blanche's surname was not DuBois but Boisseau, with the French *l'oiseau* clearly being echoed. In fact, in an earlier version "The Poker Night," Blanche recalls how, when she and Stella were young, the "chattering of birds" would descend by the thousands upon Columns (an early rendering of Belle Reve) like "a big black fan," lulling Blanche to sleep. See the opening of scene two in the unpublished typed manuscript fragment, "[A streetcar named desire]," composite Tms/inc [57 pp.] with emendations on 22 pp., n.d. Judith Thompson also traces *Streetcar*'s mythological roots where bird imagery plays an important role:

In the legend . . . Procne and Philomela are saved from Tereus' revenge by being turned into birds: Procne into a nightingale, Philomela into a swallow, . . . and

Tereus into a hawk, a bird of prey. . . . Bird images, Jungian symbols of psychological transcendence from "any confining pattern of existence," are also present in *Streetcar*, but their significance is ironic, testimony to the characters' earth-bound natures rather than symbols of liberation. (47)

See her *Tennessee Williams' Plays: Memory, Myth, and Symbol* (New York: Lang, 1987).

49. Tennessee Williams, "T. Williams's View of T. Bankhead," *New York Times*, 29 December 1963, sec. 2:3; reprinted in *Where I Live: Selected Essays*, 148-54. It is worth noting that Williams had dedicated his early draft "Go, Said the Bird!" to Tallulah Bankhead because he thought it "exciting to imagine her in the part" of Blanche Shannon. See unpublished typed manuscript fragment, "[A streetcar named desire] Go, said the bird! (A play)," T title page, n.d., pp. 1, HRHRC, University of Texas at Austin, Texas.

50. Qtd. in Phillips, 82.

No Past to Think In:
Who Wins in *A Streetcar Named Desire*?
Dan Isaac

I

You can't imagine a time when *Streetcar* didn't exist, when Blanche
DuBois wasn't with us, when Stanley Kowalski wasn't with us.

—Ted Kalem[1]

The terms of the following inquiry, involving the idea of a fictive dramatic character's winning and what that might finally mean, were suggested by a conversation between Claire Bloom and Tennessee Williams, reported by Gore Vidal, who had arranged the meeting between
the two. In his autobiography, Vidal described the encounter between the
wary playwright and the insecure actress, who was preparing for the role
of Blanche DuBois in a 1974 London production of *A Streetcar Named
Desire*. Since Williams had only reluctantly agreed to Bloom's being
cast as Blanche, she was understandably jittery. When the playwright offered her a cigarette, she said, "I don't smoke." However, she grabbed
it and inhaled deeply as he lit it, then said, "except one just before dinner always in the evening." Looking "suspiciously" at her, he inquired,

"Do you have any questions about the play?"
"Yes." Claire pulled herself together. "What happens after the final cur-
tain?"
The Bird [Williams] sat back in his chair and narrowed his eyes.
"No actress has ever asked me that question." He shut his eyes; thought.
"She will enjoy her time in the bin. She will seduce one or two of the
more young doctors. Then she will be let free to run an attractive boutique
in the French Quarter . . ."
"She wins?"
"Oh, yes," said the Bird. "Blanche wins."[2]

Ever a courtly gentleman with an actress performing in one of his plays, Williams was telling Bloom what he thought she wanted to hear, playing with her wrong-headed hypothetical just for the fun of it, to see where it might lead.

Williams's associative jumping-off point may have been Blanche's fantasy-hope for salvation through Shep Huntleigh, a former boyfriend, now a wealthy oilman, whom she says she encountered a year earlier in Miami. Trying to separate Stella from Stanley, Blanche suggests that all she need do is telegraph Shep, "Sister and I in desperate situation," and he will set them up in a shop:

> *Stella:* What kind of a shop?
> *Blanche:* Oh, a—shop of some kind! He could do it with half what his wife throws away at the races.[3]

On the other hand, Williams might have been prompted by George Bernard Shaw's response to the persistent questions about what happens to Eliza Doolittle after the curtain comes down on *Pygmalion*. Does she marry Professor Higgins—or find another mate elsewhere? In order to put these sentimental and romantic queries permanently to rest, Shaw wrote a prosaic afterword crowded with tedious incident. Finally, Eliza marries Freddie, and the two open a flower shop in the arcade of a railway station.[4] All this serves to demonstrate the wisdom of Wayne Booth's aesthetic imperative throughout *The Rhetoric of Fiction* that endings are definitive.[5]

If Bloom was actually searching for a somewhat different Blanche and another kind of resolution to the play, one in which Blanche dominates and taunts Stanley after a torrid night of love and then leaves New Orleans sans psychotic breakdown, ready to start a new life elsewhere, this request could have been easily accommodated. In fact, such a version already existed:

Stanley: I'll find out where you are and follow you there—
           because I won't be able—to help myself. (Kisses her
           roughly)

Blanche: You know what I think may happen. We'll never be
           able to get away from each other—never, never
           completely. This infernal union will keep on crashing
           us together and bumping us apart. And *I will bear
           you a son*. Oh, yes. I'll creep in some lightless corner
           or drop in a ditch somewhere and bear you a child
           that will be more beast than human.

To refer to this as a *version* may be somewhat misleading in that only a four-page last scene exists, scribbled in longhand on the blank back-side of a typed short story, "The Angel in the Alcove." One imagines a sudden revelation and Williams's reaching out for whatever was ready at hand so that he might write it down before the vision evap-orated. Working quickly, he didn't bother to assign names to the speeches, but the characters call each other Blanche and Stanley. Fur-thermore, both scene and circumstance unmistakably belong to the world of *Streetcar.*

In 1986, supported by a travel grant from the National Endowment for the Humanities to journey to the Harry Ransom Humanities Re-search Center in order to examine Tennessee Williams manuscript ma-terial, I took verbatim notes on this four-page scene, fascinated by its several unique qualities, hoping that I might someday be able to write about it (the late Maria St. Just, the literary executrix of the Tennessee Williams Trust, refused almost all requests from writers to quote from unpublished Williams manuscripts). I had not then read Sarah Boyd's splendid 1980 Ph.D. dissertation, which transcribes this scene.[6]

Boyd's breakthrough study solves a very important problem in dat-ing and chronology with regard to this untitled *Streetcar* scene. Be-cause the typed manuscript of "The Angel in the Alcove" is signed and dated "Tn Williams, October 1943, Santa Monica," one might be

Critical Insights

tempted to assign the verso *Streetcar* scene to the same period. However, the earliest certain date for Williams's work on a first draft of *Streetcar* is fixed almost two years later by a 23 March 1945 letter to his agent, Audrey Wood, in which he lists several working titles and describes the plot.[7] Boyd persuasively argues that Williams most probably wrote the scene on the verso of "The Angel in the Alcove" while he was in St. Luke's Hospital in New York during September 1946. She cites a letter from Williams to Wood of 5 November 1946 in which he refers to having turned over his manuscript copy of "Alcove" to Wood when he was at St. Luke's. In a brilliant bit of sleuthing, Boyd notes that, in a letter Williams wrote Wood from the hospital on 17 September 1946, he used the same shade of blue ink that one finds used for the holograph four-page *Streetcar* scene found on the verso of "Alcove."[8] The later date for the scene is confirmed by her demonstration that, in *Streetcar*'s long manuscript journey to a Broadway opening on 3 December 1947, the name *Stanley Kowalski* came in rather late.

The manuscript scene depicts a dominant Blanche and begins with Stanley and Blanche waking up together. Stanley, ashamed of the sexual encounter, wants to leave as quickly as possible, and, as he struggles to put on his boots, Blanche mocks him: "May I help you with it? You seem to be all fists and thumbs this morning." Stanley's response is to shove Blanche, and she explodes: "Remember you took me, it wasn't I that took you. So if you got somewhat more than you bargained for, Mr. Kowalski—If you hadn't suspected a lady could be so violent, could give such a wild performance when aroused—try to remember the way it started, not me but you, putting dynamite under the teapot! Ha-ha!"[9] Flaunting her sexual prowess, Blanche depicts the sexual act as a contest—literally an agon, a wrestling match, in which one opponent seeks to exhaust the other—and Blanche has clearly won, despite the fact that he "took" her.

Trying to reassure the shaken Stanley, Blanche informs him that, by the time he returns from visiting Stella in the hospital, she will be gone. When Stanley asks her where she will go, she refers to the bus ticket that he gave her for her birthday and declares that she will trade it in for one that will take her in another direction, to someplace where she can make "a fresh start." This reference to the birthday gift of a bus ticket indicates that this crucial plot element was already in place, in Williams's head if not on paper.

When Stanley offers Blanche money, she refuses to accept it; and here occurs the exchange, quoted above, in which Stanley declares that he will find out where she has relocated and follow her "because I won't be able to help myself." To see Stanley helplessly in love with Blanche is indeed odd, the surest sign that Williams had yet to find this character. Blanche wins—but this is a different Blanche and a different Stanley from those in the *Streetcar* we know.

The scene begins with a brief exchange between the two regarding the gender of Stella's newborn child. When Stanley indicates that it is a girl, Blanche jokes that the infant's "delinquency has been determined." Then Blanche continues to build on the idea that she will deliver a *male* child to Stanley, and her fantasy takes on wildly mythic and messianic proportions: "Because our coming together could not result in anything more than beast or less than angel. And this angelic monster coming to be, will rise out of smoke and confusion to—build! To destroy and to build! Yes, something immense and altogether unplanned for, like a new world, in which—nobody's—unfaithful." This weirdly wonderful messianic quality is worth noting, for we will never see so grandly transcendent a Blanche again. The motif of destroying and building is taken from the opening chapter of the biblical prophet Jeremiah.

When Stanley hears "the grating roar of [the] approaching streetcar," he runs out to catch it, "gesticulating and shouting, his red flannel shirt-tails flying in the faint clear morning." Blanche runs to the window and calls after him "with hysterical gaiety": "Hey, hey wait for him, street-car! Wait for my sweetheart, street-car! Run, lover! Run, Candy Man! Keep both legs moving! Fast! Fast! Oh, there! There now, you've got it! Good-bye! Good-bye!" Blanche is not just triumphant but exultant, even though the scene ends with her feeling lost and for-lorn as she comes down from her high-spirited exhilaration: "(Draws her head in. Hair falls over her face. She pushes it slowly back with a dazed expression) Goodbye. . . ." Thus, in this version, Blanche more or less wins—what she loses will be addressed below—and Stanley catches a ride on a streetcar that is probably named Desire as he rides off to visit Stella and his newborn baby in the hospital. The moralistic and commonplace idea that sexual desire leads to parental responsibil-ity is not the kind of symbolic meaning one usually associates with Tennessee Williams, although it is clearly what catching a streetcar named Desire suggests here.

What Blanche loses in this version is her moral authority, for there is no evidence of rape. Even if Stanley did initiate the sexual play—putting "dynamite under the teapot"—Blanche, by her own admission, was not simply a willing but an avid participant; and any woman who makes love with her sister's husband while the sister is delivering a baby would have to live with the knowledge of an unforgivable be-trayal. Because Blanche knows this, she feels that she must leave that very day.

Blanche's moral integrity is essential to the final version of *Street-car*, and never over the course of the entire play does Williams show us an immoral Blanche. Except for her excessive drinking, while she is in New Orleans she is very much the good, caring sister that she would like to be. Coming to New Orleans with limited options, she desper-ately strives to be on her best behavior and does indeed accomplish that goal.[10] What is most interesting about this four-page untitled last scene is the absence of something: a more volatile and articulate Stanley as a worthy adversary to Blanche; a man who can hold the stage with Blanche when they slug it out, toe to toe; a man who can destroy her, and will.

At some point during the long gestation period of *A Streetcar Named Desire*, Tennessee Williams must have realized that Blanche would have to lose if she were truly to win.

2

But me—I got no past to tink in.
—Eugene O'Neill, *The Hairy Ape*

While coming out as a homosexual in the French Quarter of New Orleans in the winter of 1938-39, Tennessee Williams used parts of himself—his exploration of new modes of sexuality and his feelings of ambiguity about it—to shape the character of Blanche DuBois, who was at the center of *Streetcar* from the very beginning. But where did Stanley Kowalski come from?

At least three influential sources can be positively identified: (a) Williams's tempestuous relationship with Pancho Rodriguez y Gonzalez; (b) the Group Theatre, specifically the plays of Clifford Odets and the performance style of John Garfield; and (c) Eugene O'Neill's *The Hairy Ape*.

Most of Stanley's poignant passion and rage came to the playwright directly from his sexual association with Pancho Rodriguez, a Mexican desk clerk he first encountered in a Taos, New Mexico, hotel in the winter of 1946. Soon after, Pancho visited Williams in New Orleans, and the two were fairly constant companions for the next two years as the playwright began to turn away from work on *The Chart of Anatomy*, which would become *Summer and Smoke*, and give most of his time and energy to *The Poker Night*, which was one of several working titles given to *Streetcar* during most of that period.

Relevant information about Williams's relationship with Pancho comes from Donald Spoto's biography, *The Kindness of Strangers*, specifically the letters to Spoto from Fritz Bultman and Elia Kazan. Bultman, a promising young artist when Williams first met him on the Cape in 1941, wrote Spoto on 30 May 1984, "Tennessee behaved very badly toward Pancho . . . and he did so by using Pancho for real-life scenes which he created—and then transfigured them into moments in *A Streetcar Named Desire*." Kazan said something close to this, but without the implication of manipulative malice in Bultman's account: "Tennessee liked Pancho for the same qualities he saw in Kowalski. That he'd break up the joint if he didn't like what was going on."[11] Pancho's persona seems to have been the direct source for both Stanley's aggressive sensuality and his destructiveness.

Earlier, however, the theater itself was an influence, and the major event in American theater during the 1930s involved the Group Theatre and the playwright the troupe fostered, Clifford Odets. One line in *Streetcar* sounds like the dialogue of Moe Axelrod in *Awake and Sing*; and one can almost hear John Garfield, the quintessential Odets actor, speaking when Stanley says, "If I didn't know that you was my wife's sister I'd get ideas about you!" (p. 281).

Williams was a close observer and admirer of John Garfield, and the surest sign of this is a stage direction in his unpublished prison play, *Not About Nightingales*, in which the playwright suggests that the character smoke a cigarette the way "Jules Garfield" does, talking at the same time that he blows smoke out of his mouth. Williams obviously knew about Garfield's work when he was still Jules and working with the legendary Group Theatre, but it is unlikely that the playwright had ever seen Garfield perform until the actor scored with one of his first movies, *Four Daughters*, in which he does indeed talk with a cigarette insolently clenched between his teeth. An obsessive moviegoer, Williams would certainly have seen this film, released in 1938, the same year he began work on *Not About Nightingales*. It was in *Four Daughters* that Garfield, newly christened John by Hollywood, first established his movie persona as a born loser, a cynical Jewish tough guy with a chip on his shoulder.[12]

Years later, as Williams and Kazan were beginning to cast *Streetcar*, John Garfield was at the top of both their lists to play Stanley Kowalski. According to Larry Swindell, Garfield apparently liked the role, but he was afraid that whoever played Blanche would overshadow him.[13] The real deal breaker, according to Irene Selznick, seemed to come when he demanded a "star" salary and would commit only to three months in the role.[14] Still, there might have been another reason. Talking with Garfield's daughter, Julie Garfield, after one of the screenings in the Film Society of Lincoln Center's August 1996 Garfield retrospective, I asked why her father did not do *Streetcar.* Her answer was immediate and angry: "Because he didn't want to work with Kazan!" She went on to indicate that even then he knew of Kazan's anti-Communist position, although the House Un-American Activities Committee hearings would not take place until 1952. Tending somewhat to confirm this is Irene Selznick's confusion and consternation with regard to Garfield's unwillingness to negotiate: "He loved the play, he loved the part, and he loved Gadge [Kazan] from their days in the Group Theatre. . . . Gadge said it would be a neat trick if we could get him. . . . A month before rehearsal and we still had no Stanley. Garfield's agent Lew Wasserman said in his opinion Garfield would not do the play."[15] Apparently, Wasserman knew something from Garfield that neither he nor Garfield would disclose. After that, Garfield made further demands that no producer could possibly meet.

Had Garfield created Stanley, he would have come closer to the character Williams wrote than did the younger, punk-like Marlon Brando. Garfield would have delivered an older man, an Othello back from the nightmare of war, who falls in love with an innocent and quietly accepting young Southern girl. As a result, the critics might well have pegged *Streetcar* as a continuation of the Group Theatre tradition and focused on the class difference between Stanley and Blanche, perhaps turning Stanley into a proletarian hero.

There is also an ideological influence on Williams vis-à-vis the evolution of Stanley's character, and it comes from Eugene O'Neill's 1922 *The Hairy Ape.* In his college years, probably 1937-38, the year he spent at the University of Iowa in the Theater Department, Williams wrote a term paper on O'Neill. Although very critical of many aspects of O'Neill's dramaturgy, Williams nevertheless thought very highly of *The Hairy Ape,* calling it "O'Neill's closest approach to writing a social drama, . . . the tragedy of the inarticulate and maladjusted individual who never exactly belongs." Williams was particularly moved by the final scene, Yank's "soliloquy of stirring poetry" when he addresses the caged ape.[16] I would like to imagine that Williams was attracted to the following lines in that last speech: "Yuh're de champ of de woild. But me—I got no past to tink in, nor nothin' dat's comin', and on'y what's now."[17] There is a great sadness in Yank's confession, the sadness of a man without either a cultural tradition or a personal past "to think in," no memories to use as guideposts or standards. It is as though the will to plan, strive, and re-create oneself were an essential quality of being human, for *The Hairy Ape* is O'Neill's depiction of an alienated industrial worker devolving.

By inscribing, I believe, some aspects of O'Neill's Yank on Stanley Kowalski's psyche, Williams was able to give Blanche the kind of antagonist she could call a caveman and denounce as subhuman when she cries out to Stella, *"Don't—don't hang back with the brutes!"* (p. 323). Even before this great rhetorical speech that explicitly articulates O'Neill's implicit argument against devolution in *The Hairy Ape*, in the very first scene Stella tries to prepare Blanche for Stanley by arguing an essential difference in his nature:

> *Stella:*   You'll get along fine together, if you'll just try not
> to—well—compare him with men that we went out
> with at home.
> *Blanche:* Is he so—different?
> *Stella:*   Yes. A different species. (pp. 257-58)

In part, Stella is referring to social class differences, but her use of the term *species* also points toward a biological subgroup. It is left to Blanche to speak the word *ape* that Stella hints at: "There's even something—sub-human—something not quite to the stage of humanity yet! Yes, something—ape-like about him, like one of those pictures I've seen in—anthropological studies!" (p. 323). There are two other instances of the use of *ape* in the first complete version of *Streetcar* that Audrey Wood thought good enough to have typed by a professional typist, but they did not survive a later edit. According to Sarah Boyd, this professionally typed version was prepared in February 1947 and still used the title *The Poker Night*, although that title was later penciled out on the title page and *A Streetcar Named Desire* written next to it.[18]

In the birthday scene of this February 1947 version, after Stanley has given Blanche a bus ticket back to Laurel, Stella launches an angry attack on Stanley that climaxes with the "a-word" (the italics are Williams's): "I always thought it was just a *man* you were being, but now I wonder if it isn't—an *ape!*" In the final scene of this February 1947 version, Blanche is off stage in the bathroom bathing and calls out to Stella for a towel, specifying "a towel the King Ape hasn't been using."[19]

Taking Yank's negative formula for himself, a creature with "no past to think in," and applying it to Stanley, to what extent do we find that Stanley Kowalski has a usable past, a past to think in that shapes both his speech and his behavior? Stella takes delight in noting that "Stanley was born just five minutes after Christmas" (p. 328)—almost a messiah! Stanley himself, however, probably reared in the Catholic church, displays no trace of religious thought or value, and his one flourish of political lore is a self-interested reference to Huey Long and the Napoleonic Code. When given an opportunity to talk about ethnicity, parents, family, he reacts defensively and tells us nothing: "I am not a Polack. People from Poland are Poles, not Polacks. But what I am is one-hundred-per-cent American, born and raised in the greatest country on earth and proud as hell of it, so don't ever call me a Polack" (p. 374).

The ring of the phone cuts him off, but would he have told us anything of his family? Admittedly a Claire Bloom question of sorts, but we are left to wonder whether his parents are living or dead and what it was like for him growing up. Unlike most major Tennessee Williams characters, Stanley has no memory speeches, none of those long, reflective flights that, like dream material, reveal a character's most deeply felt fears, regrets, and hopes; he seems to live mostly in the present, reacting instinctively to perceived threats and needs. Like O'Neill's Yank, Stanley has no past to live and think in. All we know of his life is that he likes to drink and bowl with the boys and that, during World War II, he served with the 241st Engineer Corps.[20]

Why did Williams withhold Stanley's past from public view? Perhaps the answer is located in the necessary economy imposed on a theater piece, whose time constraints are quite unlike those of the novel, in which the reader controls the intermissions. Or is that withholding an essential part of Williams's dramatic strategy, built on an ethical imperative that also serves as an aesthetic principle: "To know all is to forgive all"? To have told more about Stanley would have made him more sympathetic than Williams wanted him to be. Furthermore, Stanley is not the kind of character for whom memory and the past are precious.

One more influence must be factored into Williams's composition of Stanley Kowalski. Despite the danger of Freudian speculation, it is difficult to ignore what is on the record in every Williams biography with regard to his father, Cornelius Coffin Williams (1879-1957), a man who not only treated his wife, daughter, and son Tom with cruel and destructive contempt but was also a heavy drinker addicted to all-night poker games with a rough crowd. Lyle Leverich writes that on one occasion, when Cornelius Williams accused a man of cheating, a fight ensued, and his opponent bit off a piece of Cornelius's ear.[21]

Like Stanley Kowalski, Williams's father was a traveling salesman, and it is precisely this one aspect of Stanley's characterization that rings false. Most worth noting is the fact that, as Sarah Boyd points out, in one of the earliest versions of *Streetcar*, the brother-in-law, originally named Ralph, is a "mortuary salesman." To portray the ur-Stanley as a death merchant is a perfect symbolic equation for Williams's perception of his father. Revealing to Mitch her prescient fear about Stanley, Blanche adds, in a line that was later cut, "That man will destroy me."[22]

3

> I remember you asked me what should an audience feel for Blanche. Certainly pity. It is a tragedy with the classic aim of producing a catharsis of pity and terror, and in order to do that, Blanche must finally have the understanding and compassion of the audience. This without creating a black-dyed villain in Stanley.
>
> —Tennessee Williams to Elia Kazan[23]

On the way to writing a masterpiece, Tennessee Williams's biggest problem involved Blanche DuBois. Having created a character who was a heavy drinker, a nymphomaniac, and a pathological liar given to occasional auditory hallucinations,[24] how was he to make her both sympathetic and an acceptable center of moral reflection? The answer was to dramatize Blanche's suffering and to portray her as a courageous figure who, despite her contradictions, was imbued with a unique moral passion. Indeed, with the "don't hang back with the brutes" speech, she is inspired with the vision and passion of a biblical prophet, showing concern for the future—which is to say, the future evolution of the human species. In the penultimate line to this speech, "In this dark march toward whatever it is we're approaching . . ." (p. 323), Williams/Blanche may well be expressing some cautionary extinction anxiety.

Curiously, we know almost as little of Blanche's family history and relations as we do of Stanley's, little more than the fact that both parents are dead. (We do know that Stella left Belle Reve immediately after their father died, which permits the vague inference that she was "Daddy's girl" and had a problematic relationship with her mother; but the playwright leaves this garden untended.) Many of Williams's plays prior to *Streetcar*—the well-known *Glass Menagerie* and *Summer and Smoke*, as well as the still-unpublished *Candles to the Sun* (1937) and *Spring Storm* (1938)[25]—are at least in part about young adults' problematic relationships with their parents, while *Streetcar* represents adults who not only are without parents but also have no interest in remembering them.

Furthermore, Blanche's memory is largely restricted to two traumatic events: the suicide of her young homosexual husband, whom she married when she was sixteen, and in later years her concern and care for surviving kinfolk, ministering to them during their dying and arranging for their burial. It is worth noting that, in creating Blanche's character, Williams also created a powerful engine for getting out expository information. Whenever Blanche feels trapped by a question, she responds by delivering an account of one of these traumatic events, providing pieces to the larger puzzle of her personality.

In the very first scene, anticipating accusations from Stella for the loss of the family estate, Belle Reve, through foreclosure, Blanche delivers a great aria describing how the death of kinfolk, the cost of their illness and burial, led to bankruptcy. Revisiting this theme with Mitch, Blanche supplies contrapuntal music to the cry outside her window, "Flores para los muertos" (p. 387), and adds an important detail to her endgame situation: "I lived in a house where dying old women remembered their dead men."[26]

When Stanley accuses Blanche of having lost Belle Reve, she attributes the loss to the "epic fornications" of her ancestral forefathers, who parceled out the land to pay for their women. In this first face-off with Stanley—which Blanche later will claim to have *won* when recounting it to Stella ("I think I handled it nicely")—Blanche hands over a number of legal documents and tells him, "There are thousands of papers, stretching back over hundreds of years, affecting Belle Reve as, piece by piece, our improvident grandfathers and fathers and uncles and brothers exchanged the land for their epic fornications—to put it plainly! . . . The four-letter word deprived us of our plantation, till finally all that was left—and Stella can verify that!—was the house itself and about twenty acres of ground, including a graveyard, to which now all but Stella and I have retreated" (pp. 285, 284). This marvelous speech, which simultaneously reveals and deceives, hides from immediate sight the very truth that Stanley seeks, for, at the end of the line, Blanche herself is the last of the red-hot epic fornicators. It is she who has squandered money on clothes and jewels and luxury vacations to Miami, hoping to snare, if not a husband, at least a lover for the night.

On the deepest level, these dual accounts of the loss of Belle Reve—explaining it as the cost of death and dying to Stella and as the cost of epic fornications to Stanley—begin to establish the crucial death-and-desire nexus dominant in Blanche's mind. The nexus is first suggested in the opening scene when Blanche stands amazed, recalling that she had been told "to take a street-car named Desire, and then transfer to one called Cemeteries and ride six blocks and get off at—Elysian Fields" (p. 246). The amazement comes because these directions map out the secret neural pathways of her mind.

Contextually, these speeches function as defensive rhetoric generated by Blanche's guilt and hysteria. But this defensive modality tends to depreciate the truth that Blanche speaks as she bears witness to all the details of death and dying, details that can be absolutely verified, for Stella, who "came home in time for the funerals" (p. 261), knows as well as Blanche how many died and something of their final death throes.

In order fully to understand and feel what Blanche suffered as she tended to the dying, it is necessary to reproduce this speech in its entirety:

I, I, *I* took the blows in my face and my body! All of those deaths! The long parade to the graveyard! Father, mother! Margaret, that dreadful way! So big with it, it couldn't be put in a coffin! But had to be burned like rubbish! You just came home in time for the funerals, Stella. And funerals are pretty compared to deaths. Funerals are quiet, but deaths—not always. Sometimes their breathing is hoarse, and sometimes it rattles, and sometimes they even cry out to you, "Don't let me go!" Even the old, sometimes, say, "Don't let me go!" As if you were able to stop them! But funerals are quiet, with pretty flowers. And, oh, what gorgeous boxes they pack them away in! Unless you were there at the bed when they cried out, "Hold me!" you'd never suspect there was the struggle for breath and bleeding. You didn't dream, but I saw! Saw! Saw! And now you sit there telling me with your eyes that I let the place go! How in hell do you think all that sickness and dying was paid for? Death is expensive, Miss Stella! And old Cousin Jessie's right after Margaret's, hers! Why, the Grim Reaper had put up his tent on our doorstep!... Stella. Belle Reve was his headquarters! Honey— that's how it slipped through my fingers! Which of them left us a fortune? Which of them left a cent of insurance even? Only poor Jessie—one hundred to pay for her coffin. That was all, Stella! And I with my pitiful salary at the school. Yes, accuse me! Sit there and stare at me, thinking I let the place go! I let the place go? Where were you? In bed with your—Polack! (pp. 261-62)

Not simply a superior piece of rhetoric, this speech testifies to Blanche's courage and deep sense of familial responsibility. While it is a terrible tactical mistake for her repeatedly to accuse Stella, Blanche has certainly earned the moral right to do so.

From Williams's point of view, Blanche was performing an act of supreme virtue, the purest kind of love. It would, however, be fifteen years before the playwright gave this concept full expression in two successive plays, first in *The Night of the Iguana* (1961), and then in *The Milk Train Doesn't Stop Here Anymore* (1963). In *Iguana*, Hannah's long description of the House for the Dying comes late in the play, and I abbreviate it slightly here:

In Shanghai, Shannon, there's a place that's called the House for the Dying—the old and penniless dying, whose younger, penniless living children and grandchildren take them there for them to get through with their dying on pallets, on straw pallets. The first time I went there it shocked me. I ran away from it. But I came back later and I saw that their children and grandchildren and custodians of the place had put little comforts beside their death-pallets, little flowers and opium candies and religious emblems. . . . Sometimes only their eyes were still alive, but, Mr. Shannon, those eyes of the penniless dying with those last little comforts beside them, I tell you, Mr. Shannon, those eyes looked up with their last dim life left in them as clear as the stars of the Southern Cross . . . and lately . . . lately my grandfather's eyes have looked at me like that.[27]

Milk Train describes a young hustler, Chris Flanders, nicknamed the Angel of Death because he is known for coming to rich old ladies to tend them as they are dying. But whether Chris does this only for money or from religious conviction is left beautifully ambiguous for most of the play. Late in *Milk Train*, Chris tells Mrs. Goforth—who refuses to recognize that she is dying—how he once helped an old man end his life by taking him out beyond the waves. When Chris described this event to his Hindu teacher, this teacher told him that he had found his vocation. But, impatient to complete her memoirs and meet her deadline, Mrs. Goforth does not want to listen to Chris's words about life, death, and the meaning of silence:

> *Chris:* Oh, no, you're nobody's fool, but you're a fool, Mrs. Goforth, if you don't know that finally, sooner or later, you need somebody or something to mean God to you, even if it's a cow on the streets of Bombay, or carved rock on the Easter Islands or— . . .
>
> *Mrs. Goforth:* Go on to your next appointment. You've tired me, you've done me in. This day has been the most awful day of my life. . . .
>
> *Chris:* I know. That's why you need me here a while longer.

In this death-drenched world, there is one true act of kindness that one can perform: to help the sick and the dying die graciously by being at their side until the end. "Be here when I wake up!" says Mrs. Goforth to her companion, Chris, just as she is about to go to sleep forever.[28] Blanche has performed the obligatory acts for her elderly kinfolk, the surviving women of the clan. But acting as the family angel of death has left its scars.

The other trauma that Blanche has suffered, one that came early and profoundly shaped her relationships with men, was by her own account responsible for "many intimacies with strangers" (p. 386). Blanche fully discloses this traumatic event only to Mitch during a long, late-night discussion in which both, admitting vulnerability and need, trade confessions. Mitch's sudden question triggers a more intimate level of conversation: "How old are you?" (p. 352).

Instead of answering, Blanche cross-examines Mitch and finds that it is his mother who wants to know her age. With only a few months to live, Mitch's mother is anxious to see her son "settled down," and Blanche seems to be the only candidate available to satisfy this dying woman's last wish. Moved by Mitch's "devotion" to his mother, which she clearly sees as a neurotic attachment, Blanche feels quite suddenly a warm sympathy for him. Perhaps she recognizes a curious parallel to that wounded part of herself, and, when Blanche learns that Mitch lost a woman for whom he cared deeply, she decides to tell him of her own unaccountably strange love, setting him up with a teaser that begs to be explained:

> *Blanche:* I loved someone, too, and the person I loved I lost.
> *Mitch:* Dead? . . .
> *Blanche:* He was a boy, just a boy, when I was a very young girl. When I was sixteen, I made the discovery—love. All at once and much, much too completely. (pp. 353-54)

Blanche then relates the story of falling in love with a boy and discovering "in the worst of all possible ways" that he was homosexual, walking into a room where her husband was making love to an older man. Later, while dancing, she angrily accuses him: "I saw! I know! You disgust me . . ." (pp. 354, 355). Shortly thereafter, the young boy ran out and put a gun in his mouth, blowing his head apart. Blanche's guilt is overwhelming:

> There was something different about the boy, a nervousness, a softness and tenderness which wasn't like a man's, although he wasn't the least bit ef-feminate looking—still—that thing was there. . . . He came to me for help. I didn't know that. I didn't find out anything till after our marriage when we'd run away and come back and all I knew was I'd failed him in some mysterious way and wasn't able to give the help he needed but couldn't speak of! He was in the quicksands and clutching at me—but I wasn't hold-ing him out, I was slipping in with him! I didn't know that. I didn't know anything except I loved him unendurably but without being able to help him or help myself. (p. 354)

Some aspects of this trauma may be lost in the mist of memory, and it would have been helpful to have gotten a second opinion on the matter—which is to say, a contemporary observer's description and judgment of not only the traumatic event itself, Allan's suicide, but also significant attendant circumstances. Blanche was sixteen, but how old was "the boy"? What was Blanche's sexual experience at the age of sixteen? What was her relationship to her parents? Why exactly did she feel obliged to run away to get married?[29]

Stella might well have played the role of the observer, and she does at least confirm the general truth of the event to Stanley: "But when she was young, very young, she married a boy who wrote poetry. . . . He was extremely good-looking. I think Blanche didn't just love him but worshipped the ground he walked on! Adored him and thought him al-most too fine to be human! But then she found out— . . . This beautiful and talented young man was a degenerate" (p. 364). Curiously, Stella leaves out the suicide, probably for dramaturgic reasons, so that Blanche's completion of the story to Mitch will deliver one more punch in the guts to the audience. But surely such an event, in either Stella's or Blanche's version, would prove traumatic and formative for anyone suffering it.

4

> He shall dwell alone! Outside the camp shall be his dwelling place!
> —Lev. 13:46

Most of Blanche's rhetorical speeches contain a moral argument, coupled with compelling pleas for sympathy on the grounds of extenuating circumstances. At the same time, these speeches function subtextually as calculated, self-interested moves in a deadly game whose rules and goals are never openly expressed. Blanche and Stanley are joined in a battle to see who will win Stella and who will capture Mitch. The primal struggle at first appears to be between two sisters, a rivalry for the same man; but it is truly between two volatile and self-dramatizing people, Blanche and Stanley, for the Good Mother, Stella, who seems so calm and accepting that Blanche wonders whether she has come to adopt some "Chinese philosophy" (p. 314).

The terms of battle seem always to have an implicit moral component. For instance, if Stanley can prove that Blanche lost Belle Reve because she spent huge sums on herself, he will have won the first round early in the bout. With regard to keeping Mitch as a loyal member of his male peer group, if Stanley can demonstrate that Blanche has been lying to Mitch in order to portray herself as a woman of virtue, Stanley can destroy the relationship between Blanche and Mitch, which seems to be moving toward marriage.

As the play progresses, we begin to understand what would constitute total victory for each with regard to the primary relationship. If Blanche should be successful in separating Stella from Stanley, resulting in the two sisters' living together, working together, and rearing the new baby together, this would be total victory for Blanche. Total victory for Stanley would involve removing Blanche from the apartment with little likelihood of her return—which is exactly what he achieves in the last scene of the play.

In a grand sweep, Stanley seems to win what at first looks like total victory, retaining control of both wife and friend. But the victory is tainted, achieved by raping his sister-in-law and then lying about it to his wife. Stanley has indeed won, but only by breaking the rules that demand ethical behavior, thereby defining himself as a villain and Blanche as a sympathetic victim.

One of the most interesting questions concerned with plot resolution in *Streetcar*—and admittedly it belongs to the Claire Bloom genre— asks what happens when Stella discovers what Stanley has done to Blanche. Ancillary to that is another question: How long will it take for Stella to push for an answer?

In the professionally typed version of February 1947, Williams planted a time bomb, forcing Stella to consider material evidence. According to Sarah Boyd, Williams was so intent on vividly dramatizing this matter that he turned several lines into a full page of dialogue that was only later inserted into the February 1947 typescript. The inserted page reads as follows:

Stella: (Whispering) This—this couldn't be true, I know it
          couldn't be true, it's part of her madness.
Eunice: What?
Stella: What she accuses him of! And yet if it was true; if it
          turned out that it was—I never could touch him
          again! She says that he took her by force while I was
          in the hospital!
Eunice: You don't believe her!
Stella: I wouldn't dare believe her! But look at this!
          (REMOVES PYJAMA COAT FROM CLOSET. THE BACK OF
          THE COAT IS TORN TO SHREDS)

Stella:	The coat of his pyjamas is torn to shreds and his shoulder and back are covered with scratches as if a wildcat had clawed him.
Eunice:	What does he say? How does he explain it?
Stella:	All he says is, She's crazy. Of course she must be.— That's why I signed the paper. I had to commit her in the asylum or believe her story and I couldn't believe her story and go on living with Stanley.
Eunice:	Don't think such a thing of him. Never.
Stella:	I try not to.

In the final moment of the February version, as Steve helps the doctor *carry* Blanche out, Stella turns to Stanley and delivers a definitive judgment: "You! You did this to her!"[30]

The final stage version is obviously superior to this earlier one, precisely because there is no objective evidence or indisputable sign, only Blanche's word against Stanley's.[31] Because Blanche is given to embellishment and even outright lies—"I tell what *ought* to be truth" (p. 385)—and violates social taboos in her choice of sexual partners, her story of Stanley's rape would invite skepticism from the most impartial of observers. But this time Blanche is telling the truth! This is the reason why the scene *must* be shown! Furthermore, this dramaturgic choice to show the initial stages of the rape is not for the sake of sensationalism but so that the audience can know more than Stella, analyze her decision-making process rather than identify with her confusion, and know as well Stanley's true venality—all of which gives a certain Grecian grandeur to the play's causality system that leads to Blanche's legal placement in a snake-pit prison that may only ensure her further abuse and further deterioration, resulting in her confinement forever.

But Blanche transcends the status of mere victim in the scene in which she is at last alone with Stanley, for it is here that she defines the terms of true moral behavior, terms that are so clear and simple and absolute that Stanley stands condemned even *before* he rapes her.

Ironically, this great shining moral truth is delivered to Stanley in the context of a lie, a prime example of what "ought to be truth." In telling Stanley about Mitch's visit to her earlier that same evening, Blanche falsely claims that Mitch returned with roses begging forgiveness. As she continues building on this fiction, she announces a moral principle so self-evident that it instantly takes its place beside the golden rule: "He implored my forgiveness. But some things are not forgivable. Deliberate cruelty is not forgivable. It is the one unforgivable thing in my opinion and it is the one thing of which I have never, never been guilty" (p. 397). In this regard, both Stanley and Mitch are guilty as charged.

The accusation is irrefutable and must be considered as one more reason for a resentful Stanley to destroy Blanche. The means of destruction are delivered genitally, a rape that tears apart the moral fabric of her life, for she becomes, albeit unwillingly, a partner in the betrayal of her sister.

Blanche's final moral thrust comes in her famous last line, "I have always depended on the kindness of strangers" (p. 418). Addressed to the doctor and nurse who have come to take her away, it is obliquely aimed at Stella and Stanley,[32] for, in their disposition of her, she has gotten little kindness from them. At the end Stella has become Blanche's chief antagonist, failing either to believe or to support her. Instead, Stella, her last living kinsman, signs the commitment papers that result in Blanche's enforced placement in a state insane asylum:

Stella: I don't know if I did the right thing.
Eunice: What else could you do?
Stella: I couldn't believe her story and go on living with
             Stanley. (p. 405)

In order to preserve her marriage, Stella betrays her sister.

But did Stella and Stanley seek medical help in treating what looks like either severe depression or a psychotic breakdown, probably precipitated by Stella's failure to consider the possibility that her sister's story might be true?[33] The text is silent on this point, but we can safely presume that Blanche's sister and brother-in-law did little but seek to get rid of her as expeditiously as possible. Indeed, Stella veils the truth concerning the steps taken to place her in an asylum and encourages her desperate fantasy that Shep Huntleigh is coming to rescue her: "I— just told her that—we'd made arrangements for her to rest in the country. She's got it mixed in her mind with Shep Huntleigh" (pp. 404-5). Not telling Blanche the truth is a way of instantly infantilizing and manipulating her. In this case, the deception gains Blanche's cooperation in getting dressed and ready for her own unwished-for internment. The lie serves only Stella, making it easier for her to get rid of Blanche. Even worse, telling Blanche she is going to a green world for a little rest feeds into Blanche's pathological dream of rescue by an old beau.

When Blanche utters the little introductory phrase, "Whoever you are" (p. 418), to the famous "kindness of strangers" line, we get the glimmer of a hint that she knows she is playing a role, pretending to be happy, and just beneath the mask has a sharp sense of the awful reality. She is finally right to leave—under her own cognizance—the people who want now only to destroy her. And the "kindness of strangers" line might be translated as, "Any place better than this place!"

Stella, alas, has neither the strength nor the will to help her troubled sister. Instead, Stella joins Stanley in declaring Blanche taboo, and Blanche is cast outside the camp of familial responsibility, suffering the same biblical fate as the unclean or the leper.[34]

5

Je suis la Dame aux Camellias! Vous êtes—Armand! . . . Voulez-vous couchez avec moi ce soir?
— Blanche in *A Streetcar Named Desire*

Always ready to self-dramatize and imagine herself living out the lives of characters in nineteenth-century Romantic epics, not only is

Blanche seductive, but she also glories in her sexual lust. When she gets drunk enough and mean enough, she tells Mitch with angry, vengeful pride how she took on a whole company of men: "Not far from Belle Reve, before we had lost Belle Reve, was a camp where they trained young soldiers. On Saturday nights they would go in town to get drunk— . . . and on the way back they would stagger onto my lawn and call—'Blanche! Blanche!'—the deaf old lady remaining suspected nothing. But sometimes I slipped outside to answer their calls. . . . Later the paddy-wagon would gather them up like daisies . . . the long way home . . ." (p. 389). In the final version of *Streetcar*, this speech lacks the originally intended mood and quality of *prideful* bragging. The original range of Blanche's wantonness and how she glories in it can be recovered from material cut from the February 1947 typescript, lines that once preceded Blanche's description of making love to the army recruits:

> *Mitch:*   You know what he [Stanley] told me?
> *Blanche:* What?
> *Mitch:*   That if you laid them out feet to forehead, they'd
>   stretch all the way from here to Lake Pontchartrain.
> *Blanche:* How far is the lake? What distance?
> *Mitch:*   About three miles.
> *Blanche:* No, further! (throws back her head with a breathless
>   laugh) Further than that! His estimate was too
>   modest. The men who've enjoyed me, the strangers
>   to whom I gave pleasure, would pave a glittering
>   highway from here to—Mobile. Listen! . . . Here's
>   something unknown to even the merchant
>   Kiefaber!— . . . Not far from Belle Reve, before I
>   had lost Belle Reve, was a camp where they trained
>   young soldiers. . . .[35]

The text then continues with what we have in the final published version, the passage in which the soldiers cry out, "Blanche! Blanche!" We are left to imagine that she responded joyously, a treasure trove dumped in her lap, as she took each soldier in turn for her pleasure.

In male chauvinistic slang, this is called a *gang bang*, and such occasions are usually organized by fraternity brothers and football teams. Here, however, it is Blanche who takes advantage of the situation and controls the event and the men who are punished for it, carried off in a paddy wagon. It is finally left to Stanley to punish Blanche, not only for her sexual adventures in the past, but also for her arousing him in the present. Certainly, the lurid stories Kiefaber has told him contribute to his arousal.

6

Great traditions are extended not by imitators but by original transformers.
— Waldo Frank[36]

A Streetcar Named Desire is a modern tragedy, and Blanche DuBois's tragic flaw is hubris—pride of intellect and pride of sexual prowess—as well as wanton disregard for the sexual mores of the world in which she lives. Blanche simply wants to have sex the way men do: casually, serially, and triumphantly. A sexual Joan of Arc, who listens to the voices of her body, she is a prophet and a poet, morally superior to her adversaries.

Heroic in her suffering, Blanche DuBois is victorious in her defeat.

And the past she thinks in is the literary tradition of Romanticism in which love and striving and death are ever intertwined.

Recapitulating that Romantic tradition, she has reconfigured it for her own time and become its icon.

7

Studs Terkel:	Blanche at the very end says I will always depend upon "the kindness of strangers" and finds no kindness really . . .
Tennessee Williams:	I think people always find kindness.
Studs Terkel:	Well, did Blanche find it as that man took her away?
Tennessee Williams:	I have no idea what happens to Blanche after the play ends, I know that she is shattered.[37]

Claire Bloom was acclaimed by the London critics for her portrayal of Blanche, and they remarked on her great show of pride as she is led off to the asylum, her head held high. In noting this critical response, Gore Vidal attributed Bloom's portrayal to Williams's luncheon with her, his affirming that Blanche wins. Thus, it would seem that Bloom got it right, but for the wrong reason. Alas, that she could not find Blanche's strength and courage in the text as Williams finally came to write it, for it is assuredly there.

If there ever is a last word, let Tennessee Williams have it. In a 1977 interview, George Whitmore, responding to Williams's boast that every play he ever wrote was a revolutionary work, asked if Blanche is "a revolutionary," and the playwright responded that she certainly is: "In a small southern town like Laurel, Mississippi, to live such a life is totally revolutionary and totally honest. She was over-sexed, dared to live it out, without harming anybody."[38]

From *Louisiana Literature* 14, no. 2 (Fall 1997): 8-35. Copyright ©1997 by Southeastern Louisiana University. Reprinted by permission.

Notes

This essay is dedicated to two mentors at the University of Chicago: Professor Elder Olson, who died in 1992, and Professor Mark Ashin, who died on 6 September 1997. In the classroom, Olson argued that *showing* the rape of Blanche DuBois was gratuitous sex and violence. When I wrote a paper trying to demonstrate that it *had* to be shown, that letting the audience know what happened was necessary to Williams's dramatic strategy, Olson's response was to invite me to write a Ph.D. dissertation with him on the relation of structure to meaning in Williams's major plays.

When Olson took a teaching Fulbright in the Philippines, Mark Ashin became my first reader, and his encouragement, help, and warm friendship continued long after the completion of the dissertation in 1968, until the time of his death. I had wanted personally to present this essay to him as proof that, almost thirty years later, the work on Williams and *Streetcar* continues. His death frustrated this wish.

May the memory of both Elder Olson and Mark Ashin endure as an inspiration and a blessing to those who knew them.

Profound thanks to Kenneth Holditch, an all-time great editor, whose information, suggestions, and corrections were always helpful and on several occasions saved me from embarrassing error. If we still disagree on whether Blanche is an alcoholic and a nymphomaniac, our difference results from the fact that once precise clinical words have entered the popular language of social disapproval.

Many thanks also to June Schlueter, who not only sent me several of her articles on the film version of *Streetcar* but also checked her taped copy of the film for Stella's precise words at the end.

Profound thanks to the University of the South for generously granting permission to publish for the first time select quotations from the early unpublished versions of the play that would become *A Streetcar Named Desire*. And great thanks as well to Michael D. Remer, who serves as legal counsel to the University of the South with regard to the Tennessee Williams Literary Trust.

Thanks to the Harry Ransom Humanities Research Center (HRHRC) at the University of Texas at Austin for accepting and preserving Tennessee Williams's early papers in 1963, now known as the Tennessee Williams Collection. And thanks as well to research librarian Cathy Henderson, who, on behalf of the HRHRC, has made the early versions of *Streetcar* available for both scrutiny and publication. (See also n. 6 below.)

Thanks to Sarah Boyd for generously permitting me to quote from her "Williams's journey to *Streetcar*: An Analysis of Pre-Production Manuscripts of *A Streetcar Named Desire*" (Ph.D. diss., University of South Carolina, 1980).

Thanks to New Directions and Peggy Fox, vice president of New Directions, for granting permission to quote from *A Streetcar Named Desire* (© 1947), *The Night of the Iguana* (© 1961), and *The Milk Train Doesn't Stop Here Anymore* (© 1964).

Thanks to Speer Morgan, editor of the *Missouri Review*, for sending me a copy of the *Review*'s most recent issue, which contains the first publication of Williams's *Will Mr. Merriwether Return from Memphis?* and permitting me to quote from it.

Thanks to Jack Ott, patient friend and wise counselor, who read a draft of this essay and made his fax machine available at late hours.

On the most personal level, everything I do is dedicated to the memory of my late wife, Margaret Ann Parker Isaac, an art historian and gallery manager of the Fourcade Gallery until its closing shortly after the death of its owner. With regard to this essay, Margaret owns a very special part of it, for the spark of conception would never have been struck had she not urged me to go to the Harry Ransom Humanities Research Center in September 1986, but a week before our wedding. Margaret died in a car accident in December 1987. Our daughter, Marina Bat-Yam, survived.

Many thanks are owed to Marina for surrendering a number of play dates with her father so that this essay could be brought to term, as late as she was early.

Completing perhaps a mystical circle, Margaret's father, John C. Parker, an Episcopalian minister and editor, studied for the ministry at the University of the South.

1. Quoted in Ira J. Bilowit, "Roundtable: Tennessee Williams, Craig Anderson, and T. E. Kalem Talk about *Creve Coeur*," in *Conversations with Tennessee Williams*, ed. Albert Devlin (Jackson: University Press of Mississippi, 1986), 310-11.

2. Gore Vidal, *Palimpsest* (New York: Random House, 1995), 155-56. Vidal frequently called Williams "the Glorious Bird" or just "the Bird" as he does here.

3. Tennessee Williams, *A Streetcar Named Desire*, in *The Theatre of Tennessee Williams*, vol. 1, *"Battle of Angels," "The Glass Menagerie," "A Streetcar Named Desire"* (New York: New Directions, 1971), 317-18. (Unless otherwise specified, all quotations of *Streetcar* are taken from this 1971 edition. Page numbers for subsequent citations are hereafter given in the text.)

4. George Bernard Shaw, *Pygmalion, a Romance in Five Acts: Definitive Text* (Harmondsworth: Penguin, 1975), 122.

5. Wayne C. Booth, *The Rhetoric of Fiction* (1961), 2d ed. (Chicago: University of Chicago Press, 1983).

6. Sarah Boyd Johns, "Williams' Journey to *Streetcar*: An Analysis of Pre-Production Manuscripts of *A Streetcar Named Desire*" (Ph.D. diss., University of South Carolina, 1980). (Professor Boyd has since dropped the *Johns* from her name.) This remarkable study is an examination and classification of all the early manuscript material that led up to the final version of *A Streetcar Named Desire*. Regrettably, this very important work has never been published. I am therefore doubly appreciative that Boyd has given me permission to refer to and quote from this first-rate piece of research and analysis.

All the manuscript material that Boyd cites, including the four-page scene for *Streetcar*, is located in the Tennessee Williams Collection at the Harry Ransom Humanities Research Center, Austin, Texas, and is quoted here by special arrangement with the University of the South. © 1998 The University of the South.

7. Boyd, "Williams' Journey to *Streetcar*," 201-4.

8. Ibid., 107-8.

9. All quotations of this scene are taken from my own transcription of the manuscript.

10. Blanche comes closest to slipping in the scene in which she encounters the young newsboy "collecting for *The Evening Star*" (p. 336). Excited by the possibility of seducing him, she is aggressive and provocative. Indeed, we see her here at her lyrical, seductive best: "Don't you just love these long rainy afternoons in New Orleans

when an hour isn't just an hour—but a little piece of eternity dropped into your hands—and who knows what to do with it?" Toying with the thought of seduction, she kisses him, then backs off, talking to herself as much as to him: "Now run along, now, quickly! It would be nice to keep you, but I've got to be good—and keep my hands off children" (pp. 338, 339). This is a fine, minor example of how Blanche can control her sexual desire when she wants and needs to. The major examples involve Mitch and Stanley.

11. Donald Spoto, *The Kindness of Strangers* (Boston: Little, Brown, 1985), 123-24, 140.

12. *Four Daughters* was almost certainly released in August 1938, for a review of it appeared in the *New York Times* on 19 August 1938. Williams could not have begun *Not About Nightingales* until after 1 September 1938, for it was on this date that the *St. Louis Star* ran an article about prison inmates killed when placed in a cell block where radiators were turned up so high that four men were fried to death. A dramatization of this event is at the very center of Tennessee Williams's "Living Newspaper" play, *Not About Nightingales*. According to Lyle Leverich, Williams began to work on *Nightingales* early in the fall of 1938 as he began his one-year sojourn in the Theater Department at the University of Iowa (Lyle Leverich, *Tom: The Unknown Tennessee Williams* [New York: Crown, 1995], 270).

With regard to the film *Four Daughters* itself, in August 1996, the Film Society of Lincoln Center in New York ran a John Garfield retrospective; on 9 August I saw the film at the Walter Reade Theater and am convinced that this is the Garfield movie Williams had in mind when he referred to "Jules" Garfield in the stage direction. Perhaps some quotes from the *Times* review cited above, bylined "B.R.C." (B. R. Crisler), will convince the reader who has not seen the film: "'Four Daughters' is one of the best pictures of anyone's career, if only for the sake of the marvelously meaningful character of Mickey Borden as portrayed by John (formerly Jules) Garfield, who bites off his lines with a delivery so eloquent that we still aren't sure whether it is the dialogue or Mr. Garfield who is so bitterly brilliant. Our vote, though, is for Mr. Garfield . . . as the most startling innovation in the way of a screen character in years—a fascinating fatalist, reckless and poor and unhappy, who smokes too much, who is insufferably rude to everybody and who assumes as a matter of course that all the cards are stacked against him." In the acting style of John Garfield, as well as the film scripts written for him, Williams found his secret sharer.

Happily, *Not About Nightingales* will be published in the near future by New Directions, with Allean Hale editing the text and providing an introduction. It will also be produced at the Royal National Theatre in London, with an opening set for 3 March 1998, Trevor Nunn directing. In Mel Gussow's *New York Times* article announcing this event ("First Production for an Early Williams Play," 11 June 1997), Vanessa Redgrave claimed to have "found" the play, and Trevor Nunn was quoted to the effect that *Not About Nightingales* had never been read before. Neither of these claims is correct: *Not About Nightingales* exists in manuscript at the Harry Ransom Humanities Research Center, and a number of scholars have read it there. I have studied the play and described it briefly in "'I Rise in Flame': Tennessee Williams as a Political Writer," *Village Voice*, 7 August 1990, 98, 100.

---

13. Larry Swindell, *Body and Soul: The Story of John Garfield* (New York: William Morrow, 1975), 216.

14. Irene Mayer Selznick, *A Private View* (New York: Alfred A. Knopf, 1983), 302.

15. Ibid., 300-302.

16. Tennessee Williams, "Some Representative Plays of Eugene O'Neill and a Discussion of His Art," n.d., typescript, Harry Ransom Humanities Research Center.

17. Eugene O'Neill, *The Hairy Ape*, in *Nine Plays by Eugene O'Neill* (New York: Modern Library, 1952), 86.

18. Boyd, "Williams' Journey to *Streetcar*," 117-18.

19. Quoted in ibid., 124, 127. Clearly, Williams could have come to this iconic reference to the subhuman on his own, and, furthermore, his depiction of the ape-like Stanley, a survivor and a conqueror, is quite different from O'Neill's depiction of Yank. Still, Williams's great interest in *The Hairy Ape* is on the record and cannot be dismissed.

Williams's very early one-act play *Moony's Kid Don't Cry* (1931) may also have been influenced by *The Hairy Ape*. Although Lyle Leverich (*Tom*, 122) believes that *Moony* is "notable for its similarity to O'Neill's one-act play *Before Breakfast*," he also points out that Williams's drama teacher that year at the University of Missouri, Robert Ramsay, organized a student production of *The Hairy Ape*. In *Moony's Kid Don't Cry*, Moony's wife, disgusted with her husband's destructive behavior, complains, "Why didn't I marry an ape an' go live in the zoo?" (Tennessee Williams, *American Blues* [New York: Dramatists Play Service, 1948], 6).

One more Williams reference to *ape* must be acknowledged. An entry in Williams's private journal, dated 6 November 1943, describes a strange and frightening mystical experience; and, when I first encountered this entry at the HRHRC, I was overwhelmed by its implications. It reads, in part, as follows:

> GOD! I SEE! THE APE'S FACE! I'VE STOPPED WRITING.
>
> If I am careful this moment and from now on, I can maybe save myself from madness. It is worth doing anything to do that.

Leverich (*Tom*, 527) records this entry and its brief continuation but offers no explanation or interpretation. I regard this entry as a shorthand description of a defining religious experience in which the ape's face represents a subjectively perceived demonic presence. Surviving this experience led to Williams finding the personal strength to continue and achieve great things—despite his sense that malevolent forces both inside and outside himself threatened to destroy his sanity. A simple, self-evident conclusion can be drawn: Williams himself overcame these forces, while his sister, Rose, and his fictive creation Blanche did not.

20. Stanley does make one declaration in the middle of a poker game that might qualify as a memory speech; and both its subject matter, surviving combat in World War II, and its placement at the beginning of the last scene of the play are significant: "You know what luck is? Luck is believing you're lucky. Take at Salerno. I believed I was lucky. I figured that 4 out of 5 would not come through but I would . . . and I did. I put that down as a rule. To hold front position in this rat-race you've got to believe

you're lucky" (Tennessee Williams, *A Streetcar Named Desire*, 1st ed. [New York: New Directions, 1947], 156). This speech, which follows fast on the rape scene, serves as an authorial apologia for Stanley's treatment of Blanche: destroying the enemy is what Darwinian warriors do for a living. When *Streetcar* opened at the end of 1947, the memory of World War II was still fresh and raw in the mind of every adult in America.

21. Leverich, *Tom*, 191.

22. Boyd, "Williams' Journey to *Streetcar*," 54, 122.

23. Quoted in Elia Kazan, *Elia Kazan: A Life* (New York: Knopf, 1988), 330.

24. The auditory hallucinations are the aspect of Blanche's character with which I have the most problems. If she is psychotic, then she is pathetic, but less interesting as a dramatic character since her fate would be so determined that not even the kindness of Mitch could provide the "cleft in the rock" she seems to be seeking. This dramaturgic flaw is the result, I suspect, of Williams's attempt to merge his own character with that of his sister, Rose: his anxiety, heart palpitations, and paranoia with her intense depression, withdrawal, and confusion that left her unable to fend for herself. Psychosis may have been a more dramatic way of representing this intensity. The movie *Spellbound* (1945), in which weird electronic music signals the surfacing of repressed memory, may have been an influence.

Worth noting and probing is the fact that, after Blanche's breakdown, in the last scene of the play almost all signs of her hysteria and hallucinating have disappeared and she seems to have achieved the resignation and stoical calm of Hamlet in the fifth act—which is also the emotional affect of depression. Even her accepting the doctor's arm may be an act of rational resignation, permitting a final shot at her true enemies, Stella and Stanley. (See my interpretation of this final moment below.) Surely Blanche's "mad scene" deserves careful clinical interpretation. But as dramatic poetry it is overwhelming, the best mad scene since Lady Macbeth's fifth-act guilt-ridden ritualistic washing of her hands. Blanche imagines her own death resulting from "eating an unwashed grape" and burial at sea "sewn up in a clean white sack and dropped overboard—at noon—in the blaze of summer—and into an ocean as blue as [*chimes again*] my first lover's eyes!" (p. 410).

25. The manuscripts of *Candles to the Sun* and *Spring Storm* are held in the Harry Ransom Humanities Research Center. I am presently editing both plays for New Directions.

26. This marvelous line—"I lived in a house where dying old women remembered their dead men . . ."—suggesting a world winding down, can be found only in the first, 1947 edition of *Streetcar* (p. 142). It is *not* in the version of the play published in *The Theatre of Tennessee Williams*. According to George Crandell, the change took place when New Directions published a second edition in 1950: "The text of the play has been extensively revised (including 91 substantive variants) to reflect changes made to the play following its initial production. The revisions include cuts as well as alterations of dialogue and stage directions. As a result, the revised edition is five pages shorter than the first edition" (*Tennessee Williams: A Descriptive Bibliography* [Pittsburgh: University of Pittsburgh Press, 1995], 49).

27. Tennessee Williams, *The Night of the Iguana* (New York: New Directions,

1961), 107-8. This speech is frequently cut from productions of *Iguana*. The three times that *Iguana* was done at Circle in the Square in New York, I went and waited for it, but each time it was cut. Finally, I went to the artistic director, Ted Mann, for whom I used to work as dramaturg in the early 1970s, and asked why the "House for the Dying" speech was always omitted. He said that they always try it in rehearsal, and that it never works, and that cutting it makes the action flow faster and more smoothly.

But to cut this speech cuts the heart out of *Iguana* as an exploration of religious thought and asexual love. For a description of how Williams wrote the role of Hannah for Katherine Hepburn and their correspondence about it, see my "Love in Its Purest Terms: Williams, Hepburn, and *Night of the Iguana*," *Village Voice*, 14 May 1996, 82.

28. Tennessee Williams, *The Milk Train Doesn't Stop Here Anymore* (New York: New Directions, 1964), 111-14, 116. *Milk Train* is a play about Eastern mysticism and the acceptance of death: "Death is one moment, and life is so many of them" (p. 84). For a further exploration of some of the themes of *Milk Train*, see my "*A Streetcar Named Desire*—and Death," *New York Times*, 18 February 1968, sec. 2, 1 and 7. Even better, read the play itself, a neglected masterpiece.

29. This traumatizing marriage to Allan, followed by his suicide, raises the classical Aristotelian question, Was her marriage to him an act of chance or one of necessity? Certainly, one aspect of the question can be answered with some certainty, for we have two instances in the play—one referenced, the other shown—that demonstrate Blanche's ongoing sexual attraction to young "boys." Clearly, this is an obsession, for she is ready to risk her professional reputation for the pleasure it brings her. But exactly why remains a mystery. Is it because she desperately needs to control the sexual relationship and mistakenly believes that she can do so with a male younger than herself? Or has she become stuck in time, forever replaying her relationship with Allan, the young boy who shot himself? Whatever the cause, it is a costly obsession, for, when she loses her teaching job in Laurel because of another affair with a boy, she is propelled to New Orleans, the last stop down. However, we have no evidence that she was attracted to either homosexual or androgynous men.

We do, however, get a hint of a more sordid kind of life than we might otherwise imagine when Blanche describes to Stella her fears of growing old and losing her good looks: "But I'm scared now—awf'ly scared. I don't know how much longer I can turn the trick." "Turning the trick" is the jargon of prostitutes, and her use of it suggests that she may have at some point entered the trade—something more than selling herself for a night's shelter, which she speaks of toward the beginning of the speech. Her "That's why I've been not so awf'ly good lately" may be a veiled confession to prostitution (see *Streetcar* [1947], 91).

This raises the question with which I began this note, only in slightly different terms: To what extent is Blanche driven? To what extent free? The answer is most likely that she is driven—but struggling to be free.

30. The inserted page is quoted in Boyd, "Williams' Journey to *Streetcar*," 127-29. Aside from providing grounds for a possible breakup between Stella and Stanley, there is an additional interest in this ending, and it has to do with the 1951 film version of *Streetcar*. The film was attacked before its release by both the Catholic Legion of Decency and Joseph Breen, enforcer of the Motion Picture Production Code, Breen de-

manding that the rape scene be removed. Williams wrote Breen insisting that *Streetcar* was a moral play and that the rape was an essential element of the "truth" of the drama.

The Breen Office relented on the rape but in return demanded that Stanley be punished. Apparently, this was a deal that both Williams and Kazan could live with, so the following speech was given to Stella at the very end as Stanley moves toward her: "Don't you touch me! Don't you ever touch me again!" (This speech is cited in both Gene D. Phillips, "*A Streetcar Named Desire*: Play and Film," and June Schlueter, "Reading toward Closure in *A Streetcar Named Desire*," both in *Confronting Tennessee Williams' "A Streetcar Named Desire*," ed. Philip C. Kolin [Westport, Conn.: Greenwood, 1993], 231, 79.) But with this compromise Kazan had simply returned to the resolution of the February 1947 script, which had probably been sent to him when he was first considered as director of the stage production. If this material found on the inserted page of the February 1947 text had survived the final cut, might it have influenced the original theatrical production of *Streetcar*?

During the 24 November 1997 program "Memories of Tennessee Williams's *A Streetcar Named Desire*," sponsored by the New York Public Library for the Performing Arts at Lincoln Center and featuring Kim Hunter reminiscing about the rehearsal period and long Broadway run of *Streetcar*, in which she created the role of Stella, I described the page insert where Stella discovers the torn pajamas and marks on Stanley's back and asked Hunter if this knowledge would have changed her interpretation of Stella. Hunter smiled, was silent for a time, and then responded, "There is nothing that could have caused Stella to leave Stanley."

But one of Hunter's remarks earlier in the evening suggested a different attitude toward Stanley during the rehearsal period. Unable to imagine Stella attracted to the brutish Stanley, Hunter asked Kazan, "What does Stella see in Stanley?" Kazan snapped, "Forget Stanley! You're in love with Marlon."

31. In her conclusion, Boyd remarks about such revisions in general: "A very large portion of the *Streetcar* manuscripts is quite poor writing. Williams, however, recognized and discarded the weak material and doggedly persisted in reworking and revising—and almost without exception the revision constituted improvement" ("Williams' Journey to *Streetcar*," 141).

32. As it turned out, Kazan directed the scene in just this way, emphasizing Blanche's accusation in the "kindness of strangers" line. In Brenda Murphy's splendid and invaluable *Tennessee Williams and Elia Kazan: A Collaboration in the Theatre* (Cambridge: Cambridge University Press, 1992), there is a chapter on *Streetcar* describing how Kazan's direction influenced interpretation as well as the text itself. With regard to Blanche's accusation of Stella, Murphy reports: "In the production, Kazan had Blanche turn and look accusingly at Stella after Stanley gave her the bus ticket for her birthday, and he had her repeat this look in the closing scene when she realized that the man who had come for her was not Shep Huntleigh" (p. 60).

The one blemish of this chapter on *Streetcar* is Murphy's readiness to accept and embrace Williams's declaration that the play is but a tragedy of misunderstanding. In a letter to Kazan before Kazan had signed on to direct *Streetcar*, Williams wrote: "I will try to clarify my intentions in this play. . . . There are no 'good' or 'bad' people. Some are a little better or a little worse but all are activated more by misunderstanding than malice. . . . Stanley sees Blanche not as a desperate, driven creature backed into a last corner to make a last desperate stand—but as a calculating bitch. . . . It is a thing (Misunderstanding) not a person (Stanley) that destroys her in the end" (Kazan, *Elia Kazan: A Life*, 329-30). This idea of misunderstanding is so reductive and generalizing that it is worthless as well as incorrect. Americans under the influence of psychotherapy have come to believe that everything can be reduced to a communications problem. (If we could only have gotten Blanche and Stanley to do role reversal, everything would have come out all right!)

Toward the end of this letter, Williams went on to address the apparent breakdown in negotiations between two strong personalities, those of the producer, Irene Selznick, and Kazan. The playwright meant his theory of the inevitability of misunderstanding to apply to what was going on between Kazan and Selznick, the mutual hostility each had begun to feel for the other. Williams was trying to patch things up: "I have written all this out in case you were primarily troubled over my intention in the play. Please don't regard this as 'pressure.' A wire from Irene and a letter from Audrey [Wood] indicate that both of them feel you have definitely withdrawn yourself from association with us and that we must find someone else. I don't want to accept this necessity without exploring the nature and the degree of difference between us." Kazan then indicates that this letter won him over, that "it became the key to the production for me" (ibid., 330).

33. I have purposely echoed the last line of *Suddenly Last Summer*—"I think we ought at least to consider the possibility that the girl's story could be true . . ."—in order to call attention to the similarity of Blanche's situation to that of Catherine's: the enforced institutionalization of a woman because of a story she tells. The situation in *Suddenly Last Summer* is more dire because Catherine's adversary, Mrs. Venable, demands that a lobotomy be performed on her "to cut this hideous story out of her brain" (Tennessee Williams, *Suddenly Last Summer* [New York: New Directions, 1958], 88).

But the profound power of the doctor's open-ended refusal to judge is located in what this accomplishes. His refusal demands that the reader/spectator consider the truth value not just of Catherine's story but of the entire dramatic action. One is sent back into the text to consider the probability of her story, how likely it is to be true—a consideration to which Stella gives scant attention with regard to her own sister.

Elder Olson gives special consideration to probability systems working within the world of a play, supplying suggestive labels for such different kinds of systems as hypothetical, hyperbolic, emotional—the latter one in which "a given emotion predisposes us to believe certain things." In *Suddenly Last Summer*, the viciousness of Mrs. Venable disposes us to believe Catherine. On a closing page of Olson's chapter on probability systems, he teasingly declares, "There is probability even within the realm of accident and coincidence," but "not all accidents are equally improbable" (*Tragedy and the Theory of Drama* [Detroit: Wayne State University Press, 1966], 50, 52).

34. The subject of lepers is dealt with, albeit fantastically, in Williams's only recently published play *Will Mr. Merriwether Return from Memphis?* (*Missouri Review*, vol. 20, no. 2 [1997]). The middle-aged widow, Nora—one of two women regularly visited by apparitions—claims that there is a hidden colony of lepers living secretly in the cisterns of their small Southern town. According to Nora, they are "mostly concen-

trated along Bella Street . . . between the white and black sections of town . . ." (p. 93), which puts them geographically and sociologically where lepers have always been, in no-man's-land.

35. Quoted in Boyd, "Williams' Journey to *Streetcar*," 124-25.

36. Waldo Frank, foreword to *The Complete Poems of Hart Crane* (New York: Doubleday Anchor, 1958), xii.

37. Quoted from "Studs Terkel Talks with Tennessee Williams," in *Conversations with Tennessee Williams*, 81.

38. "George Whitmore Interviews Tennessee Williams," in *Gay Sunshine Interviews*, ed. Winston Leyland (San Francisco: Gay Sunshine Press, 1977), 1:316.

Is There a Gay Man in This Text?
Subverting the Closet in
A Streetcar Named Desire[1]

Dean Shackelford

Tennessee Williams' homosexuality manifests itself in a number of provocative, subtle, and "closeted" ways in his fiction, drama, and poetry before 1970—when he first came out publicly in an interview with David Frost.[2] Not only do his fundamental concerns in his greatest plays seem rooted in a homosexual sensibility, but also his characters call into question the whole notion of "natural" gender roles and the "naturalness" of what Adrienne Rich has referred to as "compulsory heterosexuality."[3] Furthermore, his dramas reveal the "problem" of human sexuality to an intolerant, anti-flesh society.

For an alert audience almost any work Williams wrote signifies his homosexual identity. This indicates that though contemporary gay critics sometimes damn Williams for his failure to "come out" before 1970, he may have, whether consciously or not, used his works as the means through which to "out" himself as a gay writer and to "out" homosexuality as an important cultural phenomenon in America. Williams seems to have been much more liberated about his need for self-disclosure than is commonly assumed—perhaps even more than he ever admitted to himself.

In her important book *Epistemology of the Closet*, Eve Kosofsky Sedgwick argues that, in order to protect the status and identity known as "heterosexuality," the prevailing hegemony forces gay men and lesbians to inhabit the closet and keeps heterosexuality "out of the closet" to reaffirm heterosexual normativity.[4] The heterosexual majority consistently attempts to keep gay men and lesbians closeted while at the same time makes it necessary for heterosexuals to perform their sexuality time and again. Particularly for the average male in America's heterosexist society, the masculine self must be reestablished and reinforced throughout the entire culture. Like Sedgwick, Judith Butler has written concerning the masking of heterosexuality that since the homosexual directly threatens the existence of heterosexuality by calling into question the "naturalness" of this social norm, homosexuality must of necessity be suppressed. In discussing heterosexual constructs in an influential essay entitled "Imitation and Gender Insubordination," Butler claims that heterosexuality is an identity permanently at risk: "It requires to be instituted again and again, which is to say that it runs the risk of becoming de-instituted at every interval."[5] Because Sedgwick and Butler focus on the degree to which homosexuality does not exist outside the heterosexual paradigm and emphasize that the closet and sexual orientation are both rooted in performative aspects of gender identity, these two theorists will provide a theoretical framework for discussing the central *trope* of the closet as evident in what many critics consider as Tennessee Williams' most important play, *A Streetcar Named Desire.*[6]

By definition, the "closet" may refer to a hidden secret, which may or may not be revealed to the self or others; a disguise and pretense to protect the self, a means of escape from the everyday world of harsh reality; or a shell of protection to lie to or avoid the rejection of others. The closet, in other words, raises issues about a character's and the playwright's personal secrecy and disclosure, revelation and denial, mendacity and truth—all issues which the homosexual of Williams' generation had to confront, manipulate, dodge, circumvent, negotiate, and overcome in order to survive in an intolerant, oppressive society. In a 1960 essay from *New York Times Magazine*, Williams himself raises the possibility for rereading his plays as attempts to subvert the closet when he says, ". . . the theater has made . . . its greatest artistic advance through the unlocking and lighting up and ventilation of the *closets* [my emphasis], attics, and basements of human experience."[7] As this passage suggests, the "closets" of human experience are very much a part of the theater and most especially the plays of Tennessee Williams. In each of his plays the most thoroughly operative trope is the "closet." When closely examined, the playwright's use of the closet as *trope* may be said to demonstrate his inner desire to reveal his true identity as well as his recognition of the necessary protection that must be invoked in order to hide his sexual identity. Williams' characters inhabit closets in the space of the mind and the body, in both physical and psychological space.

The protection of the closet may best be seen in the two earliest dramatic successes of Williams, *The Glass Menagerie* (1944) and *A Streetcar Named Desire* (1947), and it is most fully developed in the most homosexual ("gay") of all of Williams' major plays from his commercially successful period, *Cat on a Hot Tin Roof* (1955), and the darker *Suddenly Last Summer* (1958). In each case the main characters struggle with one another over the desire for self-protection and the fear of disclosure.

While, superficially, homosexuality is not an issue in *The Glass Menagerie*, the Wingfield family inhabit a sort of closeted existence. Laura's glass ornaments provide the necessary refuge for escape into the closet of her imagination. Amanda, too, isolates herself from the outside world, even working at home to sell magazine subscriptions. Recent productions such as Paul Newman's excellent film version of the play have hinted that Tom is a gay man. Indeed, he fights against his closeted existence: He is a part of the outside world, the shoe factory.[8] His artistic temperament and personal (and sexual, however subtly explored) desire conflict with his mother's intrusion on his imaginary and real closet. He cannot accept his rejection of family to live his own truth, but at the same time, he must reveal himself to himself and to his mother when she pressures him too hard.

As I recently argued in "The Truth That Must Be Told: Gay Subjectivity, Homophobia, and Social History in *Cat on a Hot Tin Roof*," Williams comes closest to "coming out" as a gay writer during the 1950s in this 1955 Pulitzer Prize-winning drama.[9] His prose descriptions of the "marriage bed" of Jack Straw and Peter Ochello are handled tenderly and without apology. Like Allan in *A Streetcar Named Desire*, Skipper provides the central motivation for the play's conflict and plot. Brick's entire life (his name seems appropriate for one who builds imaginary walls of protection) has been a closet. More importantly, he has inhabited a closet within the world of Big Mama and Big Daddy; they have overprotected him. While Big Daddy is dying, Brick closets himself from the family in Jack Straw and Peter Ochello's former bedroom to hide the truth from himself. Brick's secret may be one he has even kept from himself—his own gay identity. The web of secrecy and disclosure in this play is never fully revealed—suggesting perhaps that Williams could not, when dealing with a subject so personal as homosexual orientation, completely "come out" during the mid 1950s as a gay playwright—though the play strongly indicates the writer's desire to do so.

With *Suddenly Last Summer* (1958), however, the "closet" of homosexuality has turned warped and perverse in a play which is arguably the most negative portrayal of the gay poet in Williams' corpus. It may be argued that the plight of Sebastian is partly due to his own homosexual libido and his mother's failure to acknowledge the truth concerning his inclination, and it is also true that Williams appears metaphorically as the guilt-ridden homosexual poet in this play. For Sebastian is really a projection of Williams himself in a play in which he tries to "write himself out" of existence as a gay writer and "burned out" artist figure. Whereas in *Cat on a Hot Tin Roof* and *The Glass Menagerie*, Williams appears to portray himself and homosexual characters on stage in somewhat positive ways (for the time), in *Suddenly Last Summer*, the poet portrays a darker view, as though he is being punished for his "depravity." The play's central metaphor of cannibalism suggests not only that society consumes and destroys the gay artist but also that his excessive appetite is self-destructive. In this case, the gay writer cannot do himself in directly; he is destroyed by his own conflict of flesh and spirit and by a society which feeds on the flesh of sensitive souls.

As one might expect, the varying portrayals of the gay subject in these and other Williams' plays have led several commentators to criticize the playwright—at times severely. Two in particular use essentialist reasoning to argue that his plays demonstrate that he was a self-hating victim of his own homophobia. In his book *Not in Front of the Audience*, Nicholas DeJongh is critical that Williams did not write a play about "the new conceptions of gay desire and relationship in the post-Liberation period"[10] and laments the degree of self-loathing evident in Williams' plays, suggesting that his portrayal of homosexuality is thus characteristic of some "mid-century homosexuals."[11] Does DeJongh believe that only gays of the past were affected by an internalized homophobia, as this interpretation of Williams seems to suggest? Likewise, John Clum, author of *Acting Gay*, deplores Williams' negative portrayal of homosexuality in his plays. Calling *A Streetcar Named Desire* the "quintessential closeted gay play," Clum accuses Williams of writing heterosexist, homophobic dramas "built on a closeted sensibility."[12] Like DeJongh, Clum essentializes gay identity in Williams and fails to comprehend the complexity of his attitudes.

Contrary to each of these critics' anachronistic and severe criticisms regarding Williams' internalized homophobia and his failure to write openly gay plays, I will argue that in *A Streetcar Named Desire* Williams may "closet" the gay subjectivity from the repressed audience of 1940s America, but nevertheless he inscribes the gay subject and turns the play into a plea against homophobia and the social intolerance of both gay men and unconventional women.[13] As David Savran, the author of *Communists, Cowboys, and Queers* and Williams' most astute gay critic, argues, critiques of Williams generally fail to recognize the complex ways in which Williams' drama and fiction explore the homosexual subject and demonstrate the fluidity and decentralization of masculinity and femininity. Particularly, Savran argues that Williams cut "diagonally across the binary oppositions between masculinity and femininity, heterosexuality and homosexuality"[14] in plays which "redefine and reconfigure resistance."[15] Though he frequently heterosexualizes the conflicts and the characters, he nevertheless problematizes the interrelationship of sexuality, gender, and society, and courageously gives voice to gay male subjectivity in a time of widespread denial of the existence of and prejudice against homosexuals.

For the contemporary gay critic as well as for those using other approaches to interpret Williams' dramatic legacy, *Streetcar* raises several important questions. What is the connection between Blanche DuBois and gay male subjectivity? How do readers interpret the role of Allan Grey, her dead gay husband? What importance does their relationship play in arriving at the work's meaning? How does Williams represent male and female sexuality? How does he represent the male body? Is there a "gay male gaze"? If so, how does theorizing it affect readers' interpretations of the play? In what way do Stanley Kowalski and other significant characters inscribe gay male subjectivity? Addressing these fundamental questions will enable readers and viewers of *Streetcar* to recognize that the play's center is, indeed, gay male subjectivity.

Williams shows his resistance to the repressive era of the 1940s and the pre-Stonewall period through subversive means, partially by reshaping Aristotelian concepts of drama. Not directly *mimetic*, his plays, while seeming to represent a heterosexual reality, in fact encode and inscribe another, parallel reality which reflects the plight of the gay "other" in American society. In *A Streetcar Named Desire*, several key elements call into question the seeming "heterosexuality" of the play's situation and characters, and subversively explore gay male subjectivity. These elements include the character of Allan Grey, whose absence and presence through Blanche's mind voices the destruction of the gay subject in a repressive society; Blanche DuBois, who becomes the means through which Williams projects his own gay subjectivity; and Stanley Kowalski, who, by becoming the object of Blanche's gaze, surrenders his body for the gay spectator.

The play, which premiered in 1947 and which most critics consider Williams' masterpiece, concerns the plight of the outcast Blanche DuBois, a symbol of Old Southern refinement and respectability who finds herself in the hands of merciless barbarians like Stanley Kowalski, a symbol of crudity and insensitivity in the modern world. In this play the Kowalskis live in a small closet where Blanche's past is "outed" for all to see. Blanche herself uses the closet of the past to hide the truth from herself and others. She intrudes upon the closet of her lost lover, Allan, who has attempted to hide himself in heterosexual marriage. Until the appearance of the paper boy, she closets from the audience her affection for young men. Each of these closets may provide a refuge, a "safe" place for hiding—but they also create self-deception. The closet trope is in fact the primary means through which Williams offers a radical reinterpretation of American masculinity and human sexuality. It is the manner in which he, to use Butler's word, "de-institutes" heterosexual normativity.

Streetcar is clearly a play about the plight of the homosexual, the effects of the closet, the threat of loneliness, and the power of disclosure. I propose that examining the trope of the "closet" will lead to a broader context from which to read this work (and others), for while Williams maintains the distance brought about by the "closet," at the same time he illustrates the effects of secrecy, discretion, and revelation to self and others. Moreover, he shows the problem of attempting to reconstruct and dismantle the closet in a repressive era.

In *Streetcar*, Williams introduces the subject of homosexuality directly for the first time. But this is not by definition a "homosexual" play, nor is Blanche DuBois a thinly-disguised transvestite, as some limited critics have suggested.[16] However, homosexuality becomes the center around which all events and circumstances in the life of its heroine, Blanche DuBois, evolve. As a result, though not a play about homosexuality per se, *A Streetcar Named Desire* dramatizes the plight of the homosexual and becomes a metaphor for homosexuality—a bold action for a gay playwright in the late 1940s.

The initial intrusion into Blanche's closeted existence occurs when she is a young woman in love deeply for the first time. She describes her devotion to Allan in this manner: "When I was sixteen, I made the discovery—love. All at once and much, much too completely. It was like you suddenly turned a blinding light on something that had always been half in shadow, that's how it struck the world for me."[17] As this passage might suggest, the light and dark imagery throughout the play has been the subject of critical discussion for years. In this key scene of the play, Blanche ironically comments on her own failure to recognize her husband as a gay man as well as her own predicament as a "closeted" and "fallen" woman. Critic Joseph Allen Boone, in his recent book *Libidinal Currents*, has written concerning the role of homosexuality in presumably heterosexual discourse: "Whether literally embodied in specific characters or presented as a recurring motif, the shadowy presence of homosexual desire becomes a site of threatening otherness. . . ."[18] Keeping in mind Boone's comments, I see Blanche's reference to the "half-shadow" as a commentary on the partial disclosure of homosexuality and the gay subject throughout the play—as a part of the "closet" trope.

Trapped in her imaginary "closet" of perfect love and ideal Southern womanhood, Blanche, as we learn later in the same speech, accidentally opens the closet door on her own world of illusions as she clearly finds Allan Grey, her beloved, in bed with another man. When Allan's closet is accidentally opened, he finds the resulting exposure too horrible for him to handle. He cannot face the rejection and judgment of Blanche and thus kills himself. It is almost as if the playwright is commenting on his own desire to be "out" yet at the same time his fear of a rejecting public were he to acknowledge his homosexual orientation openly.

After Allan's death, Blanche opens her own eyes to the problem of "desire" (for which Allan is punished and rejected) which has been the root of her marital difficulty and the deceptions of a society where homosexuality, because it is hidden, does not exist. Until this point she has in effect always lived in the closet of Southern gentility. However, she now exchanges this deceptive place of hiding for a secret life of forbidden sex, prostitution, and seduction. When Blanche escapes this world by entering the "closet" of the Kowalskis in Elysian Fields, she not only tries to hide the truth of her "fallenness" from Stella and Stanley, but she also attempts to deny her true identity.

This conflict, which is common among gay men and lesbians who first recognize their homosexuality, suggests that the closet not only operates to hide the self from others, but it also helps one hide from one's self. Ironically enough, Blanche, after opening the closet which Allan has inhabited, assumes his role as a closeted subject—and is thus forced to become the same as her gay husband and the gay playwright. She assumes Allan's role of presumed heterosexual for the rest of her life, playing out the script of heterosexuality while undermining its naturalness. Her conflict and guilt are rooted in her mistreatment and rejection of her gay husband, and for this reason, homosexuality is not only important to a full comprehension of the play, it also shapes the play's outcome.

Because of the importance Allan plays in the work, he is, contrary to critical consensus, the most important character of *Streetcar*—a gay subject who never appears on stage, but his presence is always signified. For it is Allan who best represents the gay playwright's condemnation of American homophobia, and it is he whose suicide shapes the entire play's plot and is the root of the heroine's downfall. As a result, his presence is constantly within the mind of Blanche DuBois, through the haunting music which she (and the audience) hears in her head and can never forget. Without Allan's character, there would be no tragedy, there would be no failed Southern idealism, and there would be no need for a villain to destroy Blanche's illusions. While Blanche does, as numerous critics have acknowledged, receive the playwright's sympathy, and while she is, in many ways, a female projection of Tennessee Williams, she is clearly both villain and tragic heroine, for she destroys the homosexual poet (a projection of Williams himself). In one of her most famous lines, Blanche tells Stanley, "Deliberate cruelty is not forgivable. It is the one unforgivable thing in my opinion and it is the one thing of which I have never, never been guilty."[19] Therefore, applying her own (and the playwright's own) concept of justice to her character, Blanche must, in turn, receive the punishment of all those who are guilty of "deliberate cruelty" to the marginalized homosexual. As Thomas P. Adler has written, Blanche recognizes "her complicity in Allan's death, her violation of Williams's first commandment to accept what is human about the other. . . ."[20] Heterosexuality thus is undercut in the play through Blanche's tragic downfall and by the figurative representation of the gay subject, Allan.

As a married, presumably heterosexual man, Allan's mere existence as a gay subject calls into question the heterosexual norms of American society and thus opens the closet door for the homosexual. He illustrates how gender and heterosexual orientation may be nothing more than a form of masquerade. During her eloquent speech to Mitch, Blanche tells the audience that "There was something different about the boy, a nervousness, a softness and tenderness which wasn't like a man's, although he wasn't the least bit effeminate looking—still—that thing was there."[21] Such tenderness and nervousness, while stereotypes of the gay male, appear to indicate that gender is nothing more than a mask, for if Allan, a male, can possess, to use Williams' words, "that thing" and still not be "the least bit effeminate looking" so can other men.[22] Through Blanche's recollection of Allan and the constant playing of the "Varsouviana," Williams positions the audience as intruders into the closet of gay experience, destabilizing the notion of heterosexual normativity.

Moreover, Blanche speaks for and embodies the gay subject, for it is within Blanche's "body" that Allan continues to exist. The closet, for Allan and Blanche both, protects them from having others intrude upon their "true" identity. As characters who are "married" to the illusion of heterosexual normativity, Allan and Blanche share subjectivities which at times seem difficult to distinguish from each other. Having been in her in the literal sense, Allan becomes one with her for life. Like Allan, Blanche cannot face the world of reality. Like Allan, she cannot publicly confess her attraction to men. Nor can she admit her true orientation personally or to others.

When she confesses to Mitch her disappointment over the discovery of Allan's homosexuality, she refers to the "blinding light" which she cannot face. As mentioned earlier, the light and dark imagery refers to truth, including the presence of homosexuality within the heterosexual subject. The "blinding light" represents her problem of self-delusion and idealism—a conflict which Blanche, and her poet husband, have also shared. This unbearable light of truth—a central metaphor used throughout the canon of Tennessee Williams—has, like homosexuality and the other secrets of a repressed society, been kept, in the playwright's words, "half in shadow."[23] When the "shadow" and the "light" are stripped away (witness Mitch's hostile removal of the pink lamp shade covering the light bulb which Blanche has been unwilling to face), all that is left is truth, the harshness of reality, the severity of stripped illusions, the pain of failed idealism, and the inevitable presence of homosexuality.

As the primary vehicle through whom Williams projects the plight of the gay subject, Blanche contains within her both the "closet" of homosexuality and the threat it presents to heterosexual normativity. In her most famous speech, Blanche blames herself for Allan's suicide: "It was because—on the dance floor—unable to stop myself—I'd suddenly said—'I saw! I know! You disgust me! . . .'"[24] Blanche gazes upon Allan to discover the truth of his homosexuality. Her revulsion is not at all uncommon to the reaction when heterosexual families even today learn that a beloved brother or sister is "one of those." On the surface, Blanche's revulsion would seem to undercut the play's subversive representation of homosexuality and support John Clum's view that *Streetcar* is a heterosexist, homophobic drama "built on a closeted sensibility."[25] But as earlier suggested, the play's emphasis on the closet trope continues to subvert heterosexual hegemony and thus calls into question the truthfulness and purpose of the closet.

In addition, Blanche's reaction to the discovery of Allan's affair with his older friend would seem to indicate the reinscription of heterosexual and masculine norms for men while at the same time acknowledging the presence of what is supposed to be absent and thus undercutting heterosexuality as well. Judith Butler's "Melancholy Gender/Refused Identification" suggests that "Heterosexuality is cultivated through prohibitions, where these prohibitions take as one of their objects homosexual attachments, thereby forcing the loss of those attachments."[26] Allan's closet is, like Blanche's reaction to her husband's homosexuality, the means through which "compulsory heterosexuality" is maintained. Therefore, Blanche embodies both the gay male subject and the "closet" by paradoxically empathizing with and simultaneously feeling guilty about her participation in society's destruction of the homosexual. She also undermines the heterosexuality which her marriage and her liaisons with men might suggest. At the same time what she embodies becomes destabilized when she rejects Allan as well as when she desperately tries to "save" all young men from the plight of homosexuality. She neither represents a gay transvestite, as some critics have argued, nor does she become, in a *mimetic* sense, the heterosexual woman. Her role, like her character, is ambiguous, representing Williams' desire to open the "closet" for gay representation on stage and his participation in capitulating, probably for commercial and career reasons, to the reinscription of illusory heterosexual norms—one of which is the closet.

Ironically, though, Blanche's seemingly homophobic reaction is undercut by her own self-doubt and guilt over having destroyed her beloved gay husband. Allan cannot voice his own anger and disgust at American society's rejection of him as a gay man—which Blanche's confession represents—but he can haunt the soul of Blanche, causing her to believe she must "prove" her own desirability as a woman through one-night stands and substitutes for Allan, her "perfect" poet-spouse. By playing out the role of sexually promiscuous female, Blanche embodies the violator of social taboos, the "fallen woman," as well as the gay male, for to her mind she must sleep with other young men in the hopes that she will save them from homosexuality since she failed so miserably in doing so with her husband. As she says in her famous speech, "I didn't find out anything till after our marriage when we'd run away and come back and all I knew was I'd failed him in some mysterious way and wasn't able to give the help he needed but couldn't speak of!"[27]

While a seemingly homophobic, heterosexist reaction, Blanche's need to "save" Allan and other young men may be rooted in her own unconscious recognition that heterosexuality as a "natural phenomenon" has been undermined but also that *her own* sexuality has been called into question. Metaphorically, then, Blanche may be a female projection of the male Don Juan figure out to "prove" his masculinity and heterosexuality—and perhaps even a woman whose own "closeted" lesbianism is implicit in her future actions. In her unusual marriage to a gay man and in her subsequent violations of Southern social and sexual codes for the female, Blanche becomes an "other"—a woman who is pretending to be a lady who is pretending to be a heterosexual. Ultimately, she does not comfortably fit at either pole (heterosexual/homosexual or woman/man). Her complexity as a character reveals clearly that despite Blanche's homophobic reaction to Allan, Williams again subversively strips away the illusion of heterosexual normativity by his ambiguous presentation.

As a quasi-gay subject herself, Blanche becomes the playwright's alter ego. At the same time she projects the gaze of the gay playwright. This is where Williams' challenge to heterosexuality and patriarchy becomes most subversive. For the play centers on the male, not the female, body. Despite Blanche's attempts to maintain her beauty and youth, Williams clearly indicates she has not; her beauty has faded just as the ideal of heterosexual normativity has been diminished. Despite Stanley's occasional gaze upon her, he is in fact the principal object of the gaze—the projection of Tennessee Williams' desire to write about his attraction to the male body. Through, Blanche, Williams is able to gaze upon the male without having to out himself as a gay playwright. His use of the gaze destabilizes traditional masculinity, subverts the closet, and forces the audience (even if they are unaware of it) to participate in an undermining of its own assumptions about the "naturalness" of heterosexuality and males' attractions to women.

In his book *The Arena of Masculinity*, Brian Pronger argues that "When a gay man looks at another man in the showers or locker room, it is never from the position of power that straight men have when they look at women at the beach or on the street. In fact, the erotic world that is invoked in homosexual voyeurism is one of equality in the gender myth and the paradoxical *violation* of masculine power rather than the orthodox, heterosexual *confirmation* of power difference that is fundamental to heterosexual desire. . . ."[28] Like the heterosexual male's gaze, the gay gaze, in the words of Susan Bordo, "shares with orthodox masculinity a celebration of masculine power" by giving it "intense erotic meaning."[29] Nevertheless, there is, as Bordo suggests, a "'deconstruction' of the icons of male power, even as they are worshipped."[30] When Williams employs the seeming reversal of the heterosexual male gaze by having Blanche DuBois gaze upon Stanley Kowalski and the lovely paper boy, he is both celebrating and subverting traditional masculinity—and, by implication, heterosexuality. Gay men clearly do not share equality with heterosexual men; instead, they transgress by calling into question the normativity of heterosexuality and conventional masculinity.

For if the gay man dares gaze upon the heterosexual male, he destabilizes heterosexual normativity and de-naturalizes the heterosexual male gaze, opening the door not only for the female gaze but also the opportunity to "de-institutionalize" heterosexuality, patriarchy, the objectification of women, and the stability of the heterosexual male's sexual desire. As Pronger and Bordo imply, the gay gaze upon the heterosexual male allows the gay man to participate in a subversive act in a heterosexist society and becomes a source of empowerment and defiance of those rules by which he has become imprisoned and oppressed. By desiring to possess that which is forbidden to him (the presumably heterosexual male's body), the gay male defies the very patriarchal masculinity and heterosexuality which has disempowered him. There is power in the gaze for the gay man—albeit short-lived. Many a gay man's look on a presumably heterosexual male's body has inspired anxiety and even called into question the masculinity and sexual orientation of the object of the gaze. Undoubtedly, Williams uses his plays to gaze upon the male body. In his introduction to the *Collected Stories*, Gore Vidal points out that Williams said he could not write "'any sort of story . . . unless there is at least one character in it for whom I have physical desire.'"[31] Through Blanche's gaze, Williams demonstrates clearly that his attraction to and desire for the male body—the presumed heterosexual body of Stanley Kowalski—is the center of the play.

Blanche's subversive gaze, her defiance of heterosexual norms for women, most reflects her gay subjectivity. For when she centers her life on attraction to—desire for—the male body, Williams is able to write his own desire for the audience. Blanche's desire for male bodies occurs throughout the play. She tries to seduce a teenage male student (an action stereotypically associated with closeted gay men of Williams' generation and not heterosexual women) and is fired for having corrupted a minor (a charge often launched against gay men in the past when they are caught with an underage teenager or young adult just coming out *and* a social sanction which reinscribes the norm of compulsory heterosexuality). With the paper boy, she expresses erotic yearning toward his innocent adolescent body when she says, "You make my mouth water"[32] and talks of a cherry soda. Her character clearly establishes the play's erotic center on the gay playwright's attraction to his own sex.

Nevertheless, because of his aspirations of becoming a commercially successful playwright, Williams could only project his sexual attraction for men through the play's overt heterosexual dimensions. Blanche is a woman and therefore can be attracted to a man without arousing the suspicion of an unknowing American audience that the gay male (and the author himself) is the real subject of the play and that his erotic attraction toward members of his own sex is embodied through a female projection. Unlike the traditional male gaze as described by Laura Mulvey and Kaja Silverman, Blanche, on the surface, reverses it—with the female gaze itself becoming an equalizing element.[33] As a female projection of a male homosexual, Blanche enables the gay male to gaze upon the male body in front of the audience and makes viewers participate in a subversion of their own concepts of normality and empowers both women and gay men to look defiantly upon that which traditional male subjectivity will not allow in film and drama.

To suggest female subjectivity (and I am extending this to gay subjectivity and its emphasis on the male as object) without the male gaze does, as Silverman suggests, "challenge every conception by means of which we have previously known her [him], since it is precisely as *body* that she is constructed."[34] Peter Lehman writes in *Running Scared*, a study of filmic representations of the male body: ". . . the silence surrounding the sexual representation of the male body is itself totally in the service of traditional patriarchy. . . ."[35] Although Lehman is directly concerned with film, Williams' plays, by representing the male as sexual object, undercut and destabilize patriarchy. And even though Williams could not represent the penis, the most taboo part of the male anatomy, on stage during the 1940s, he could nevertheless suggest that the male body is an object of the gaze.

While Stanley clearly gazes on Blanche, he becomes the primary object of the gaze for her, and by extension for the gay playwright, and thus the audience. Therefore, Blanche's role is that of both woman and homosexual. Known for his display of raw masculine sensuality, Stanley, especially as played by Marlon Brando on stage and in the film, frequently appears without his shirt and arouses the gaze of the heterosexual women and homosexual men in the audience—and perhaps even the admiration of a few heterosexual men and lesbians. Shirtless, he becomes the fetishized object of the gaze. Representing the ideal masculine body, Stanley threatens both the sensitivity and sexual identity of the poet/homosexual and the ideal Southern lady,

Blanche DuBois, for the heterosexual male's body/his masculinity is what she and Williams himself as transgressors desire. Stanley's eroticism also produces an ambiguity for spectators which calls into question the "closet" or mask of heterosexuality and subversively destabilizes heterosexual and masculine normativity. Through accomplishing this goal, Williams participates in the form of power associated with the heterosexual male gaze by desiring to possess the heterosexual man.

The "closeted" gaze does not, however, go without punishment for Blanche DuBois, but interpreting the heroine's fall within a gay context is also problematic and called into question—substantiating Savran's claim about the complex nature of Williams' radicalism. Although Stanley is in many respects the play's villain because he destroys the sensitive soul, Blanche DuBois, he ironically serves as Williams' embodiment of the ideal man, who celebrates his sexuality and represents an earthy sensuality. At the same time he destroys the sensitive souls of the world like Blanche DuBois and, by implication, her husband, the artist-homosexual. He will make Blanche the submissive woman just as society forces gay men into submission by imposing the "closet," reasserting heterosexual normativity, and emasculating men who do not adhere to a heterosexual male-centered social construct. Furthermore, Stanley, the epitome of the "out" heterosexual man who is perpetually self re-outing as per Sedgwick and Butler, becomes the destroyer of the "closet"—leading to Blanche's demise. It seems that, in Williams' view, homosexuality for men, like unconventional gender identities for women, cannot exist in an oppressive patriarchal society. They become too threatening to the established power of the Stanley Kowalskis and heterosexual men in the world. Thus, the outcome of the play calls attraction to the male body into question—but not without irony.

When Blanche becomes the victim of Stanley Kowalski, her role and Allan's are reversed. As critics have sometimes observed (see Arthur Ganz, for example), Stanley becomes the destroyer of Blanche and as a result functions to avenge the death of the gay poet.[36] Because her masculine behavior and gaze—her transgressive behavior—have upset the patriarchal male gaze, she must become the "feminine" to Stanley's "masculine" sexuality. Though Stanley is comfortable with the body and the flesh, ironically, at the same time, he is not comfortable with Blanche, who has so clearly violated the very terms upon which male heterosexuality must be based. His forced submission—rape—of her results, then, from his attempt, through violence, to destroy and control both the "feminine" impulses in men and the "masculine" impulses in women. More importantly, he can deny the same impulses in his own nature. Through Stanley's violations of the norms, the social and sexual taboos against female promiscuity and male homosexuality which Blanche embodies are punished.

Curiously, at the same time, Stanley's mask as a heterosexual male remains problematic. On the one hand, he masquerades as heterosexual; on the other hand, he willingly becomes the object of the female, and, by implication, the gay male's gaze. Like gay men, he embodies the masculinity and male physical beauty which attracts the gay male's gaze, for it is as body that gay men have been written in America's homophobic society. Gay men offend traditional American society by being attracted to the male body. In fact, many Americans focus on the sex act between homosexuals when they consider gay identity. To some extent, Williams' focus on his own sexual attraction plays into this mythos, but at the same time Stanley's roles as surrogate gay male and sex object enable the playwright to violate the very norms Stanley seems to represent. Embodying both gay male desire and female transgression, he rapes Blanche to prove that he is an object for her sexual attraction, her female gaze, but not a conquered one. His violence against her, while villainy of the highest order, enables Williams to punish Blanche for her transgressive behavior in the same way she had punished Allan for his/their attraction to the taboo male body.

Since neither Blanche's female sexuality nor Allan's heterosexuality is authentic, it is no surprise that the image of masculinity and heterosexuality which Stanley represents is not real either. He embodies the subjectivity of Allan when becoming the punisher for Blanche's single sin of "deliberate cruelty." When he rapes the woman masquerading as a gay man, he becomes one with the gay man for whom he wields justice. And when he is inside Blanche (enclosed by her) as Allan has been inside her, he, like all of Blanche's other "conquests," becomes, metaphorically speaking of course, a gay man. By being in Blanche, Stanley has been in the gay male and, as a result, participates in his own de-naturalization of heterosexuality. By becoming one with the pseudo-gay male, he undermines his own normativity. Thus, Williams destroys the illusion of masculine heterosexuality when Stanley stands in for Allan and the playwright's gay subjectivity. He metes out justice the gay way.

Stanley's relationship with Stella also may be read as another means by which Williams projects his own desire for the male body as well as by which he problematizes the social constructs of heterosexuality, masculinity, and femininity. When Blanche criticizes Stanley for his barbaric abuse of her, Stella defends him in this way: "But there are things that happen between a man and a woman in the dark—that sort of make everything else seem—unimportant."[37] Drawing attention to her attraction to Stanley as sexual being, Stella reiterates the playwright's fascination with the male as lover. The play seems to indicate that the primary reason Stella remains with Stanley is that he is a great lover. This fact not only reinforces Blanche's frequent gazing on Stanley but also indicates that the roles of men and women have been reversed. Traditional Southern women even today are not generally encouraged to express openly their sexual desires for men.

Stanley's abuse of Stella and Blanche may also be read as his attempt to reestablish traditional heterosexual normativity. As he tells Blanche early in the play, upon his discovery that Belle Reve was lost, "You see, under the Napoleonic code—a man has to take an interest in his wife's affairs. . . ."[38] Such lines indicate that Stanley does not like change—that he wants the roles of men and women to be clearly defined and that Blanche clearly threatens his view of manhood since she is to him a transgressor. His abuse of Stella and Blanche during the poker nights and the "clearing the table" scene clearly shows the problem of women and conventional marriage in postwar American society. In the latter scene he says: "What do you two think you are? A pair of queens? Remember what Huey Long said—'Every Man is a King!' And I am the king around here, so don't forget it!"[39] This passage not only is important because it is one example of Williams' use of camp (and Blanche is a "campy" character herself) in the play but also because it indicates clearly that Stanley becomes the enforcer of heterosexual normativity in the play. Stanley's outbursts represent conventional American society's reaction to the threat of otherness—an otherness that not only includes women like Blanche who are in his opinion playing and trying to usurp the roles of men but males who reflect a sensitive and thus gay nature which is not suppressed. He illustrates what Boone considers as the conservative reaction to the increasing fluidity of male and female identities after World War II:

> . . . [T]he unprecedented sexual freedom experienced by *both* men and women in the postwar period . . . proceeded hand-in-hand with a retrenchment of traditional gender ideals. Ironically, this conservative reaction can be seen as the outcome of the destabilization of accepted social assumptions about 'masculine' and 'feminine' behavior occasioned by a new era of sexual permissiveness. . . . In the process homosexuality increasingly became the scapegoat for an array of sexual, gender, and textual anxieties, its status as the 'other' face of heterosexuality never far beneath the surface of the dominant . . . discourse of sexuality in England and America.[40]

For Stanley his own norms should be the basis of society, and his relationships with his peers and women are a way of reinscribing heterosexual, masculine idealism. Ironically, his own exaggerated male behavior is virtually impossible for even his peers to live up to, most especially Mitch, whom Stanley considers different from him.

To reinforce the possibility that Stanley's own "out" heterosexuality is perhaps a mask for homosexuality, Williams also disguises his gay subjectivity through the character of Mitch while the playwright simultaneously cracks open the door. For Mitch is a mama's boy, which, in the 1940s and even to some extent today, might be read as code for a gay man or sissy. When he first appears, he explains to Stanley why he doesn't stay at home: "She says to go out, so I go, but I don't enjoy it. All the while I keep wondering how she is."[41] Stanley, true to form, belittles Mitch for his lack of masculinity: "Hurry back [from the bathroom] and we'll fix you a sugar-tit."[42] As Vito Russo has shown in his important book *The Celluloid Closet*, the sissy in films and popular culture as a whole represented the stereotypes of the gay man and thus reinforced a homophobic reaction in the audience.[43] Stanley's response to Mitch's whining about going home to his mother functions similarly to the "sissy" in American films in the first half of the century: "Early sissies were yardsticks for measuring the virility of the men around them."[44] This suggests that Stanley feels he must perform as heterosexual masculine male by elevating his own gender status above those around him, most notably Mitch. The latter desires to belong to the brotherhood of male heterosexuality but is stigmatized and thus is not completely "male" in the world of Stanley Kowalski.

As his frustration with Stanley might suggest, Mitch is different from his peers; he is a sensitive soul. This is made clear early in the play when Blanche opens his cigarette case to discover lines from Elizabeth Barrett Browning. During this scene he tells her about the young girl who has given him the case: "She knew she was dying when she give me this. A very strange girl, very sweet—very!"[45] Like the "strange" girl who haunts Mitch, Allan is, to use the phrase from gay camp, a "girl" who haunts Blanche. In this passage and throughout the rest of the play, Williams emphasizes Mitch's association with "otherness," thus linking him with Blanche and Allan. As noted scholar C. W. E. Bigsby says, Blanche is "drawn to another man whose sexuality seems in some way suspect, a mother's boy, weak enough, she supposes, to be made to enact the essentially adolescent fantasies which she stage-manages with such care."[46]

Similarly, Father Gene D. Phillips says of Mitch: "Given the parallels between Mitch and Allan, it is not surprising that it is to Mitch alone that Blanche recounts the tale of her husband's death."[47] After Blanche's famous scene which "outs" her gay husband (and her resulting problems with her own sexual identity), Mitch declares, "You need somebody. And I need somebody, too."[48] Traditional men in American society generally have not openly admitted their need for anyone outside themselves. Like Allan and Blanche, Mitch is an "other," a metaphorical gay man.

When he discovers the truth about Blanche, Mitch parallels her own realization when she became aware of Allan's closeted self. Superficially, he plays the conventional male role by getting drunk (like Stanley) and treating Blanche roughly. But his stability as a heterosexual man has been challenged. Through his act of deliberate cruelty, he becomes like Blanche, who embodies gay subjectivity. Moreover, he rejects Blanche because she fails to live up to her illusion—to the ideal he has for her. Most importantly, however, Blanche is rejected because "You're not clean enough to bring in the house with my mother."[49] In this scene Williams again reinscribes the "otherness" of Mitch as a mama's boy. At the play's closing when Mitch expresses his anger over Stanley's destruction of Blanche, he has returned to the homosocially acceptable world where women need to be defended. But he is attacking its extreme representative, Stanley. Mitch is still a part of (as well as apart from) Stanley's homosocial circle, which ends the play with the game of "seven-card stud"—a pun for the "stud" Stanley, who has destroyed Blanche, and the symbol of the privileged masculine heterosexual world which does the same to all women and gay men (and even presumably heterosexual men like Mitch) who cross binary boundaries.[50] Mitch's gender identity as heterosexual and masculine, like Stanley's, remains problematized—suggesting, once again, the fluidity of these social constructions.

Outlining the "structure of homosexual discourse," critic David Bergman points out that "homosexuality—even as conceived by homosexuals—cannot be viewed outside of the constructs of heterosexuality."[51] He particularly outlines the characteristic elements of the homosexual writer's rhetoric: the separation of sexual identity and sexual practice; the awareness of otherness; the recognition that homosexuality is "a lifelong condition"; the "genuineness of [the] experience" of being homosexual; the "equality of its relations."[52] In line with Bergman's observations about gay discourse, *A Streetcar Named Desire* is an attempt to call into question not only the plight of the gay "other" and his counterpart, the aggressive female sexual being, but also the problem of the "closet" for homosexuality and its forced submission into a heterosexual male's paradigm for normativity. Gender identity and sexual orientation are both destabilized in Williams' works.

Through all his major characters, both on- and off-stage, Williams projects his own gay subjectivity and undermines the very norms of gender identity and sexuality which his audience may share. However, at the end, the prevailing hegemony is, on the surface, reinforced through Blanche's madness and through Mitch's (a feminine "mama's boy") rejection of all that she embodies. The ending allows the very normative behavior of which Blanche and Allan are victims to be reinscribed. But it does not do this without clearly calling into question the norms which Stanley Kowalski and Blanche, in her earlier days at Belle Reve and her sham of a marriage to a gay man, appear to represent. Stanley's punishment for Blanche is "deliberate cruelty" just as her behavior towards her sensitive gay husband and Mitch's reactions toward her are similarly destructive. This deliberate cruelty becomes central to the play's theme of the effects of society on the individual and particularly its devastating intolerance of gay men. Stanley's overt action of destroying Blanche parallels the average heterosexual male's desire to destroy the gay "other." Without Blanche's homophobic actions toward Allan, the play's paradigm of sin, punishment, and retribution would not have taken place.

The plight of Blanche DuBois and Allan, her husband, may thus be read as a metaphor for the homosexual of the 1940s—an individual rejected by society, fearful of his own nature and truth, afraid of being ostracized. Like the psychologist Evelyn Hooker in her early studies of gay subjects during the 1950s, Williams implies that such qualities are not inherent to the status of being homosexual but forced upon the gay subject by an intolerant society. As he told John Hicks in an interview of 1979, "I think that society has imposed upon homosexuals a feeling of guilt. . . ."[53]

Because Williams circumvents the "closet" of homosexual subjectivity and questions the norms upon which heterosexual normativity and masculinity are based, *A Streetcar Named Desire* is a subversive play. Through the curious and ambiguous use of gay subjectivity and the gay male gaze, Williams attempts to open a space for the homosexual in American culture. As the closeted gay subtext of this play suggests, Williams, like most gay men before the Stonewall era, presumed he was expected to remain silent about his identity in order to gain success in a heterosexist culture all too fearful of its own ambivalence concerning the issues of gender identity, sexual relations, and same-sex unions. While superficially silent until 1970 about his identity, Williams created in the tragedy of Blanche DuBois a struggle that allowed a brief glimpse inside the closeted world of homosexuality. Attacking Williams for internalized homophobia, as several gay critics have done, therefore fails to account for Williams' accomplishment of conveying gay subjectivity through his subtle, though paradoxical, depiction of vulnerable men and women, and through images and symbols which suggest that repression of the "other" may not be in the best interest of America.

Notes

1. This essay will be part of my full-length book project, *Subverting the Closet: Tennessee Williams and the Evolution of Gay Theatrical Representation*, which is currently in progress. I wish to acknowledge the assistance of the West Virginia Humanities Council for a Summer 1997 grant to work on this essay and the project as a whole. I presented a shorter version of this essay for the 50th anniversary celebration of *Streetcar* at the Modern Language Association Convention in Toronto in December 1997.

2. Tennessee Williams, "Will God Talk Back to a Playwright?," interview by David Frost, in *Conversations with Tennessee Williams*, ed. Albert J. Devlin (Jackson and London: University Press of Mississippi, 1986), 146.

3. Adrienne Rich, "Compulsory Heterosexuality and Lesbian Existence," in *Adrienne Rich's Poetry and Prose*, ed. Barbara Charlesworth Gelpi and Albert Gelpi (New York: Norton, 1993), 203-224.

4. Eve Kosofsky Sedgwick, *Epistemology of the Closet* (Berkeley: University of California Press, 1990).

5. Judith Butler, "Imitation and Gender Insubordination." *Inside/Out: Lesbian Theories, Gay Theories*, ed. Diana Fuss (New York: Routledge, 1991), 24.

6. For recent and alternative readings of Williams' play other than those mentioned in the text, see Philip C. Kolin's *Confronting A Streetcar Named Desire: Essays in Critical Pluralism* (Westport, CT: Greenwood P, 1993)—especially Laurilyn Harris' essay "Perceptual Conflict and the Perversion of Creativity in *Streetcar*." For other sources, see also Dan Isaac's "No Past to Think In: Who Wins in *A Streetcar Named Desire?*" *Louisiana Literature* 14 (Fall 1997): 8-35. Isaac argues that Blanche is the moral center of the play, thus making her tragedy possible. In addition, see Philip C. Kolin's "'It's only a paper moon . . .': The Paper Ontologies in Tennessee Williams's *A Streetcar Named Desire*," *Modern Drama* 40 (1997): 454-467, in which he traces the images of paper in the play signifying Stanley's "hidden and revelatory" legalism and Blanche's hidden history. See also Dianne Cafagna, "Blanche DuBois and Maggie the Cat: Illusion and Reality in Tennessee Williams," *Critical Essays on Tennessee Williams*, ed. Robert A. Martin (New York: G. K. Hall, 1997), 119-131. Another essay, Nancy Tischler's "Sanitizing the *Streetcar*" uncovers information about the film of *Streetcar* and Lillian Hellman's suggestions for altering the gay content which seem similar to her own alteration of the lesbian content of *The Children's Hour* and *We Three*, its original film version. The essay appears in *Louisiana Literature* 14 (Fall 1997): 48-56.

7. Tennessee Williams, "Tennessee Williams Presents His Point of View," *New York Times Magazine*, 12 June 1960; reprint, *Where I Live: Selected Essays*, ed. Christine R. Day and Bob Woods (New York: New Directions), 116-117.

8. In Paul Newman's faithful film version John Malkovich portrays Tom as a gay man by using stereotypical mannerisms and giving his voice an effeminate quality. There should no longer be doubt as to the validity of a gay reading of *The Glass Menagerie*.

9. Dean Shackelford, "The Truth That Must Be Told: Gay Subjectivity, Homo-

phobia, and Social History in *Cat on a Hot Tin Roof*," *Tennessee Williams Annual Review* 1 (1998): 103-118.

10. DeJongh, Nicholas, *Not in Front of the Audience* (New York: Routledge, 1992), 72.

11. DeJongh, 69.

12. John M. Clum, *Acting Gay: Male Homosexuality in Modern Drama* (New York: Columbia University Press, 1992), 166.

13. For another gay-oriented reading of this and other Williams plays, see Mark Lilly, *Gay Men's Literature in the Twentieth Century* (New York: New York University Press, 1993). Robert J. Corber's *Homosexuality in Cold War America* (Durham: Duke University Press, 1997) includes an excellent essay on the closet in Williams' short story "Hard Candy" and play *Cat on a Hot Tin Roof.*

14. David Savran, *Communists, Cowboys, and Queers: The Politics of Masculinity in Arthur Miller and Tennessee Williams* (Minneapolis: University of Minnesota Press, 1992), 116.

15. Savran, 81.

16. Stanley Edgar Hyman, "Some Notes on the Albertine Strategy," *Hudson Review* 6 (Autumn 1953): 417-422; Stephen S. Stanton, "Introduction," *Tennessee Williams: A Collection of Critical Essays* (Englewood Cliffs, NJ: Prentice-Hall, 1977), 1-16.

17. Tennessee Williams, *A Streetcar Named Desire. The Theatre of Tennessee Williams*, Vol. 3 (New York: New Directions, 1971), 354. All references to this play are from this edition.

18. Joseph Allen Boone, *Libidinal Currents: Sexuality and the Shaping of Modernism* (Chicago: University of Chicago Press, 1997), 359.

19. Williams, 397.

20. Thomas P. Adler, *A Streetcar Named Desire: The Moth and the Lantern* (Boston: Twayne, 1990), 45.

21. Williams, 354.

22. Williams, 354.

23. Williams, 354.

24. Williams, 355.

25. Glum, 166.

26. Judith Butler, "Melancholy Gender/Refused Identification," in *Constructing Masculinity*, ed. Maurice Berger, Brian Wallis, and Simon Watson (New York: Routledge, 1995), 25.

27. Williams, 354.

28. Brian Pronger, *The Arena of Masculinity: Sports, Homosexuality, and the Meaning of Sex* (New York: St. Martin's Press, 1990), 205-06.

29. Susan Bordo, "Reading the Male Body," in *The Male Body: Features, Destinies, Exposures*, ed. Laurence Goldstein (Ann Arbor: University of Michigan Press, 1994), 284.

30. Bordo, 285.

31. Gore Vidal, "Introduction," *Tennessee Williams: Collected Stories* (New York: New Directions, 1985), xxiii.

32. Williams, 338.

---

33. Laura Mulvey, "Visual Pleasure and Narrative Cinema," *Screen* 16.3 (1975): 6-18; Kaja Silverman, "Dis-Embodying the Female Voice," in *Revision: Essays in Feminist Film Criticism*, ed. Mary Ann Doane, Patricia Mellencamp, and Linda Williams (Los Angeles: American Film Institute, 1984), 131-149.

34. Silverman, 135.

35. Peter Lehman, *Running Scared: Masculinity and the Representation of the Male Body* (Philadelphia: Temple University Press, 1993), 4. Little has been written concerning the gay gaze, but one especially good essay on the representation of the male body and its challenges to masculinity is William G. Doty, "Baring the Flesh: Aspects of Contemporary Male Iconography," *Men's Bodies, Men's Gods: Male Identities in a (Post-) Christian Culture*, ed. Bjorn Krondorfer (New York: New York University Press, 1996), 267-308.

36. Arthur Ganz, "Tennessee Williams: A Desperate Morality," *Tennessee Williams: A Collection of Critical Essays*, ed. Stephen S. Stanton (Englewood Cliffs, NJ: Prentice-Hall, 1977), 123-137.

37. Williams, 321.

38. Williams, 284.

39. Williams, 371.

40. Boone, 360.

41. Williams, 288.

42. Williams, 288.

43. Vito Russo, *The Celluloid Closet: Homosexuality in the Movies* (New York: Harper & Row, 1981).

44. Russo, 16.

45. Williams, 298.

46. C. W. E. Bigsby, *Modern American Drama, 1945-1990* (Cambridge: Cambridge University Press, 1992), 45.

47. Gene D. Phillips, S.J. "Blanche's Phantom Husband: Homosexuality on Stage and Screen." *Louisiana Literature* 14 (Fall 1997), 40.

48. Williams, 356.

49. Williams, 390.

50. Williams, 419.

51. David Bergman, *Gaiety Transfigured: Gay Self-Representation in American Literature* (Madison: University of Wisconsin Press, 1991), 26.

52. Bergman, 31.

53. Tennessee Williams, "Bard of Duncan Street: Scene Four," interview by John Hicks, in *Conversations with Tennessee Williams*, ed. Albert J. Devlin (Jackson: University Press of Mississippi, 1986), 322.

Works Cited

Adler, Thomas P. *A Streetcar Named Desire: The Moth and the Lantern.* Boston: Twayne, 1990.

Bergman, David. *Gaiety Transfigured: Gay Self-Representation in American Literature.* Madison: University of Wisconsin Press, 1991.

Bigsby, C. W. E. *Modern American Drama, 1945-1990.* Cambridge: Cambridge University Press, 1992.

Boone, Joseph Allen. *Libidinal Currents: Sexuality and the Shaping of Modernism.* Chicago: University of Chicago Press, 1997.

Bordo, Susan. "Reading the Male Body" in *The Male Body: Features, Destinies, Exposures.* Edited by Laurence Goldstein. Ann Arbor: University of Michigan Press, 1994.

Butler, Judith. "Imitation and Gender Insubordination" in *Inside/Out: Lesbian Theories, Gay Theories.* Edited by Diana Fuss. New York: Routledge. 1991.

Butler, Judith. "Melancholy Gender/refused Identification" in *Constructing Masculinity.* Edited by Maurice Berger, Brian Wallis, and Simon Watson. New York: Routledge, 1995.

Cafagna, Dianne. "Blanche DuBois and Maggie the Cat: Illusion and Reality in Tennessee Williams" in *Critical Essays on Tennessee Williams.* Edited by Robert A. Martin. New York: G. K. Hall, 1997.

Clum, John M. *Acting Gay: Male Homosexuality in Modern Drama.* New York: Columbia University Press, 1992.

Corber, Robert J. *Homosexuality in Cold War America.* Durham: Duke University Press, 1997.

DeJongh, Nicholas. *Not in Front of the Audience.* New York: Routledge, 1992.

Devlin, Albert J., ed. *Conversations with Tennessee Williams.* Jackson and London: University Press of Mississippi, 1986.

Doty, William G. "Baring the Flesh: Aspects of Contemporary Male Iconography" in *Men's Bodies, Men's Gods: Male Identities in a (Post-) Christian Culture.* Edited by Bjorn Krondorfer. New York: New York University Press, 1996.

Ganz, Arthur. "Tennessee Williams: A Desperate Morality" in *Tennessee Williams: A Collection of Critical Essays.* Edited by Stephen S. Stanton. Englewood Cliffs, NJ: Prentice-Hall, 1977.

Hyman, Stanley Edgar. "Some Notes on the Albertine Strategy." *Hudson Review.* 6 (1953): 417-422.

Isaac, Dan. "No Past to Think In: Who Wins in *A Streetcar Named Desire?*" *Louisiana Literature.* 14 (1997, 2): 8-35.

Kolin, Philip C., ed. *Confronting A Streetcar Named Desire: Essays in Critical Pluralism.* Westport, CT: Greenwood Press, 1993.

Kolin, Philip C. "'It's Only a Paper Moon . . .': The Paper Ontologies in Tennessee Williams's *A Streetcar Named Desire.*" *Modern Drama.* 40 (1997): 454-467.

Lehman, Peter. *Running Scared: Masculinity and the Representation of the Male Body.* Philadelphia: Temple University Press, 1993.

Lilly, Mark. *Gay Men's Literature in the Twentieth Century*. New York: New York University Press, 1993.

Mulvey, Laura. "Visual Pleasure and Narrative Cinema" in *Revision: Essays in Feminist Film Criticism*. Edited by Mary Ann Doane, Patricia Mellencamp, and Linda Williams. Los Angeles: American Film Institute, 1984. First published in *Screen* 16 (3): 6-18.

Phillips, Gene D., S.J. "Blanche's Phantom Husband: Homosexuality on Stage and Screen." *Louisiana Literature*. 14 (1997, 2): 36-47.

Pronger, Brian. *The Arena of Masculinity: Sports, Homosexuality, and the Meaning of Sex*. New York: St. Martin's Press, 1990.

Rich, Adrienne. "Compulsory Heterosexuality and Lesbian Existence" in *Adrienne Rich's Poetry and Prose*. Edited by Barbara Charlesworth Gelpi and Albert Gelpi. New York: W.W. Norton, 1993.

Russo, Vito. *The Celluloid Closet: Homosexuality in the Movies*. New York: Harper & Row, 1981.

Savran, David. *Communists, Cowboys, and Queers: The Politics of Masculinity in Arthur Miller and Tennessee Williams*. Minneapolis: University of Minnesota Press, 1992.

Sedgwick, Eve Kosofsky. *Epistemology of the Closet*. Berkeley: University of California Press, 1990.

Shackelford, Dean. "The Truth That Must Be Told: Gay Subjectivity, Homophobia, and Social History in *Cat on a Hot Tin Roof*." *Tennessee Williams Annual Review*. 1 (1998): 103-118.

Silverman, Kaja. "Dis-embodying the Female Voice" in *Revision: Essays in Feminist Film Criticism*. Edited by Mary Ann Doane, Patricia Mellencamp, and Linda Williams. Los Angeles: American Film Institute, 1984.

Stanton, Stephen S. Introduction to *Tennessee Williams: A Collection of Critical Essays*. Edited by Stephen S. Stanton. Englewood Cliffs, NJ: Prentice-Hall, 1977.

Tischler, Nancy. "Sanitizing the *Streetcar*." *Louisiana Literature*. 14 (1997, 2): 48-56.

Vidal, Gore. Introduction to *Tennessee Williams: Collected Stories*. New York: New Directions, 1985.

Williams, Tennessee. *A Streetcar Named Desire* in *The Theatre of Tennessee Williams. Vol. 3*. New York: New Directions, 1971.

Williams, Tennessee. "Tennessee Williams Presents His Point of View" in *Where I Live: Selected Essays*. Edited by Christine R. Day and Bob Woods. New York: New Directions, 1978. First published in *New York Times Magazine*.

A Streetcar Named Desire:
Spatial Violation and Sexual Violence_____

Anne Fleche

> We see from the outside what could not be seen within.
>
> —Tennessee Williams on *Streetcar*

In *A Streetcar Named Desire*, Williams confronts directly the violence implicit in *The Glass Menagerie*. Once again he experiments with space, but in *Streetcar* he examines meaning in its relation to *desire*, that structure of inside and outside, of image and object, that produces the subject. The relation of inside to outside—essence to appearance—is one of representation's great disputes. It is also, more or less, the relation of expressionism to realism. Expressionism's optical distortions, its emphasis on childhood, madness, crime—on emotion as truth's medium—break the connections set up to be analyzed in realism. Realism depends on a stable space and a stable perspective, as we have seen, that enable its mimetic exertions to seem effortless, "natural." What makes the play go is inferred from its surfaces: the past from the present, the inner life from the character, the inner rooms from the visible spaces. The critic's analytical talent is given plenty to work on in this inductive, part-for-the-whole structure. But like cinema, and far more deliberately, expressionism imploded realism's composition, blowing up the inner life until its outer frames snapped. While the principal distinction of "inner-outer," which underlies both dramatic forms, remained firmly in place theoretically, expressionism ended up undermining it in practice. After all, it was an unstable mixture of impression and expression, for how could we have a "pure" expressionist play? How would we be able to *see* it?[1]

The vestiges of realistic space are theoretically behind expressionism, or before it, rather, acting as the reference for "inner" life, providing the objective language for it. Criticism and analysis can never only look at one thing: the comparison implied by mimetic practice is simply reproduced at another level of abstraction. To see something we have always to be looking past something else, as realism teaches us to look past a curtain, then *past* the fourth wall, "into" the scene (chapter 4). Yet this desire to see beyond, as well as into, surfaces *is* somewhat of the truth this gaze is searching for. It's not an object but a propulsion with a theoretically endless trajectory that won't stop to be analyzed, nor to respect boundaries, but pushes on blindly far out—and in—to space.

Realism is the drama of sexual life: its representation of social and family surfaces via the voyeurism of the fourth wall is designed to get at the hidden behavior of the individual psyche, what people think but don't say, what they do "in private." The omnivorous discourse of realism subsumes every desire into a promised fullness bent on keeping the unspeakable under moral control. But the moral code is elaborated in language, language that proliferates the more it reaches for power. The moral imperative of desire is this: that "you will seek to transform your desire, your every desire, into discourse" (Foucault, *History* 21). As discourse, desire becomes an inexhaustible fountain of metaphor. Realism's repression and secrecy, far from silencing sexual desire, incite a discourse of sexuality. "What is peculiar to modern societies, in fact [Foucault writes], is not that they consigned sex to a shadow existence, but that they dedicated themselves to speaking of it *ad infinitum*, while exploiting it as the secret" (Foucault, *History* 35, italics Foucault's). And this is a difficult plot to escape—Foucault has to spend lots of time talking about what he isn't talking about. The strategy of inexhaustible revelation is fixity—realism sets representational limits so as to assure truth the bright light of scrutiny.

Meanwhile realism's analytical structure assures the sexual act its pastness, its remoteness: its always-already is reassuringly repetitious, in a code that, promising sex its full revelation, nevertheless prohibits its return. If realism is *the* bourgeois dramatic form, then sex is *the* bourgeois dramatic subject. What can be more crucial than the survival and enrichment of the species, the harnessing of energies for production, the containment of the threat of disorder? Incest, homosexuality, and other "perversions" are completely off the track of realism's linear, evolutionary development, as surely as eugenics, adaptation, and heterosexuality provide its strategic security. "Through the themes of health, progeny, race, the future of the species, the vitality of the social body, power spoke of sexuality and to sexuality" (Foucault, *History* 147). Yet as the word "desire" implies, sexuality has an ambiguous power in language; it is both empirical "truth" and symbolic "representation"—it is "sex" but also more than sex, for sex is "able to function as a unique signifier and as a universal signified" (Foucault, *History* 154). Desire is both bodily sexuality and its "spiritual" tendency, an all-inclusive guide to the smallest points of connection between the hidden and the visible.

> Discourse, therefore, had to trace the meeting line of the body and the soul, following all its meanderings: beneath the surface of the sins, it would lay bare the unbroken nervure of the flesh. Under the authority of a language that had been carefully expurgated so that it was no longer directly named, sex was taken charge of, tracked down as it were, by a discourse that aimed to allow it no obscurity, no respite. [Foucault, *History* 20]

Realism has its roots in the confessional. At the intersection of the (hidden) soul and the (visible) body, a discourse of desire weaves back and forth between flesh and its inner truth, in a language whose subject is "no longer directly named." The language of materiality and the language of ideas are the same.[2] "They told me to take a street-car named Desire, and then transfer to one called Cemeteries and ride six blocks and get off at—Elysian Fields!" (246).

Language's metaphor of experience, spun out, is allegory, as it leaves implicit the comparison it is making between life and life's equivalent expression. Unlike simile, or symbol, metaphor and allegory do not try to enter experience but keep their distance, paralleling life, not intersecting it (cf. de Man 191-92). The fact that the "allegori-

---

cal" language here describes real places, cars, and transfers has the effect of making its doubleness the more apparent. ("[A]ll desires," de Man warns, "fall prey to the duplicities of expression" [12].) Realism's language is the metaphor of experience; allegory, as de Man reminds us, maintains this doubleness, the "desire for a unity toward which . . . thought and poetic strategy strive" (195). The moment in *The Glass Menagerie* when the unicorn is broken suggests a rupture that makes the representation what it is—the excision of what is uncontainable, of what cannot be "measured" or "copied" from pattern (both related meanings of the word "norm"). The scene enacts the severed connection between image and copy, the containment of desire's excess in the recognizable form. What this broken image offers, then, is not a criticism of reality, nor of artistic representation—the arguments for and against mimesis, respectively—but a reflection on the desire for their union, which is never satisfied.[3] The desire for the union of reality and representation is maintained in allegory, which, rather than merely representing "a meaning that it does not itself constitute," establishes the distance "between the representative and the semantic function of language" (de Man 189). The allegorical thus tends to seem inorganic, apart from experience, "purely mechanical, an abstraction whose original meaning is . . . devoid of substance . . . ; it is an immaterial shape" (ibid. 191-92). The "mechanistic" argument against allegory is telling: form and function must seem indigenous, not forced, empirical, not "abstract." Truth is a found unity, not a sophisticated invention of the mind. We cannot be seen to be making our meanings up.

Through allegory the desire for unity with the real loses none of its indefinite yearning. Williams's plays, with their allegorical language, seem to have a tentative, unfinished character. The ending of *A Streetcar Named Desire* compares the cycle of fertility (spring to fall, pregnancy to birth) with the poker players' game of bluff and chance. These rhythms are not resolutions. Williams's plays thus continually reveal the desire for an ending. Memory or recollection, a sense of its pastness, is crucial to representation and, consequently, as we have seen, to realism, which creates order through the temporalizing of events. Realism's analytical structure starts from a proposed shape or vision of totality and then works backward, breaking it down into re-formable segments. The "future" toward which it tends is in fact its starting point. Realism represents desire as something with a goal—"eyes on the finish" (Brecht 37), something that looks past a present into a consoling "future," where a sense of the past and a sense of the future amount to the same thing. In *The Glass Menagerie*, for instance, Amanda's optimistic speeches to Laura, apparently rooted in an idyllic past, are echoed by the Gentleman Caller, who raves about the future. We are used to this parallel in Chekhov: one longing looks pretty much like another. Revealed as a repetitious wandering between body and soul, visible and invisible—unrecapturable—desire loses its sense of an object: it is constantly on the move, "a fundamental pattern of being that discards any possibility of satisfaction" (de Man 17).

The metalanguage of desire seems to preclude development, to deny progress. And yet it seems "natural" to read *A Streetcar Named Desire* as an allegorical journey toward Blanche's apocalyptic destruction at the hands of her "executioner," Stanley. The play's violence, its baroque images of decadence and lawlessness, promises its audience the thrilling destruction of the aristocratic southern Poe-esque mothlike neurasthenic female "Blanche" by the apelike brutish male from the American melting pot. The play is full in fact of realism's developmental language of evolution, "degeneration," eugenics. Before deciding that Stanley is merely an "ape," Blanche sees him as an asset: "Oh I guess he's just not the type that goes for jasmine perfume, but maybe he's what we need to mix with our blood now that we've lost Belle Reve" (285). The surprising thing about this play is that the allegorical reading also seems to be the most "realistic" one, the reading that imposes a unity of language and experience to make structural sense of the play, that is, to make its events organic, natural, inevitable. And yet this reading feels false, because allegorical language resists being pinned down by realistic analysis—it's always only half a story.

But it is possible to close the gap between the language and the stage image, between the stage image and its "double" reality, by a double forgetting: first we must forget that realism is literature, and thus already a metaphor, and then we must forget the distance between allegory and realistic "unity." To say that realism's empiricism is indistinguishable from its metaphor is to set *Streetcar* on a course that is one with a moral, natural ordering of events. Stanley is wrong and Blanche is right, the moralists agree. But the hypocrisy of the "priggish" reading is soon revealed in its ambivalence toward Blanche/Stanley: to make a unity of the play, to order events sequentially, requires a reading that finds Blanche's rape inevitable, a condition of the formal structure: she's the erring woman who gets what she "asks" for (her realistic antecedents are clear). For the prigs, this outcome might not be unthinkable, though it might be—what is worse—distasteful. But Williams seems deliberately to be *making* interpretation a problem: he doesn't exclude the prigs' reading; he invites it. What makes *Streetcar* different from *Glass Menagerie*, let alone O'Neill's late plays, is its constant self-betrayal into and out of analytical norms. The realistic setups in this play really *feel like* setups, a magician's tricks, inviting readings that leave you hanging from your own schematic noose. Analytically, this play is a trap; it's brilliantly confused; yet without following its false leads, there is no way to get anywhere at all. *Streetcar* has a map, but it's changed the street signs, relying on the impulse of desire to take the play past its plots. In a way it's wrong to say Williams doesn't write endings. He writes elaborate *strings* of them.

Williams has given *Streetcar* strong ties to the reassuring rhetoric of realism. Several references to Stanley's career as "A Master Sergeant in the Engineers' Corps" set the action in the "present," immediately after the war. The geographical location, as with *Glass Menagerie*, is specific, the neighborhood life represented with a greater naturalistic fidelity—"Above the music of the 'Blue Piano' the voices of people on the street can be heard overlapping" (243). Lighting and sound effects may give the scene "a kind of lyricism," but this effect seems itself a realistic touch for "The Quarter." Even the interior set, when it appears (after a similar wipe-out of the fourth wall), resembles *Glass Menagerie* in layout and configuration: a ground floor apartment, with two rooms separated by portieres, occupied by three characters, one of them male.

Yet there are also *troubling* "realistic" details, to which the play seems to point. The mise-en-scène seems to be providing too much enclosure to provide for closure: there's no place for anyone to *go*. There is no fire escape, even though in *this* play someone does yell "Fire! Fire! Fire!" (sc. 9)—in fact, heat and fire and escape are prominent verbal and visual themes. And the flat does not, as it seems to in *Glass Menagerie*, extend to other rooms beyond the wings but ends in a cul-de-sac: a doorway to the bathroom that becomes Blanche's significant place for escape and "privacy." Most disturbing, perhaps, is not the increased sense of confinement but this absence of privacy, of analytical, territorial space. No gentleman caller invited for supper invades this time, but an anarchic wilderness of French Quarter hoi polloi who spill onto the set and into the flat as negligently as the piano music from the bar around the corner. There doesn't seem to be anywhere to go to evade the intrusiveness and the violence; when the flat erupts, as it does on the poker night, Stanley's tirade sends Stella and Blanche upstairs to Steve and Eunice, the landlords with, of course, an unlimited run of the house ("We own this place so I can let you in" [248]), whose goings-on are equally violent and uncontained. "You know that one upstairs? (more laughter) One time (laughing) the plaster—(laughing) cracked—" (294). The violence isn't an isolated climax but a repetitive pattern of the action, a state of being—it doesn't resolve anything.

> Blanche: I'm not used to such—
> Mitch: Naw, it's a shame this had to happen when you just got here. But don't take it serious.
> Blanche: Violence! Is so—
> Mitch: Set down on the steps and have a cigarette with me. [308]

Anxiety and conflict have become permanent and unresolvable, inconclusive. It isn't clear what, if anything, they *mean*. Unlike realistic drama, which produces clashes in order to push the action forward, *Streetcar* refuses its events a clarity of function, an orderliness.

The ordering of events, which constitutes the temporality of realism, is thus no less arbitrary in *Streetcar* than the ordering of *space*: the outside keeps becoming the inside, and vice versa. Williams has done more to relativize space in *Streetcar* than visualize the fourth wall: the outer wall appears and disappears more than a half-dozen times, often in the middle of a "scene," drawing attention to the spatial illusion rather than making its boundaries absolute. The effect on spatial metaphor is that we are not allowed to forget that it is metaphor and consequently capable of infinite extensions and retractions. As we might expect, the struggle over territory between Stanley and Blanche ("Hey, canary bird! Toots! Get OUT of the BATHROOM!" [367]), which indeed results in reasserting the male as "King" (371; Stanley is quoting Huey Long) and pushes Blanche off-stage, punished, defeated, is utterly unanalytical and unsubtle. "*She'll go!* Period. PS. She'll go *Tuesday!*" (367). While the expressionistic sequence beginning in scene 6 with Blanche's recollection of "The Grey boy" relativizes space and time, evoking Blanche's memories, it also seems to drain her expressive power until when Stanley is about to rape her she mouths the kinds of things Williams used to put on screens: "'In desperate, desperate circumstances! Help me! Caught in a trap'" (400). She is establishing her emotions like signposts: "Stay back!" "I warn you, don't, I'm in danger!" (401). What had seemed a way *into* Blanche's character has had the effect of externalizing her feelings so much that they become impersonal. Space doesn't provide an objective mooring for Blanche's psychology; it keeps turning inside out, obliterating the spatial distinctions that had helped to define the realistic character as someone whose inner life drove the action. Now this driving force of emotion replaces the subtlety of expectation, leaving character out in space, dangling. "There isn't time to be—" Blanche explains into the phone (399);

faced with a threatening proximity, she phones long distance and forgets to hang up.

The expressionistic techniques of the latter half of the play abstract the individual from the milieu, and emotion begins to dominate the representation of events. In scene 10, where Blanche and Stanley have their most violent and erotic confrontation, the play loses all sense of boundary. The front of the house is already transparent, but now Williams also dissolves the rear wall, so that beyond the scene with Blanche and Stanley we can see what is happening on the next street.

> A prostitute has rolled a drunkard. He pursues her along the walk, overtakes her and there is a struggle. A policeman's whistle breaks it up. The figures disappear.
>
> Some moments later the Negro Woman appears around the corner with a sequined bag which the prostitute had dropped on the walk. She is rooting excitedly through it. [399]

The mise-en-scène exposes more of the realistic world than before, since now we see the outside as well as the inside of the house at once, and yet the effect is one of intense general paranoia: the threat of violence is "real," not "remembered," and it is everywhere. The walls have become "spaces" along which frightening, "sinuous" shadows weave—"lurid," "grotesque and menacing." The parameters of Blanche's presence are unstable images of threatening "flames" of desire, and this sense of sexual danger seems to draw the action toward itself. So it is as though Blanche somehow "suggests" rape to Stanley—it is already in the air; we can see it being given to him as if it were a thought. "You think I'll interfere with you? Ha-ha! . . . Come to think of it—maybe you wouldn't be bad to—interfere with" (401).

The "inner-outer" distinctions of both realistic and expressionistic representation are shown coming together here. Williams makes no effort to suggest that the "lurid" expressionistic images in scene 10 are all in Blanche's mind, as cinematic point of view would: the world outside the house is the realistic world of urban poverty and violence. But it is also the domain of the brutes, whose "inhuman jungle voices rise up" as Stanley, snakelike, tongue between his teeth, closes in. The play seems to swivel on this moment, when the logic of appearance and essence, the individual and the abstract, turns inside out, like the set, seeming to occupy for once the same space. It is either the demolition of realistic objectivity or the transition point at which realism takes over some new territory. At this juncture "objective" vision becomes an "outside" seen from inside; for the abstraction that allows realism to represent truth objectively cannot itself be explained as objectivity. The surface in scene 10 seems to be disclosing, without our having to look too deeply, a static primal moment beneath the immediacy of the action: the sexual taboo underneath realistic discourse.

> *Blanche:* Stay back! Don't you come toward me another step
> or I'll—
> *Stanley:* What?
> *Blanche:* Some awful thing will happen! It will!
> *Stanley:* What are you putting on now?
> (They are now both inside the bedroom.)
> *Blanche:* I warn you, don't, I'm in danger! [401]

What "will happen" in the bedroom doesn't have a name or even an agency. The incestuous relation lies beyond the moral and social order of marriage and the family, adaptation and eugenics, not to mention (as Williams reminds us here) the fact that it's unmentionable. Whatever words Blanche uses to describe it scarcely matter. As Stella says, "I couldn't believe her story and go on living with Stanley" (405).

The rape in *Streetcar* thus seems familiar and inevitable, even to its "characters," who lose the shape of characters and become violent antagonists as if on cue. "Oh! So you want some roughhouse! All right, let's have some roughhouse!" (402). When Blanche sinks to her knees, it's as if the action is an acknowledgment. Stanley holds Blanche, who has become "inert"; he carries her to bed. She is not only silent but crumpled, immobile, while he takes over control and agency. He literally places her on the set. But Williams does not suggest that Stanley is conscious and autonomous; on the contrary the scene is constructed so as to make him as unindividuated as Blanche: they seem, at this crucial point, more than ever part of an allegorical landscape. In a way, it's the *impersonality* of the rape that is most telling: the obliteration of individuation and the spatial distinctions that allow for "character." Expressionistically, then, character dissolves into an overwhelming mise-en-scène that produces emotion as a landscape. The rape scene ends without words, without conflict, without characters.

Perhaps *Streetcar*—and Williams—present problems for those interested in Pirandellian metatheater. Metatheater assumes a self-consciousness of dramatic form; but Williams makes the "form" *everything*. It isn't arbitrary, or stifling: Stanley and Blanche are not characters struggling to get out of their "plot." Character is the expression of the form; it is not accidental or originary. Like Brecht, Williams does not see character as a humanist impulse raging against fatal abstractions. (In a play like *The Good Person of Setzuan*, for example, Brecht makes a kind of comedy of this "tragedy.") Plays are not about people. They're about thought and feeling; they represent these things. If this seems to suggest that the rape in *Streetcar* is something other than a rape, and so not a rape, it also suggests that it is as much a rape as it is possible for it to be. While exposing the essence of appearances, as Williams says, seeing from outside what can't be seen from within, the scene exposes its own scenic limitations for dramatizing that which cannot be in the scene: namely, the act it represents.

Both the surface "street scene" and the jungle antecedents of social order are visible, outside and inside, thoroughly violating the norms of realism's analytical space. When Stanley "springs" at Blanche, overturning the table, it is clear that a last barrier has been broken down, and now there is no space that is outside the jungle. "We've had this date with each other from the beginning!" (402). We've regressed to some awful zero point (or hour). "A fetid swamp," one critic said of Williams's plays, by way of description. We are also back at the *heart* of civilization, at its root, the incest taboo, and the center of sexuality, which is oddly enough also the center of realism: the family, where "sexuality is 'incestuous' from the start" (Foucault, *History* 108-109). At the border of civilization and the swamp is the sexual transgression whose suppression is the source of all coercive order. Through allegory, Williams makes explicit what realism obscures, forcing the sexuality that propels discourse into the content of the scene.

The destruction of spatial boundaries visualizes the restless discourse of desire, that uncontainable movement between inside and outside, soul and body. "Desire," Williams writes in his short story "Desire and the Black Masseur," "is something that is made to occupy a larger space than that which is afforded by the individual being" (Williams, *Stories* 217). "Desire" derives from the Latin word for "star" ("Stella for Star!"); an archaic sense is "to feel the loss of": the individual is a sign of incompleteness, not self-sufficiency, whose defining gesture is an indication of the void beyond the visible, not its closure. The consciousness of desire as a void without satisfaction is the rejection of realism's "virtual space," which tries to suggest that its fractured space implied an unseen totality. Realism's objectivity covered up its literariness, as if the play were not created from nothing but evolved out of a reality one had but to look to see. But literature answers the desire for a fullness that remains unfilled—it never intersects reality, never completes a trajectory; it remains in orbit. The nothing from which literature springs, whole, cannot be penetrated by a vision, even a hypothetical one, and no time can be found for its beginning. As de Man reasons in his discussion of Lévi-Strauss's metaphor of "virtual focus," logical sight lines may be imaginary, but they are not "fiction," any more than "fiction" can be explained as logic:

> The virtual focus is a quasi-objective structure posited to give rational integrity to a process that exists independently of the self. The subject merely

fills in, with the dotted line of geometrical construction, what natural reason had not bothered to make explicit; it has a passive and unproblematic role. The "virtual focus" is, strictly speaking, a nothing, but its nothingness concerns us very little, since a mere act of reason suffices to give it a mode of being that leaves the rational order unchallenged. The same is not true of the imaginary source of fiction. Here the human self has experienced the void within itself and the invented fiction, far from filling the void, asserts itself as pure nothingness, our nothingness stated and restated by a subject that is the agent of its own instability. [19]

Nothingness, then, the impulse of "fiction," is not the result of a supposed originary act of transgression, a mere historical lapse at the origin of history that can be traced or filled in by a language of logic and analysis; on the contrary, fiction is the *liberation* of a pure consciousness of desire as unsatisfied yearning, a space without boundaries.

Yet we come back to Blanche's rape by her brother-in-law, which seems visibly to reseal the laws of constraint, to justify the logic of lost beginnings. Reenacting the traumatic incestuous moment enables history to begin over again, while the suppression of inordinate desire resumes the order of sanity: Stella is silenced; Blanche is incarcerated. And if there is some ambivalence about Blanche's madness and her exclusion, it is subsumed in an argument for order and a "healthy" redirection of desire. In the last stage direction, Stanley's groping fingers discover the opening of Stella's blouse. The final setup feels inevitable; after all, the game is still "Seven-card stud," and aren't we going to have to "go on" by playing it? The play's return to realistic (and we might also say, heterosexual) logic seems assured, and Williams is still renouncing worlds. He points to the closure of the analytical reading with deft disingenuousness. Closure was always just next door to entrapment; Williams seems to be erasing their boundary lines.

Madness, the brand of exclusion, objectifies Blanche and enables her to be analyzed and confined as the embodiment of nonbeing, an expression of something beyond us and so structured in language (Foucault, *Madness* 100). "There isn't a goddam thing but imagination! . . . And lies and conceit and tricks!" Stanley says (398). The containment of desire's excess through the exclusion of madness creates, as Foucault has argued, a conscience on the perimeters of society, setting up a boundary between inside and outside ("[The madman] is put in the interior of the exterior, and inversely"; Foucault, *Madness* 11). Blanche is allegorically a reminder that liberty can also be captivity, just as her libertinage coincides with her desire for death (her satin robe is a passionate red, she calls Stanley her "executioner," etc.). And Blanche senses early on the threat of confinement; she keeps trying (perversely) to end the play. "I have to plan for us both, to get us both—out!" she tells Stella, after the fight with Stanley that seems, to Blanche, so *final* (320).

But in the end the play itself seems to have some trouble letting go of Blanche. Having created its moving boundary line, it no longer knows where to put her; what "space" does her "madness" occupy? As the dialogue suggests, she has to go—somewhere; she has become excessive. Yet she keeps coming back: "I'm not quite ready." "Yes! Yes, I forgot something!" (412, 414). Again she is chased around the bedroom, this time by the Matron, while "The 'Varsouviana' is filtered into a weird distortion, accompanied by the cries and noises of the jungle," the "lurid," "sinuous" reflections on the walls (414). The Matron's lines are echoed by other "mysterious voices" somewhere beyond the scene; she sounds "like a firebell." "Matron" and "Doctor" enter the play expressionistically, as functional agents, and Blanche's paranoia is now hers alone: the street is not visible. The walls don't disintegrate; they come alive. Blanche is inside her own madness, self-imprisoned: her madness is precisely her enclosure within the image (cf. Foucault, *Madness* 94). In her paranoid state, Blanche really cannot "get out," because there isn't any longer an outside: madness transgresses and transforms boundaries, "forming an act of undetermined content" (ibid. 94). It thus negates the image while remaining imprisoned within it; the boundaries of the scene are not helping to define Blanche but reflecting her back to herself.

Blanche's power is not easy to suppress; she is a reminder that beneath the appearance of order something nameless has been lost. "What's happened here? I want an explanation of what's happened here," she says "with sudden hysteria" (408, 407). It is a reasonable request that cannot be reasonably answered. This is the same problem posed at the end of *The Glass Menagerie*: how to escape from the image when it seems to have been given too much control, when its reason is absolute? Expressionism threatens the reason of realistic mise-en-scène by taking it perhaps too far, stretching the imagination beyond limits toward an absoluteness of the image, a desire of desire. The "mimetic" mirror now becomes the symbol of madness; the image no longer simply reflects desire (desire of, desire for) but subsumes the mirror itself into the language of desire. When Blanche shatters her mirror (391), she (like Richard II) shows that her identity has already been fractured; she doesn't see herself in the mirror; she sees the mirror as herself. And she cries out when the lantern is torn off the lightbulb, because there is no longer a space between the violence she experiences and the image of that violence. The inner and the outer worlds fuse; the reflecting power of the image is destroyed as it becomes fully *self*-reflective. The passion of madness exists somewhere in between determinism and expression, which at this point "actually form only one and the same movement which cannot be dissociated except after the fact" (Foucault, *Madness* 88).

But realism, that omnivorous discourse, can subsume even the loss of the subjective-objective distinction—when determinism equals expression—and return to some quasi-objective perspective. Thus at the very moment when all space seems to have been conquered, filled in and opened up, there is a need to parcel it out again into clearly distinguishable territories. Analysis normalizes desire. At the end of *A Streetcar Named Desire*, there is a little drama. Blanche's wild expressionistic images are patronized and pacified by theatricality: "I—just told her that—we'd made arrangements for her to rest in the country. She's got it mixed up in her mind with Shep Huntleigh" (404-405). Her family plays along with Blanche's delusions, even to costuming her in her turquoise seahorse pin and her artificial violets. The Matron tries to subdue her with physical violence, but Blanche is only really overcome by the Doctor's politeness.

Formerly an expressionistic "type," having "the unmistakable aura of the state institution with its cynical detachment" (411), the Doctor "takes off his hat and now he becomes personalized. The un-human quality goes. His voice is gentle and reassuring as he crosses to Blanche and crouches in front of her. As he speaks her name, her terror subsides a little. The lurid reflections fade from the walls, the inhuman cries and noises die out and her own hoarse crying is calmed" (417). Blanche's expressionistic fit is contained by the Doctor's realistic transformation: he is particularized; he can play the role of gentleman caller. Straitjacket, Doctor? the Matron asks him. He smiles. It won't be necessary (417-18). As they exit, Blanche's visionary excesses have clearly been surrendered to him; "She allows him to lead her as if she were blind" (418). Stylistically, here, realism replaces expressionism at the exact moment when expressionism's "pure subjectivity" seems ready to annihilate the subject, to result in her violent subjugation. At this point the intersubjective dialogue returns, clearly masking— indeed, blinding—the subjective disorder with a reassuring form. If madness is perceived as a kind of "social failure" (Foucault, *Madness* 259), social success is to be its antidote.

Of course theater is a cure for madness: by dramatizing or literalizing the image one destroys it. Such theatricality might risk its own confinement in the image, and for an instant there may be a real struggle in the drama between the image and the effort to contain it. Using illusion to destroy illusion requires a forgetting of illusion, of the representational break illusion has to deny. "The artificial reconstitution of delirium constitutes the real distance in which the sufferer recovers his liberty" (ibid. 190). In fact there is no return to "intersubjectivity," just a kind of formal recognition of it: "Whoever you are—I have always depended on the kindness of strangers" (418). *Streetcar* makes the return to normality gentle and theatrical, while "revealing" much more explicitly than *The Glass Menagerie* the violence that is thereby suppressed. This violence isn't "reality" but yet another theater underneath the theater of ruse; the cure of illusion ironically is "effected by the suppression of theater" (Foucault, *Madness* 191).[4]

The realistic containment at the end of *Streetcar* thus does not quite make it back all the way to realism's objective "historical" truth. History, structured by relations of power, not relations to meaning (Foucault, *Power/Knowledge* 114), sometimes assumes the power of reality itself, the platonic Form behind realism, so to speak. When it becomes the language of authority, history also assumes the authority of language, rather naively trusting language to be the reality it represents. The bloody wars and strategic battles are soon forgotten into language, the past tense, the fait accompli. History is the waste of time and the corresponding conquest of space, and realism is the already conquered territory, the belated time with the unmistakable stamp of authenticity. It gets applause simply by being plausible; it forgets that it is literature. To read literature, as de Man says, we ought to remember what we have learned from it—that the expression and the expressed can never entirely coincide, that no single observation point is trustworthy (11). *Streetcar*'s powerful explosion of allegorical language and expressionistic images keeps its vantage point on the move, at a remove. Every plot is untied. Realism rewards analysis, and Williams invites it, perversely, but any analysis results in dissection; to provide *Streetcar* with an exegesis seems like gratuitous destruction, "deliberate cruelty." Perhaps no other U.S. writer since Dickinson has seemed so easy to crush.

And this consideration ought to give the writer who has defined Blanche's "madness" some pause. Even the critical awareness of her tidy incarceration makes for too tidy a criticism. In Derrida's analysis of Foucault's *Madness and Civilization*, he questions the possibility of "historicizing" something that doesn't exist outside of the imprisonment of history, of speech—madness "simply says the other of each determined form of the logos" (Derrida, *Writing* 58). Madness, Derrida proposes, is a "hyperbole" out of which "finite-thought, that is to say, history" establishes its "reign," by the "disguised internment, humiliation, fettering and mockery of the madman within us, of the madman who can only be the fool of a logos which is father, master and king" (60-61). Philosophy arises from the "*confessed* terror of going mad" (62); it is the "economic" embrace of madness (61-62).

To me, then, Williams's play seems to end quite reasonably with a struggle, at the point in the play in which structure and coherence must assert themselves (by seeming to)—that is, the end of the play. The end must look back, regress, so as to sum up and define. It has no other choice. The theatrical ending always becomes, in fact, the real ending. It cannot remain metaphorically an "end." And what is visible at the end is Blanche in trouble, trapped, mad. She is acting as though she believed in a set of events—Shep Huntleigh's rescue of her—that the other characters, by their very encouragement, show to be unreal. There is a fine but perhaps important distinction here: Blanche's acting is no more convincing than theirs, but, and Derrida makes this point about madness, she is thinking things before they can be historicized, that is, before they have happened or even have been shown to be likely or possible (reasonable). "Is not what is called finitude possibility as crisis?" Derrida asks (62). The other characters, who behave as if what Blanche is saying were real, underline her absurdity precisely by invoking reality.

Blanche's relation to history and to structural authority are laid bare by this "forced" ending, in which she repeatedly questions the meaning of meaning: "What has happened here?" The question implies the relativity of space and moment and so of "events" and their meanings, which are at this point impossible to separate. For this reason it's important that the rape suggest an overthrow of meaning, not only through a stylized emphasis on its own representation but also through its strongly relativized temporality. (Blanche warns against what "will happen" while Stanley says the event is the future, the fulfillment of a "date" or culmination in time promised "from the beginning.")

Indeed, the problem of madness lies precisely in this gap between past and future, as we have seen in chapters 2 and 3, in the structural slippage between the temporal and the ontological. For if madness, as Derrida suggests, can exist at all outside of opposition (to reason), it must exist in "hyperbole;" in the excess prior to its incarceration in structure, meaning, time, and coherence. A truly "mad" person would not objectify madness—would not, that is, define and locate it. For that reason all discussions of "madness" tend to essentialize it, by insisting, like Blanche's fellow characters at the end of *Streetcar*, that it is *real*, that it *exists*. And the final stroke of logic, the final absurdity, is that, in order to insist that madness *exists*, to objectify and to define and to relate to it, it is necessary to *deny* it any history. Of course "madness" is not at all amenable to history, to structure, causality, rationality, recognizable "thought." But this denial of the history of madness has to come from within history itself, from within the language of structure and "meaning." Blanche's demand to know "what has happened here"—her insistence that something "has happened," however one takes it—has to be unanswerable. It can't go any further. In theatrical terms, the "belief" that would make that adventure of meaning possible has to be denied, shut down. But this theatrical release isn't purifying; on the contrary, it's gotten up close to the plague, to the point at which reason and belief contaminate each other: the possibility of thinking madly. Reason and madness can cohabit with nothing but a thin curtain between. And curtains aren't walls; they don't provide solid protection.[5]

Submitting Williams's allegorical language to realistic analysis, then, leads to conclusions: the imprisonment of madness, the redirection of desire. The moral meaning smoothes things over. Planning to "open up" *Streetcar* for the film version with outside scenes and flashbacks, Elia Kazan found it wouldn't work—he ended up making the walls movable so they could actually close in more with every scene (Kazan 384). Williams's dramatic language is too free, too wanton; it's a trap, it's asking to be analyzed, it lies down on the couch. Kazan saw this perverse desire in the play—he thought *Streetcar* was about Williams's cruising for tough customers: "The reference to the kind of life Tennessee was leading at the time was clear. Williams was aware of the dangers he was inviting when he cruised; he knew that sooner or later he'd be beaten up. And he was" (351).

But Kazan undervalues the risk Williams is willing to take. It isn't just violence that cruising invites; it's death. And that desire, as O'Neill found in the end of *Iceman*, can't be realized. Since there's really no way to get what you want, you have to put yourself in a position where you don't always want what you get. In pursuing desire beyond "reason"— psychoanalytic, theatrical, or otherwise—Williams exposes the violence of representation. The complicitousness of art and violence (or submission to violence) is not lost on him, as he makes clear in the end of "Desire and the Black Masseur." Anthony Burns is cannibalized by the masseur, who has already beaten him to pulp, and thus, consumed by his desire, Burns makes up for what Williams calls his "incompletion." For violence, like art, masks the incompletion, the inadequacy, the hole or gap, through which desire, like representation, seeks closure. "Yes, it is perfect," thinks the masseur, whose manipulations have tortured Burns to death. "It is now completed!"

From *Mimetic Disillusion: Eugene O'Neill, Tennessee Williams, and U.S.Dramatic Realism.* Copyright ©1997 by the University of Alabama Press. Reprinted by permission.

Notes

1. I am indebted to my student Laurie Widdenstrom for this brilliant question. I isolate one underlying assumption of expressionism here—that of inner-outer space—in order to consider it as a formal point of comparison between expressionism and realism. The implications of invoking these two terms, however, and in such close association, are much broader. As an avant-garde style in the literary and visual arts, expres-

sionism was specifically antirealist and antinaturalist. As a political art it was also antimaterialist and antiscientific (anti-"objectivity"). Expressionism's politicization made it especially vulnerable to attack for its "subjectivity," detachment, and idealism. The Lukács-Block debate in *Das Wort* 1938 shows that, by the Popular Front period, expressionism's political position was crucial to its viability as a style; compared with realism it appeared "decadent," "immature," flimsy. "[B]ecause of the specifically anti-realist bias in Expressionism . . . [the Expressionists] had no firm artistic hold on reality which might have corrected or neutralized their misconceptions. . . . [I]t intensified the dangers which inevitably accompany all such attempts to stabilize an essentially transitional ideology" (Lukács 51). Lukács's treatment of expressionism here is both ideological and dismissive; as a political movement it has for him simply "collapsed" (52). Texts on dramatic theory do not necessarily give the political resonance of expressionism more than a passing reference. Such concerns are often left to chapters on epic theater. The Lukács-Block arguments are reprinted in *Aesthetics and Politics*, however, and there is some discussion of the subject in both Levine chap. 2; and Vajda.

   2. Compare Austin's realization, in *How to Do Things with Words* (148), that all language is "performative," that is, active and unpredictable, that it cannot simply be declarative, factual, "constative": "[T]he traditional statement is an abstraction, an ideal, and so is its traditional truth or falsity" (ibid.).

   3. What is repeated in the mimetic is, thus, something like the ongoing process of subjectivation as Lacan represents it. Subjectivation occurs through the rupture of the imaginary into the symbolic, where desire endlessly pursues the reparation of that rupture. As Judith Butler has shown, this means that the process of sexuation, too, is ongoing, continually failing, perhaps open to subversion. Lacan and Butler's ideas seem especially relevant to *Streetcar*. See my article "When a Door Is a Jar; or, Out in the Theatre: Tennessee Williams and Queer Space" for a discussion of *Streetcar* and queer theory.

   4. William Kleb, too, suggests that in the final scene Blanche is transformed into a Foucauldian docile body. Others have noted the strain in the play's sense of closure. See June Schlueter, "We've had this date with each other from the beginning"; and Anca Vlasopolos.

   5. The problem of literalizing and of localizing madness took on a new horror in medical practice in the United States during the thirties and forties, when psychosurgery became a relatively common means of tranquilizing those diagnosed with emotional disorders. Madness was seen to occupy the prefrontal lobes, and its cure was to sever them from the rest of the brain. The procedure, random and dangerous, was most often performed on patients in state institutions as a way of rendering them less violent and thus easier and cheaper to care for. Williams's sister Rose was one of many women in the United States who were lobotomized in this way. In his *Memoirs* Williams dates the lobotomy "in the early thirties" and recalls that Rose, who had been diagnosed with "dementia praecox," was removed from a Catholic sanatorium to the state asylum in Farmington, Missouri, in 1937 (*Memoirs* 158, 153). For a history of psychosurgery in the United States during this period, especially lobotomy, see Elliot S. Valenstein.

References

Austin, J. L. *How to Do Things with Words*. 2d ed. Ed. J. O. Urmson and Maria Sbisa. Cambridge, Mass.: Harvard University Press, 1978.

Brecht, Bertolt. *Brecht on Theatre*. Trans. and ed. John Willett. New York: Hill & Wang, 1964.

Butler, Judith. "Imitation and Gender Insubordination." In *inside/out: Lesbian Theories, Gay Theories*. Ed. Diana Fuss. New York: Routledge, 1991.

de Man, Paul. *Blindness and Insight: Essays in the Rhetoric of Contemporary Criticism*. 2d ed., rev. Minneapolis: University of Minnesota Press, 1983.

Derrida, Jacques. *Writing and Difference*. Trans. Alan Bass. Chicago: University of Chicago Press, 1978.

Fleche, Anne. "When a Door Is a Jar; or, Out in the Theatre: Tennessee Williams and Queer Space." *Theatre Journal* 47:2 (May 1995), 253-67.

Foucault, Michel. *The History of Sexuality*. Vol. 1. *An Introduction*. Trans. Robert Hurley. New York: Vintage Books, 1978.

_____. *Madness and Civilization: A History of Insanity in the Age of Reason*. Trans. Richard Howard. New York: Vintage Books, 1965.

Kazan, Elia. *Elia Kazan: A Life*. New York: Alfred Knopf, 1988.

Kleb, William. "Marginalia: *Streetcar*, Williams, and Foucault." In *Confronting Tennessee Williams's "A Streetcar Named Desire": Essays in Critical Pluralism*. Ed. Philip C. Kolin. Westport, Conn.: Greenwood Press, 1993.

Lacan, Jacques. *Ecrits*. Trans. Alan Sheridan. New York: W. W. Norton, 1977.

Levine, Ira A. *Left-Wing Dramatic Theory in the American Theatre*. Ann Arbor: UMI Research Press, 1980.

Lukács, Georg. "Realism in the Balance." In *Aesthetics and Politics*. New York: Verso, 1988.

O'Neill, Eugene. *The Iceman Cometh*. New York: Vintage Books, 1957.

Schlueter, June. "'We've had this date with each other from the beginning': Reading Toward Closure in *A Streetcar Named Desire*." In *Confronting Tennessee Williams's "A Streetcar Named Desire": Essays in Critical Pluralism*. Ed. Philip C. Kolin. Westport, Conn.: Greenwood Press, 1993.

Vajda, György M. "Outline of the Philosophic Backgrounds of Expressionism." In *Expressionism as an International Literary Phenomenon*. Ed. Ulrich Weisstein. Budapest: Akademiai Kiadó, 1973.

Valenstein, Elliot S. *Great and Desperate Cures: The Rise and Decline of Psychosurgery and Other Radical Treatments for Mental Illness*. New York: Basic Books, 1986.

Vlasopolos, Anca. "Authorizing History: Victimization in *A Streetcar Named Desire*." *Theatre Journal* 38 (October 1986): 322-38.

Williams, Tennessee. *Collected Stories*. New York: Ballantine Books, 1986.

_____. *The Glass Menagerie*. In *The Theatre of Tennessee Williams*, vol. 1. New York: New Directions, 1971.

_____. *Memoirs*. New York: Bantam Books, 1975.

_____. *A Streetcar Named Desire*. In *The Theatre of Tennessee Williams*, vol 1. New York: New Directions, 1971.

The Artful Rerouting of
A Streetcar Named Desire

Linda Costanzo Cahir

A Streetcar Named Desire should have made a smooth transition from stage to screen. The play is heightened realism, a visual style highly amenable to cinematic representation. The same writer (Tennessee Williams), the same director (Elia Kazan), and roughly the same cast (Marlon Brando, Kim Hunter, and Karl Malden) provided the film with the same creative alliance as the highly successful New York stage production. Kazan's proclivity to both theater and film allowed the camera to create a new affinity between cinema and stage, a hybrid of filmed theater and radical adaption. *Streetcar* was a commercial and critical success, but its screen transition was a struggle on three fronts as the body politic of the Motion Picture industry's censorship board, the Legion of Decency, and the film's own producers appeared as formidable opponents. All three forces lodged inappropriate, possibly destructive demands during the production of *Streetcar*. The success of the film, oddly, is due in part to the way in which Kazan and Williams turned the tables and made potentially destructive constraints work constructively in the movie.

Against Kazan's objections, the producers of *Streetcar* insisted that Vivien Leigh play the leading role of Blanche DuBois. In a 1971 interview with Michel Ciment, Elia Kazan discussed how opposed he was and remained to the casting of Leigh. Kazan had wanted his original New York cast, which would have included (in the role of Blanche) the thirty-eight-year-old Jessica Tandy. However, Charlie Feldman,[1] one of the producers, insisted that the film "have one movie star in it. Brando was not a star in those days" (Kazan in Ciment 68), and in hyperbole it was argued that "hardly anyone west of 10th Avenue knew who she [Tandy] was" (Nash 3176). Thus, Leigh was cast—or in Kazan's view miscast—as Blanche DuBois. In that 1971 interview, recorded some twenty-one years after the making of *Streetcar*, Kazan still held:

The main problem I had with that production was that Vivien Leigh ... had played the part in England under the direction of her husband, Laurence Olivier. He is a fine theater artist, but still, what I saw in the play was something an Englishman would see from a distance, and was not what I saw in the play. (Ciment 70)

Like Blanche stepping off the streetcar and into the Latin Quarter, Vivien Leigh came to the set of Kazan's film as something of an outsider. Leigh was from a different part of the world, England not New York; as Kazan argued above, Leigh's way of seeing was British, her sensibilities had been conditioned by a culture as different from New York as Blanche's Belle Reve was from Stanley's New Orleans.

Leigh's presence on the set was clearly unwanted and it repeatedly disrupted the status quo harmony of a group of actors who had all worked together before in the same play. Gossip surrounding the production of *Streetcar* always centered on disturbances provoked by Leigh. As flagrantly disruptive off camera as her character was on camera, she unsettled things. Thus Vivien Leigh was to the cast and set of the film what Blanche DuBois, herself, was to the Kowalskis and New Orleans. What Stanley Kowalski says of Blanche DuBois could have been said of Leigh during the filming of *Streetcar*: "And wasn't we happy together? Wasn't it all okay? Till she showed here."

A clash of acting techniques seemed to pit Leigh against the others from the start. Marlon Brando, Kim Hunter, and Karl Malden, like Kazan himself, were trained in The Method of Stanislavsky. Leigh, in contrast, came from an antithetical tradition: Stylized/Classical Acting, a tradition which, at the time, the Method Actors had rejected as formulated, as rigid.[2]

Though initially the conflicts between Leigh and Kazan were considerable, animosity grew most severe between Brando and Leigh. Consistent with his acting tradition, Brando lived the role of Stanley Kowalski, both on and off camera. In response to this, Leigh was quoted in print as having said that Brando was "a slob";[3] the tension between them on the set was rumored to be as "thick as New Orleans humidity" (Nash 3176). Yet, Leigh, who repeatedly dismissed the merits of Method Acting, essentially began to live the role of Blanche DuBois during the entire filming of *Streetcar*, while Brando ironically found her "becoming Blanche" a rather annoying activity.

Yet, the tension worked on screen. Leigh's more stylized performance, a method Stanislavsky described as "full-toned acting," pitted against Brando's method acting, heightened the distinction between Stanley Kowalski, as reality pared to its dynamic essentials, and Blanche DuBois, the skilled purveyor of illusion. As well, Leigh's full-toned acting in combination with the essential theatricality of Williams's dialogue deepened the film's heightened realism. Throughout the movie we watch the fixed, unglossed bestiality of Brando's Stanley pitted against the ever-shifting facade called Blanche. Unlike the raw corporeality of Stanley, Leigh's Blanche amorphously dons a series of masks, as she conjures persona after persona, as she constructs character after character. "I don't want realism," Blanche dramatically admits. Essentially, the *character* Blanche DuBois is an actress in the classical tradition; she assumes, rather than subsumes, a series of roles. Thus, in paradox, Leigh's classical acting, thought to be inappropriate, speaks to the essence of Blanche DuBois, and in this odd circumstance could be argued to constitute a form of method acting.

We see this specifically in Leigh's work at the beginning of the film, in those same two or three reels which Kazan, twenty-one years later, still criticized. Kazan's appraisal of those opening reels indicts Leigh's performance as so disharmonious with the others that it causes her acting to show (i.e., we see Vivien Leigh playing Blanche DuBois). The acting does show in those opening scenes, Kazan is right; but it is Blanche's acting, not Leigh's, that seems artificial, disharmonious, contrived; Blanche whose tone is unsteady, whose gesturing is overblown. Blanche hasn't had time to gauge her audience. She hasn't seen Stella in several years and has never met Stanley. Elysian Fields, literally and symbolically, is alien terrain for her, and Blanche simply doesn't know how to act, what role to perform, what face to assume, so she flits in and out of several, in a nervous longing to find the fitting form, to be accepted. Blanche has survived all these years by being an impersonator extraordinaire. What makes Leigh's performance so powerful in these opening scenes is that we see Blanche, drawn and tired from the years of laborious performance, make a last ditch effort to find the role of a lifetime, the role which will let her rest.

Vivien Leigh's performance, in a sense, serves as a metaphor for the stage-to-screen success of *A Streetcar Named Desire*. What Williams and Kazan thought would prove appropriate to the film worked and worked well; but they also turned the tables and made much of the inappropriateness forced upon them by producers and censors work for the film, too.

Inappropriate to both Kazan and Williams were the alterations demanded (even before a first script was drafted) by those guardians of decency, the Breen office. Central to Williams's play are issues that the Breen Office found de facto censorious: noisy, pleasurable lovemaking; unsanctioned promiscuity; homosexuality; and rape. Even the first filmscript, drafted largely by Oscar Saul and in accordance with Breen's recommendations, had to be emended:

> In the sixty-eight major and minor changes from the Broadway version, the dominant concern was to satisfy the demands of the Breen Office. During the initial flurry of interest in *Streetcar*, Paramount had sounded out Joseph Breen on what sort of changes would be required to get the seal of approval that most exhibitors would demand before they would show the film. Breen responded that the homosexuality and rape would both have to be eliminated. In other words, the film would have to do without the cornerstones to Blanche's behavior. (Pauly 131)

These cuts could have crippled the movie, reduced it to melodrama, diminished Blanche, and emptied characters of their most compelling and complex motivations. Instead, the film's three most hazardous alterations, i.e., the deletion of homosexuality, the ambiguity of the rape, and the addition of a penitential ending, changes that Kazan and Williams knew to be painfully inappropriate, are worked to enrich the film by appropriately dislodging it from Williams's play.

In Williams's stage version, explanations of characters and their motivations are somewhat less oblique. In the play, for example, we are *told* why Blanche carries tragedy within her. Blanche tells us herself; she comes out from behind her mask long enough to confess to Mitch the unpardonable sin of her past: Years ago, in a moment of potent cruelty, Blanche lashed out at her young husband with her condemnation of his homosexuality:

> He came to me for help. . . . He was in the quicksands and clutching at me. . . . I didn't know that. I didn't know anything. . . . Then I found out. In the worst of all possible ways. By coming suddenly into a room that I thought was empty, but had two people in it . . . the boy I had married and an older man who had been his friend for years. . . . Afterwards we pretended that nothing had been discovered. . . . We danced the Varsouviana. Suddenly in the middle of the dance the boy I had married broke away from me and ran out of the casino. A few moments later a shot. . . . It was because—on the dance floor—unable to stop myself—I'd suddenly said—"I saw! I know! You disgust me . . ." (Scene 6)

The experience of this single event, participation in the titanically destructive power of cruelty, burrowed into Blanche's soul and irreversibly changed her from what she once was. Whether or not we think that she was cruel and that her words provoked her husband's suicide, Blanche believes—as her words "It was because" tell us—that his death was caused by something that she said.

Thus, Blanche is looking for redemption, for forgiveness, in the arms of boys—young like her husband—and in her confession to Mitch. She wants Mitch to absolve, forgive, release her from the great cruelty of her past, because like her husband Allan Grey, Blanche wants to be loved for who she is. (One of Blanche's many illusions is that she claims to want *only* illusion.)

Thus, this stage Blanche is a woman of considerable moral complexity. She has a dissolute history, a soul-distorting past that Kazan's Blanche does not have. With Scene 6 softened to satisfy the demands of the Breen Office, the Blanche DuBois of the movies becomes a purified, rarified creature, lovely and fragile. She is the ethereal beauty whose past transgressions—some moments of indiscriminate sex—are understood as momentary stays against the death that permeates her Laurel, Mississippi world. Both a libidinous profligate and a devout companion to the dying (her parents, Belle Reve, the Southern Tradition), Blanche embodies the mythic image of the virgin whore. We like her even more for her transgressions; the revisionist mythologizing of Blanche works. Thus, this Blanche is Blanche DuBois, not Blanche Grey, an ironic name she guiltily shunts in the play. (In fact, in the film Blanche's and Allan's marriage hardly seems to have happened at all.) Far more sinned against than sinning, Blanche is Kazan's delicate, trapped butterfly. (He has described her in those terms.) Throughout the film, Kazan's images support this benevolent interpretation of Blanche and, in contrast, intensify the brute force and sinful cruelty of Stanley. Of course, it is more appropriate that this sanitized Blanche have no past so fulsome and cruel as to include culpability in her husband's death.[4]

It is equally important that this purified Blanche have no share in her own rape. Deleted from the film is Stanley's line, "We've had this date with each other from the beginning," a line which (at the very least) implies that in Stanley's mind the great provocateur, Blanche, induced the attack. As well, the play's stage directions call for Blanche to be an "inert figure" whom Stanley "carries . . . to the bed"—directions which could create the impression that submerged desire caused Blanche to yield too easily to Stanley's "sexual" aggression.[5]

This is not the case in the film. Blanche's moral and spiritual integrity is never called into question: She cannot possibly fight back; she has passed out. A quick cut-away denotes the violence of the rape in the image of a beer bottle smashing a mirror. This obliqueness works. It connects with the virgin/whore image of Blanche that Kazan creates throughout the film. Stanley's symbol, a powerful beer bottle earlier made to spurt its contents in Stanley's playful hands, shatters the mirror, Blanche's dualistic symbol of the virginal hymen and of purity as illusion. And, though the movie audience is never quite as certain about the rape as the stage audience would have been, the poetry of the images—the powerless Blanche in her sad rag-bag finery carried off by the sweaty, hard-fleshed Stanley—makes whatever violence that did occur (Kazan keeps the violence lyrical not literal) so much more potent. The scene achieves what Williams (in a letter to Breen) most hoped for: That the rape be understood as "the ravishment of the tender, the sensitive, the delicate, by the savage and brutal forces of modern society. . . . It is a poetic plea for comprehension" (Pauly 132). Thus, Kazan's directorial wizardry found a way to make the absurd requirements of the Breen Office work in his favor. Their foolishly inappropriate demands resulted in an aesthetically appropriate, lyrically cinematic scene, that added to rather than detracted from *Streetcar*'s stage to screen transition.

In his screen version, despite the censors, Kazan creates scenes that explode like fireworks and we see that Stanley is not the only force that has defiled Blanche; life has ravished her. In the metaphor of her life as the route the rattly streetcar takes to the Kowalski's tenement—a movement from Desire (life) to Cemeteries (death, "the opposite of desire") to Elysian Fields (paradise)—Stanley is just another stop, albeit a significant stop. But, Kazan is careful to show us that Stanley is not the only one who has raped Blanche, who has taken her desire to live, to love and perverted it. Mitch does this also, as does the Matron who comes for Blanche at the end of the film.

Mitch's abuse of Blanche takes place a short time before Stanley returns to rape her. In a moment where physical violence is undercut by emotional violence, Mitch grabs Blanche and forces a harsh light on her face. The movie has been so dimly lit throughout that we sense the sting of the light as Blanche does and we feel the violence against her as Mitch tears the flimsy paper lantern (again, her dual symbol of ruptured purity and the ruptured illusion of purity) off the plain, hard lightbulb inside of it (his symbol). Kazan's symbology here is much more complex than Williams's, which tends to reduce the Chinese lantern to Blanche's avoidance of reality. Here, as in the rape scene, the violence is subsumed in a series of phallic images. Visually, the two scenes are established as parallels. In the play, Mitch's cruelty in shining the light on Blanche is an act which parallels Blanche's cruelty in symbolically shining the light on her young husband. (Blanche's account, fraught with images of darkness and light, even includes a reference to turning "a blinding light on something that was always in the shadows.") However, since in the film Blanche's cruelty was deleted along with the deletion of the homosexuality theme, Kazan had no way of creating the tenuous parallel between those two scenes. Sensing the need to retain the interconnected harmony of Williams's scenes,[6] Kazan appropriately anchored Mitch's return by paralleling his defilement of Blanche with that of Blanche by Stanley.

All this violence is conveyed in a series of covert images which make the overtness of the final act of violence, the Matron's forcible taking of Blanche, so much more conspicuous. Here, in a furor of images, Kazan establishes his theme of Blanche as a beautiful trapped butterfly. Just as she is about to be taken to the state hospital, Blanche flies to the window where she bats against it again and again in a series of panicked flutters. Her arms become tangled in curtains that move like gossamer. The images in this scene, something lovely and fragile devastated by something solid and harsh, parallel those established in the preceding two scenes of violence; and like those, this final defilement is fraught with sexuality. As the Matron forces Blanche down, pins, and partially mounts her, we wonder how *this* could have slipped by Joe Breen and, later, the Legion of Decency!

It slipped by them because wily Elia Kazan understood the literal-mindedness of his censors and used it to his advantage.[7] The censors required that the rape not go unpunished; Stanley must not be allowed to escape reproof. Yet, to punish Stanley by having him lose Stella and his baby worked against the entire vision, meaning, and emotional charge of the play. Breen's demand would empty Williams's work of its essential theme. The two positions seemed irreconcilable.

Williams and Kazan reconciled them, though. Williams wrote the ending in which Stella, speaking to her baby, literally says: "We're not going back in there. Not this time. We're never going back. Never, never back, never back again." But, Kazan caps her lines by having Stella go where she always goes when she and Stanley have a serious fight: up the stairs to Eunice's. "Thus the twelve-year-olds [and Joe Breen] could believe that Stella was leaving her husband. But the rest of the audience would realize it was just an emotional outburst of the moment" (Schumach 76). Stella must come back down those stairs. As the movie ends with a close-up of Stella cradling her baby and moves to a long-shot of the seedy tenement, we *see*—even before she does—that Stella will return to Stanley . . . she doesn't have much of a choice.

The ending scene is poignant in its subtlety. It succeeds in the one way that Williams's play fails. The ending is delicate and elusive where (like so much of his writing) Williams's ending is heavy-handed and obvious. In this ending, Kazan scores a cinematic *coupe de maître*: He satisfies the literal-minded insolence of his censors while simultaneously preserving what is best in Williams: the tender ambivalence that does torturous battle within his characters.

The constraints imposed upon Kazan's cinematic *Streetcar* both by the censors and by his producers not only were absurdly inappropriate, but also worked against the aesthetic needs of the film. And, though the greatness of the movie must ultimately be judged by how it works when the house lights go down, how these destructive constraints came to be used constructively adds a worthy aesthetic subtext to Kazan's film.

Notes

1. Feldman's part in bringing *Streetcar* to production, overall, must be lauded. When all other studios, including Paramount, avoided the project as dangerously censorable, Charles Feldman "Determined to take a chance . . . persuaded Warner Brothers to join him in the project" (Schumach 74)

2. In Ciment's study, Kazan is quoted as having said: "It took several weeks to break her [Leigh] down. So, in my opinion the first two or three reels of the film are not that good." But, those beginning reels are good, and perhaps Kazan never really broke Leigh. Kazan's choice of words here, vis-à-vis Leigh as DuBois, are starkly ironic; they could have been spoken by Stanley Kowalski. Perhaps, like Blanche at Belle Reve, Leigh simply gave her man, Elia Kazan, the illusion of her that he wanted, while remaining faithful to her Classical Method of acting.

3. Compare these words by Vivien Leigh about Marlon Brando with Blanche DuBois's Scene Four speech about Stanley Kowalski and his "animal habits." Compare them to Kazan's filming of the "dismal birthday supper" where both Stanley's slovenly "animal habits" and Blanche's disgust over his behavior are registered most potently in visual terms. The point is clear: On the set Leigh was living Blanche as much as Brando was living Stanley.

4. In a letter to Joseph Breen, Kazan claimed, "I wouldn't put the homosexuality back into picture if the code had been revised last night and it was now permissible" (Pauly 131-32). Although Kazan's comment to Breen may have been just one more move in a game of chess, played Hollywood style, in that letter Kazan provides a rather lengthy explanation of why he thinks the ambiguity surrounding Allan Grey's sexuality ultimately works in the film. Thomas Pauly holds that this muting of what censors saw as a sexual taboo, by translating it into "meritorious sensitivity," is a strand which runs through Kazan's work, most notably *Tea and Sympathy, On the Waterfront,* and *East of Eden.*

5. Speaking to a reporter for the *New York Times,* Brando asserted that in compliance with Breen's demands regarding the rape scene, he originally was not even going to be allowed to pick Blanche up ("Pressure Problem" II, 5).

6. Like the music so central in his play, William's scenes are often variations on a theme.

7. Kazan takes an irascible delight in lampooning his censors. He blatantly thumbs his nose at their callow demands by inserting ribald imagery in the film; Mitch fondles an excessively large pole as Blanche rouses him, Stanley's beer gets excited and foams in spurts, a dripping garden hose tags the rape scene.

Works Cited

Ciment, Michel. *Kazan on Kazan*. New York: Viking, 1974.

Devlin, Albert J., ed. *Conversations With Tennessee Williams*. Jackson: UP of Mississippi, 1986.

Dowling, Ellen. "The Derailment of *A Streetcar Named Desire*." *Literature/Film Quarterly* No. 4, Vol. 9 (1981): 233:40.

Kael, Pauline. *Kiss Kiss Bang Bang*. Boston: Little, Brown, 1968.

Kazan, Elia. "Pressure Problem: Director Discusses Cuts Compelled in 'A Streetcar Named Desire.'" *New York Times* 21 Oct. 1951, sec. II: 5:7.

Nash, Jay Robert and Stanley Ralph Ross. *The Motion Picture Guide*. Vol. VII. Chicago: Cinebooks, 1987.

Pauly, Thomas H. *An American Odyssey: Elia Kazan and American Culture*. Philadelphia: Temple UP, 1983.

Schumach, Murray. *The Face on the Cutting Room Floor: The Story of Movie and Television Censorship*. New York: William Morrow, 1964.

"Some Mailed Opinions on 'Streetcar' Cuts." *New York Times* 28 Oct. 1951, sec. II: 5:2.

Williams, Tennessee. *A Streetcar Named Desire*. New York: New American Library, 1984.

Stanley Kowalski's Not So Secret Sorrow:
Queering, De-Queering, and Re-Queering
A Streetcar Named Desire as Drama, Script,
Film, and Opera_____

Keith Dorwick

Not surprisingly, homosexuality and homoeroticism have been a
subject of much critical inquiry in the analysis of Tennessee Williams'
plays. As clearly, the plays themselves are full of homosexual characters, whether on or offstage, though most of Williams' major queer
characters are discussed or mentioned in other characters' dialogue, or
otherwise appear without speaking. One thinks of Skipper in *Cat on a
Hot Tin Roof*, of Blanche's "young man" in *A Streetcar Named Desire*;
or of Sebastian Venable in the film version of *Suddenly Last Summer*,
who is literally seen in flashback but not heard, a character entirely unseen in the stage version of that work. All these queer characters are
dead before the actions of the plays that mention them, but all remain
central, often in devastating ways, to the conflicts between the major
onstage characters.

In addition to the long list of dead gay men, many of whom commit
suicide as a result of the discovery of their homosexuality, there is another kind of homoerotic tension. Though overtly heterosexual, Stanley and the other "boys," the poker players of *A Streetcar Named Desire*, exist as an example of Eve Kosofsky Sedgwick's category of the
homosocial, that is, of the "social bonds between persons of the same
sex." This category is simultaneously "distinguished [by Sedgwick]
from 'homosexual'" yet one which "hypothesize [s] the potential un-
brokenness of a continuum between homosocial and homosexual . . ."
(1-2). Throughout *Streetcar*, inexactly the way Sedgwick describes,
Williams consistently places Stanley and his poker-playing boys in a
liminal position in which the homosocial operates. Of course, Stanley
is presented as the very epitome of the hypermasculine, especially in
Marlon Brando's performance, which he originated in the first Broad-

way production, a performance preserved in Kazan's 1951 film version of *A Streetcar Named Desire*. However, in its earliest version of 1947, this masculinity is itself undercut through various means in the play's text, especially in the initial description of Stanley as a "gaudy seedbearer," a description linked as much to the men he socializes as with the women he desires (481); the men's clothing, including the bright colors of the bowling shirts worn by the poker players (492, 513); and Mitch's depiction throughout *Streetcar* as a momma's boy. All these serve as textual elements of a conflicted conception of men that, one might say, "goes both ways."

As *Streetcar*'s production and textual history continues to unfold over the years, however, the homosociality between Stanley and his boys, simultaneously rich in homoerotic tension and a visible if problematic masculinity, is gradually stripped from the three major dramatic editions of *Streetcar* and its subsequent 1951 film version (with the exception of the highly homoerotic shower scene). If the dramatic versions of *Streetcar* become progressively *less* queer from 1947 to 1953, they do so through the use of costumes and movements ("blocking") of the characters. The homoerotic tension present in the 1947 text is then, in some ways, restored in the 1997 operatic version premiered at the San Francisco Opera with music by André Previn and libretto by Philip Littell, perhaps not least through the very act of turning it into a opera, an art form that is often identified with and consumed by gay men in ways that border on the obsessive.

This "de-queering" of *Streetcar* is particularly problematic in a play that centers around the offstage and antecedent suicide of a young gay male character, a death pictured by its narrator, Blanche DuBois, as justified. That same suicide is the cause of her own psychological destruction, the heart of the conflict between Stella; Stella's husband, Stanley; and her sister and Stanley's sister-in-law, Blanche. The occlusion of the suicide's motive (entirely absent from the film version, a change that makes little dramatic sense) arises as a response to the censorship of stage and screen in the 1940s and 50s. Nonetheless, even as the homosocial is deliberately erased from Williams' play, and the film adapted from it, that very excision places the play and film squarely in the middle of societal anxiety about the ways men act out both their sexualities and their friendships in literature from these years.

Williams himself was famously, if not infamously, gay, of course, and often wrote about gay men. His depiction of gay men is informed by a long tradition of homosexual literature, especially in plays and films. To be gay is to be unhappy or dead; to be straight is to be both happy and married. Readers and play-goers and film audiences alike will not find this an unusual pattern. It is seen as early as Christopher's Marlowe's 1592 *Edward II* in which the king is killed with a hot poker in the anus, a fate intended to replicate the transgressive act that so outraged his courtiers, and it is present in the suicide of a young lesbian schoolteacher by hanging in Lillian Hellman's *The Children's Hour* (1953), a play roughly contemporaneous with 1947's *Streetcar.*

The gay characters in Williams' works often follow this pattern of death for the unhappy homosexual. He had certainly dramatized homosexual characters from his earliest days as a playwright. His second full-length play, *Not About Nightingales*, a wonderfully lurid prison drama from 1938, includes a highly colorful (if highly homophobic) gay character known only as "the Queen" who describes him/herself as "sensitive" and "refined," recognizably code words in American culture and literature for the feminized homosexual; his/her hypochondria serves to mark him/her as a hysteric and therefore as stereotypically quasi-female. In addition, s/he is self-hating: "Sometimes I wish I was dead. Oh, Lord, Lord, Lord, I wish I was dead" (115). Indeed, the Queen, in what is both literal and textual overkill, manages to achieve that first-act death wish in a particularly grotesque fashion, and, notably, by not one means but two. S/he stumbles into a stream of deadly and vastly overheated steam in the prison steam room, a result of having been confined there following a food strike, and subsequently has his/her head pounded into a cement floor by Butch, a straight man who demonstrates a conventional homophobia from his very first speech:

"Ahh, yuh fruit, go toot yuh your horn outa here" (108). As always with Williams, however, gender and sexuality are complicated. The name "Butch," of course, is slang in the gay male community for a masculine homosexual, a position much less challenged in popular culture than that of the effeminate man; "butch" gay men, as men, often fare much better than do their feminized counterparts, especially if their loves go unnamed.

It's not until Skipper names his love for Brick that he is shamed into suicide. As Williams' audiences and readers know, Skipper and Brick in *Cat on a Hot Tin Roof* were boyhood friends and maintained some contact until the night Skipper drunkenly confessed his love for Brick, then threw himself to his death out of a hotel window, a sequence of events that sends Brick into impotence and alcoholism. Blanche's young husband in *Streetcar* commits suicide by gunshot at a dance, not directly as a result of her discovery of his homosexuality when she finds him in the arms of an older man in a room she thought was empty, but only later when she reveals her disgust at his "weakness." Sebastian Venable, in *Suddenly Last Summer*, is literally eaten by the boys from whom he has been buying sex. In all of these cases, homosexuality has its price. Thus, Williams presents the consequences of homosexuality as a culturally common *quid pro quo*: it is rarely possible to be happy and in love with another man. Jack Straw and Peter Ochello, the happily partnered male couple and original owners of Big Daddy's estate in *Cat on a Hot Tin Roof*, may be an exception to the homophobic rule. However, David Savran has noted how the sins of these two gay men may have fallen onto the heads of the next generation. In a fascinating article, he links their homosexuality to Big Daddy's cancer and Brick's general malaise. Straw and Ochello may have been happy, but their happiness appears to have blighted the men in subsequent generations at Big Daddy's home (64-66).

However, in *Streetcar*, this apparently paradigmatic situation is complicated by the textual history of Williams' play. Notably, the presence, absence or rewriting of a given stage direction in a given edition

---

deeply affects the portrayal or interpretation of one of the central tensions of that play, the role of homoerotic and homosocial tension between heterosexual men—especially since the real life counterparts of any of the poker players might be "trade" (and therefore potentially available for non-passive homosexual activity) as the scholarship, for instance, of John D'Emilio has demonstrated,[1] and in the men that Williams himself knew.

Thus, the textual history of *Streetcar* is critical to my thesis: though Williams' own stage directions and stage actions in that first edition are very concerned with the tensions between machismo and effeminacy, and with being a man and being a boy, the performance tradition (especially as recorded in the Dramatists Play Service edition) presents a much less ambiguous portrayal and much more negative picture of male homoeroticism (in its absence) which then affects later versions.

The first edition of *Streetcar* is pre-performance: it was completed in March 1947, and used to arrange the Broadway premiere on December 3, 1947. It was published very soon after on December 22 of that year. It currently forms the basis of most literary editions of *Streetcar*, that is, it is the basis for texts that are intended not so much for production (though this is not a hard or fast rule), but for critical study and classroom work. Thus, the 1947 text is currently available in the Library of America two-volume edition of Williams' collected plays, in the 1997 Norton anthology *Literature of the American South*—a textbook—and in the Signet single-volume trade edition, the one with Marlon Brando on its cover.

The second edition is English (as opposed to American), printed in 1949 and essentially the text of the 1947 edition save that, as Claude Coulon has noted in an online article, "the British edition avoids the reference to Allan Grey's homosexuality found in the American text [due to] the Lord Chamberlain's censorship. . . ."

The third edition (1950) is Williams' own adaptation of his work; it includes his cuts and alterations in the onstage action and his changes to the stage directions. For the most part it has been subsumed into the fourth edition of *Streetcar* (1953, the date of another copyright held by Williams) which follows Williams' dialogue from the 1950 edition (Gussow and Holditch 1032). However, its stage directions, set and costumes descriptions are largely taken from the Broadway production and may represent a version of its prompt book. This Dramatists Play Service edition (DPS) serves in some ways as a record of Kazan's own production, and is now largely used as an inexpensive text by amateur and student productions. Thus, roughly speaking, the differences between the first and fourth editions serve to illuminate both Williams' initial vision of his play and his adaptation of *Streetcar* on stage and screen. The fact that the DPS, the flattest and least gay of all the available texts, is the standard edition for amateur performances in some ways accelerates the de-queering and normalization of this quite conflicted text.

The 1947 first edition is the most literary of the various extant versions, and I am reading this text as closest to Williams' intentions, though his role in the production of the third edition complicates what would otherwise be an obvious matter. It includes an excerpt from Hart Crane's poem "The Broken Tower" before the text of the play proper:

> And so it was I entered the broken world
> To trace the visionary company of love, its voice
> An instant in the wind (I know not whither hurled)
> But not for long to hold each desperate choice.

The next half line, *not* quoted by Williams in the 1947 edition, is "My word I poured [. . .]." Clearly, the choice of this text and of Crane, another poet known to be homosexual, is not insignificant. If one reads this inclusion of Crane's text, an allusion to authorship, in reference to any of the characters in *Streetcar*, it must be to the polyglot Blanche, who is seen writing Stanley's rude language in her journal and who speaks French. But one could also arguably read that stanza as a reference to Williams: Crane's poem is written in the first person and both

Williams and Crane are male and homosexual. That link is, in fact, a critical commonplace. For instance, Crane's homosexuality is referenced in a footnote to the *Streetcar* text in the Norton *Literature of the South*. However, while one may argue the meaning of that connection in the 1947 edition, the absence of the poem stanza in the 1953 edition absolutely severs the link between Crane and Williams in that edition, thus breaking any possible tie between their sexualities.

In the same way, the literary stage directions of the earlier editions, the ones in which Williams describes scenes or characters in a wonderfully poetic language, are often lost in the much more prosaic 1953 edition. Thus, the description of the night that Blanche first arrives in Williams' original text demonstrates the difference between the 1947 and the 1953 editions:

> It is first dark of an evening early in May. The sky that shows around the dim white building is a peculiarly tender blue, almost a turquoise, which invests the scene with a kind of lyricism and gracefully attenuates the atmosphere of decay. You can almost feel the warm breath of the brown river beyond the river warehouses with their faint redolences of bananas and coffee. (469)

That lovely description? Absent in the DPS. We see instead the Kowalski apartment: "Lights come up slowly, revealing the two rooms of the Kowalski apartment in the French Quarter of New Orleans . . . two steps lead up to a closed door that leads to bathroom," and so forth (5).

When we first meet Stanley, Blanche's brother-in-law, in Williams' original text, we find a rich description of him that invokes Sedgwick's category of the homosocial:

> . . . the center of his life has been pleasure with women, the giving and the taking of it, not with weak indulgence, dependently, but with the power and pride of a richly feathered male bird among hens. Branching out from this complete and satisfying center are all the auxiliary channels of his life,

such as his heartiness with men, his appreciation of rough humor, his love of good drink and food and games, his car, his radio, everything that is his, that bears his emblem of the gaudy seedbearer. (481)

The language of this stage direction is occluded or shadowed as a text only available to readers, directors, designer and actors but not to the audience at large. This shadowing then allows for subtle changes in the performance of the play by its performers and designers that can present a wider or a narrower range of allowable human behaviors and sexuality in Williams' work than a less ambiguous text would allow. That is, different actors, directors and designers who have or lack access to the literary stage directions of the 1947 edition will make different stage choices that will highlight or undercut the homoerotic in any given production. As with "don't ask, don't tell," transgressive behavior is more acceptable when unacknowledged. It may be tempting for readers—and actors—with access to this literary description to read Stanley and his male friends' behavior as examples of an unacknowledged homoerotic tension.

However, when that same description of Stanley, the famous—and somewhat fey—description of him as a "gaudy seedbearer," is missing from the DPS, that double reading is no longer possible. This is the totality of his first appearance in the DPS: "*Stanley enters D.R*" (16), that is, "down right," the entrance nearest the audience on their left side. The abbreviation indicates that this is a notation taken directly from a stage directions prompt book; its flatness takes away the liminal edge to Stanley's character, to that sense of a very masculine sensibility that is, nonetheless, a tad overwrought and overheated.

One might argue that the DPS is simply an inferior edition, or more charitably, a mere performance edition, and that critics should ignore the DPS; however, if this is a record of the first production, traces, one might say, of Kazan's original direction, then this may well be a record worth noting, and changes in the action may in fact be quite significant.

And there is one such significant change: the 1947 edition records a different version of the traumatic poker night when Stanley strikes Stella. The setup is the same: Blanche has turned on a radio and Stanley has become infuriated with her. He throws the radio out a window, and Stella cries out "*Drunk—drunk—animal*, thing, you." To calm him down, and to sober him up, Mitch orders Stanley's friends to throw him into the shower. Then Williams includes this direction:

> *Stanley is forced, pinioned by the two men [Steve and Pablo], into the bedroom. He nearly throws them off. Then all at once, he subsides and is limp in their grasp.*
> *They speak quietly and lovingly to him and he leans his face on one of their shoulders.* (501)

Clearly, this is a moment that, at the very least, is a tender moment, a moment, to borrow the title of Sedgwick's book, that is "between men." It verges on the homoerotic. It requires a passivity of Stanley, the one who takes his pleasure from women, to rest and to be content to be held by his friends. Indeed it almost echoes, or could echo, images from art of the figure of the Christ being taken off the cross and placed in his grave by the (male) disciples, an event known as the deposition of Christ in liturgical and theological circles. This is all the more relevant than it might at first seem, given that the relationship between Christ and his disciples forms another example of homosociality. The loving nature of this scene is extended as the men "talk quietly" and lead Stanley into the bathroom, where he explodes only as they put him in the shower. The quiet moment is over: Stanley yells out, "Let the rut go of me, you sons of bitches," and begins fighting with the two men, the party breaks up and we next hear Stanley "bellowing" for Stella (502, 42).

In the DPS edition, one that follows Kazan's blocking, we do not see the quiet moment referenced in this rich way. It is included but reduced to the flatter verb *holds*. It is also conflated with text that is seven lines down from its placement in the 1947 text:

Pablo:	(Holding Stanley up): He's ok now.
Steve:	(Holding Stanley up): Sure, my boy's ok.

While both versions preserve Steve's referring to Stanley as a "boy" (Blanche's favorite descriptor for her dead and queer husband, Allan[2]), we lose two details in the DPS—the leaning of Stanley's head on one of their shoulders, and the description of the men talking to Stanley and with him. More importantly, because the holding is shifted down in the text, the time during which Stanley is held by Steve and Pablo has been greatly compressed. The 1947 edition has the three men taking a quiet moment to talk, what would surely be a lovely moment on stage. The DPS places this quiet moment much closer in time to Stanley's final explosion and the subsequent breakup of the poker party. The DPS version also has the men talking past Stanley to Mitch, not talking with Stanley, a significant switch in tone.

It is also interesting to note the site of the homoerotic moment: in both versions, the action begins in the bedroom, after a poignant scene between Mitch and Blanche in which they dance to a radio playing "Wiener Blut." Stanley rushes into the bedroom, throws the radio into the street, and strikes Stella "behind a door." This is the same in both texts. However, the compression of the DPS version means that Stanley's quiet moment with his "boys" takes place by the living room couch and the poker table; the DPS explicitly has Stanley collapse on the couch, the public space of the two-room apartment (40-41). But in the 1947 version, Stanley throws the radio out the bedroom window, races across the stage to Stella by the poker table, strikes her offstage on that side of the stage and then—this is different—is brought by the men into the bedroom. In both cases, Mitch says exactly the same thing ("Bring him here, men"), a contrast to Steve's description of Stanley as a boy. This makes the placement of the actors very different. In the 1947 text, that extended homoerotic moment occurs immediately juxtaposed to and in ironic contrast with Stella and Stanley's marriage bed, not to the couch found in the living area of the Kowalski apartment, a piece of furniture not so clearly symbolic of the Kowalskis' sexual attraction to one another.

This proximity to the marriage bed not only makes symbolic sense, but, given the set, it also puts the actors immediately next to the bathroom, a short cross to Stanley's forced shower scene, which eliminates the need for Mitch to cross to the poker table and then to cross back two lines later. In other words, the blocking as it exists in the 1953 edition is both less symbolically charged and clumsier; why then block actors in this lax fashion? One could reasonably argue that it desexualizes the tension between Steve, Pablo, Mitch and Stanley, by moving the action away from the bed.

Finally, there is another detail that is different, one which, again, adds to the homoerotic element of the 1947 text. In both texts, Stanley is thrown under the shower by Steve and Pablo. However it is only the 1947 version that records that they stripped him of his street clothes: "After a moment, Stanley comes out of the bathroom dripping water and still in his clinging wet polka dot drawers" (502). The "still" indicates that the two men presumably took off his clothes; the only other reading possible is that Stanley took off his pants and shoes and shirt following the shower scene. In contrast, the DPS version reads "Stanley, after a moment, comes from bathroom" (41). The matter of clothes is left silent, but the performance tradition, seen in the movie version directed by Kazan, and in the operatic version at San Francisco Opera, has Stanley come out, soaked in his pants, not his boxers. In any case, there is a loving touch in the detail that Stanley's "drawers" are "clinging," a physical detail present in the stage directions of the 1947 version, but absent in the film and opera versions.

Indeed, clothing often makes the men in *Streetcar*. Williams is quite careful to describe the way the men dress. And critics have been glad to write on this subject, most seeing the bright colors that Stanley and the boys wear as emblems of a hyper-masculinity. Thus, while noting the use of "nondescript clothes" in the original production of *Streetcar*, Brenda Murphy also discusses the use of "bold primary colors of his bright silk bowling shirt and jacket and the red silk pajamas he wore in the rape scene" (32) as an example of Stanley's "aggressive masculinity" associated in the stage directions of the 1947 edition with Van Gogh's "The Night Café." There are like analyses by any number of critics, and indeed, Williams associated these bright primary colors with the "gaudy seedbearer" and the male plumage of birds—more colorful than their mates.

However, an analysis of men's and women's clothing advertisements from New Orleans' major newspaper, the *Times-Picayune*, the newspaper both Stanley and Tennessee Williams himself would have read in 1947,[3] the year of *Streetcar*'s genesis, and the city in which it was both written and set, may reveal a more complex gendering of these colors than critics have, to date, allowed.

It is women's clothing, not men's sportswear, that is wildly colored. For instance, an advertisement from local merchant Mayer Israel's dated January 3, 1947 offers stylish young ladies Basque berets in "copen, grey, tweed grey, coffee, gold, pink, navy, black, white, red, kelly green, [and] aquatone." Two days later, on January 5, 1947, women could buy "softly pleated gabardine [dresses] designed by Ann-Peri, with shining gold metal buttons. Sizes for the junior figure in assorted pastel shades" from Keller-Zander.

Men, on the other hand, had a much more limited palette available to them, at least in dress wear: Mayer Israel's offered the well-dressed man worsted flannels from Kuppenheimer with "solids, stripes and plaids in tans, blues, grey and browns." That color combination is seen in many of the advertisements I read from 1946-1948. Indeed, in some cases the palette was even more limited, as in the case of "Sharkskin All-Wool Worsteds." This advertisement from October 8, 1948, noted that sharkskin "lends itself easily to the varied weaves and color patterns that make it standard in every man's wardrobe," though the colors available in this case are only "the new soft grays, browns and blues."

And there was worry about the influx of new colors among men's fashions. Jay Richter, writing in a syndicated column from New York dated January 5, 1947, is sticking to his high standards: "I am an old clothes-horse whose natty blue, all-purpose pin-stripe with matching tailgate glow has long been the object of envious comment when my back was turned. As I pass them in the street, silly girls giggle, the way they do. And what is good enough for them is good enough for me." Still, Richter identified a casual approach to dressing that distressed him deeply: "A salesman in a Fifth avenue [sic] clothing store said that many business men are buying sports clothing for office wear even though they have plenty of suits." Though Richter's article went on to note that veterans returning from the war were demanding more color, the widest range of color *names* I noted for both men and boys was for sports shirts from Sears: "powder blue, brown, navy and tan" (January 14, 1947). Indeed the one depiction of a highly colored loud suit from this period was not in an advertisement, but in a comic strip from October 7, 1948: it was worn by the comic's title character, Joe Palooka. As a "palooka," of course, he is marked as a vulgar, low-class character.

Thus, color becomes doubly representational for men; primarily, color is marked as an attribute of casual or sports wear, and a marker, in some ways, of class. In this light, Richter's concern of business men wearing sports wear to the office then becomes almost a recounting of, even a charge, of slumming, of dressing down. More importantly, in spite of Williams' attempt to match the idea of brightly colored male clothing with the highly colored male plumage of birds and the animal kingdom (and therefore with masculinity), the fact that wide ranges of colors exist only as options for women feminizes the men who wear them, at least for the audience who watches them onstage, if not for the male characters of *Streetcar* itself.

It is not just the men whose class is marked by the colors of their clothing, as the "Joe Palooka" comic makes clear. Stella's bright clothing indicates her new class position, one that Blanche unsuccessfully challenges with her little Japanese lamps over the bare bulbs of the Kowalski place, her carefully maintained clothing in subdued colors and her expensive perfume. Stella's use of color is particularly note-worthy in this context: while she is originally of Blanche's class, she has managed to eke out a very happy life so long as Stanley continues to remain married to her and continues to fulfill her sexually, even though he abuses her. For Stella, the need to be married to Stanley is so strong, so overwhelming a need, that she refuses to be depicted as un-happy by Blanche even after Stanley viciously beats Stella, causing his friends to intervene. This is in stark contrast to the play's norm: the Elysian Fields neighborhood of the New Orleans of *Streetcar* is quite used to abusive relations between men and women. When there is a hush immediately after Blanche and Stella overhear Eunice, the Ko-walskis' upstairs neighbor, yell out, "You hit me! I'm gonna call the police!" Blanche asks, "brightly," "Did he *kill* her?" thus making a joke of the attack (512). But Stella knows what she wants: when Blanche suggests they both leave Elysian Fields, Stella remarks, "You take it for granted I am in something that I want to get out of" (509). Her bright colors are thus a sign of the allegiance she feels to her new class posi-tion.

If the clothing of this play indeed serves as a feminizing marker, as well as a class marker, it's interesting to know that Stanley's literary predecessor, Lucio, found in an early version of *Streetcar* set in Chi-cago's Little Italy, is marked by the stage directions in that draft as not entirely masculine. Vivienne Dickson has noted that the text in that early version of *Streetcar* pictures a sexually ambiguous analogue for Stanley: "Lucio, the brother-in-law, is described as a 'weakly good-looking young man. He has a playful tenderness and vivacity which would amount to effeminacy if he were not Italian'." She goes on to add that Stanley's "behavior does indeed suggest he is a man who fears the feminine in his nature" (163-64). Given Stanley's effeminate past in an early draft of *Streetcar*, the coded use of feminine color—in spite of the author's own attempts to link brightly colored clothing to the masculine—may indicate a place where there is an ambiguity, the kind of ambiguity that, in Sedgwick's formulation, always exists between men, and which is best seen in that quiet moment in which Stanley rests his head wearily on Steve's shoulder.

It is *Blanche* who exhibits a lack of feminine color in her clothing, which is mostly, in Williams' original 1947 version of *Streetcar*, blues, whites and lavenders (the blue evokes the Virgin, of course). Dickson has also pointed out that Blanche's literary antecedent in the version set in Atlanta, "The Primary Colors," is a Blanche that is not in the least afraid of taking on "Ralph," that version's variation on Stanley, and wins, ending up in bed with "Howdy," the Mitch analogue (164). I read the Blanche/Bianca of "The Primary Colors" as masculine. She then transmits an echo of her masculinity to *Streetcar*'s Blanche; hence, the lack of feminine colors in Blanche's clothing in *Streetcar* echoes her literary antecedents in just the way Stanley wears feminized colors as a result of echoes from Lucio's past. They implicate him in same-sex desire that is at least present if never acted upon.

For the most part, the 1951 film version follows the descriptions of clothing throughout,[4] except in one significant place. As directed by Kazan, the film version follows the use of Williams' descriptions of bright clothing for the men of the Elysian Fields throughout, except for the most homosocial moment of all, the poker game that is central to the action of *Streetcar* and the source for the name of the second version of *Streetcar*, "The Poker Night." In Kazan's film version of the poker game, three of the men are wearing light grey or white t-shirts (one so-called "wife beater" or "dago-tee" and two standard t-shirts); Mitch is wearing a shirt and tie. The colored shirts are entirely absent in this scene until the moment Stella (played by Kim Hunter) wishes to throw the men out. At that point she gathers up the shirts, which have been out of the frame, and throws them at the poker players. There the shirts are on the screen for a second or two, just as they were described in Williams' original text. Thus, for the film version, at least, the bright colors that have implicated the men of the 1947 stage version in Sedgwick's category of the homosocial, if my reading of color is correct, are suppressed and occluded.[5] Nonetheless, in a kind of erasure, even in the black-and-white palette of the 1951 film version, the colors and patterns of the shirts are, for that second or two, very visible and thus remain, for that brief moment, as a marker of both class and homosociality, but one that cannot be allowed to remain in sight of the audience.

If the homosociality and its linked erotic tensions between the men are obscured in the poker game itself, the transposition of the shower scene, in which Stanley is calmed by being put under a cold shower by the boys, increases the visibility of that homosociality and makes it even more apparent to movie-goers. In the play, the bathroom is off-stage; in the movie, the voyeuristic camera takes the viewers into the bathroom and lets them gaze as Stanley is held under the shower. The hands of all the other poker players are clearly visible, wrapped around Brando's chest in what becomes a very loving moment, the substitution of that quiet moment in which he leans his head on the shoulders of the men in the 1947 version, though that itself is absent in the film. Stanley's passivity is, however, increased in Kazan's direction. The stage version has him awake, but quiet, till the moment he becomes enraged again; the movie version has him clearly passed out as the water flows over him, soaking both Stanley and his boys, making him available to their touch and to our gaze in ways which the stage Stanley is not. Our ability to stare at Kazan's male "bodice ripper" (Stanley's t-shirt has been torn in the fight and his skin shows through the rip in this and the next scene which includes the famous cry of "Stellaaaa!") is problematized in the film criticism that talks about the double-edged nature of the musculature of the body builder:

> As signifiers of masculinity, muscles present a paradox since they bring together the terms of naturalness and performance. . . . The performance of a muscular masculinity within the cinema draws attention to both the restraint and the excess involved in "being a man," the work put into the male body [. . .] there is a sense in which bodybuilding does trouble the categories through which sex, as well as gender, is designated in our culture. (Tasker 119)

Brando's clearly crafted body "troubles" his performance of Stanley in just this way, especially when gallons of cascading water plaster his already tight t-shirt to his musculature, and especially when it is only through the mechanism of the camera that the viewer can see the transformation of tight clothing to skin, next to nothing at all.

* * *

What, then, of the operatic version of *Streetcar*? First, unlike plays and film, opera is—or has been claimed to be—an art form especially linked to gay men, a link that obviously becomes even more important in the case of an adaptation of a play by Tennessee Williams:

> In many ways, [Williams] is the true successor to Oscar Wilde in gay literature. Like Wilde, Williams made it impossible for his audience and his critics to separate author from creation. He was the poet as performer, the playwright as celebrity. [. . .] Williams would [. . .] become a figure of depravity, as his works would become shocking and dirty, his sexuality a justification for the vicious assaults of homophobic critics in the fifties and sixties. (Clum 32)

Streetcar in particular became especially associated with gay male culture; as Marlon B. Ross noted, "Williams' early plays . . . accrued a large 'camp following' because gays recognized that he [Williams] was writing about them, and because they understood that he was 'playing around' with sacred cows like the family, gender roles, and the purity of the American dream" (120).[6]

But opera itself is the province of many urban gay males. For instance, Wayne Koestenbaum has written about this connection at length in his *The Queen's Throat: Opera, Homosexuality, and the Mystery of Desire*. He sees a link between gay male sexuality and the opera connoisseur:

We don't have much choice about our sexual feelings. Nor can we choose our race. Nor, in most cases, our class. But for the collector, the drama of choice is supreme. [. . .] The collector dismisses poor taste, even considers it diseased. A Franco Corelli disc receives dismissal in a 1961 *Opera News*, and the language used to criticize this handsome tenor's record reflects a homophobic distaste for the desires that might have led gay fans to purchase it.

After detailing the homophobic language of the review, a description of Corelli's "lisping," Koestenbaum goes on to say, "One would think that opera were a sterile solution infected by the desires of gay fans" (63-4). Or again, "For three dark winter months I studied opera scores and salivated as I beheld sharps, flats, naturals, the concrete materials from which singers conjure song. As I held the *Carmen* score aloft, I pretended that I was [Maria] Callas or even just a dull upstart preening before a hallway mirror, a nobody, practicing for an impossible role" (198).

Indeed, it's not just opera-goers that implicate opera in gay culture. Opera *subjects* (if not always composers and singers) have become increasing queer as well, perhaps beginning with the literary source for Richard Strauss' 1905 *Salome*. Though Strauss himself was happily heterosexual, he adapted Oscar Wilde's play, originally written in French (1892) and then translated into English in 1894 by Wilde's lover, Lord Alfred Douglas. There is also Benjamin Britten's adaptation of Melville's *Billy Budd* (1951), a prime example of the homosocial in novella and opera alike; and his adaptation of Thomas Mann's *Death in Venice* (1973), both written for his long-term companion, tenor Peter Pears; *Streetcar* itself with its queer subtext restored from the 1947 edition, an effort made necessary by the librettist's decision to include "the sleazy side of the play, which is the half that gives the heft" (Myers 40)[7]; *The Life and Times of Harvey Milk*, an operatic version of the assassination of gay City of San Francisco Supervisor Harvey Milk; and many gay composers of opera and musicals, including Leonard Bernstein, Ned Rorem and Gian Carlo Menotti.

In order to include that "sleazy side," librettist Philip Littell has gone back to the 1947 edition. Thus, the 1997 operatic version of *Streetcar* re-queers the production history of this complex play by revisiting Williams' original version of his "literary" first edition. Following the author's original version (a matter as much of estate rights as it is composer and librettist's intent), we revert to the position of the 1947 text, one in which the homosociality is reinstated with an ambiguous sexuality restored; indeed, it might even be heightened as the poker players' lines are now sung and associated with an always queer opera/operatic art form, rather than spoken and thus incorporated in Williams' own mix of naturalistic and impressionistic theatre.

Opera-goers also found the colorful clothing of the 1947 version restored (including a brilliant scarlet kimono worn by soprano Elizabeth Futral as Stella Kowalski), and thus the masculinity of Blanche's rather muted palette and the femininity of Stanley's bright clothing is at least potentially available to the opera's patrons. This reading of fashions may have changed in the fifty years between *Streetcar*'s premiere and the operatic version, however. The very meaning of color, very gendered in the forties, not nearly so gendered in the nineties, reduces the sexual coding of the costumes from a telling point (I hope) to a mere recreation of Williams' own stage directions and description, one that exists as homage to an icon of the American theatre rather than as a monument to a challenged sexuality.

In one case, the homoerotic tensions are deeply reduced: since the design of the opera set follows the 1947 stage design, a result of the choice to revert to the 1947 text, the bathroom of the opera set is, unlike the bathroom in the 1951 movie version, once again offstage. This moves the shower scene offstage as well. In fact, the shower scene is so reduced that one can barely tell Stanley's hair is wet in the San Francisco Opera (SFO) production, at least in the video that followed the commission and world premiere of Previn's new opera, though Rodney Gilfry's chest is almost as built as Brando's. However, some critics found Gilfry's vocal production lacking: "Baritone Rodney

Gilfry was hunky as Stanley, but not volcanic enough vocally" (Ames online).

Still, when the fight scene is reduced to just a few minutes on stage (with a Stanley on the edge of collapse, not entirely passed out, as in the film version), the opera's blocking reduces the homoerotic tensions of the 1947 stage version to almost nothing, when one considers that the moment when everything stops on stage and Stanley rests his head on Steve's shoulder is, in the SFO production, absent. The librettist has stated his desire in many venues to remain faithful to the "text" of *Streetcar*, to the point of a fault, perhaps: "it may be that the restrictions imposed by Littell by the Williams estate ultimately hamstrung Previn" (Mermelstein online). A comparison of the 1947 edition and the opera libretto on video makes it clear that Littell was working from the first edition. In that case, in an art form associated with gay men, in a play associated with gay men written by a notoriously gay man, one would expect that moment of affection between men to be still present, but it is not. If this is a contested moment, it is because the cultural anxiety that has always surrounded productions of *Streetcar* still prevails.

Of course, it may be that opera is not all that gay, after all: Robert Hofler took on that idea in an essay written for the national gay and lesbian news magazine, the *Advocate*, in no uncertain terms:

> Even looking back at my rather extensive career of opera-going, the art form has never seemed so much a gay thing as a kid thing. Opera is expensive and time-consuming and people with children simply have other ways to spend their time and money. Almost all of the heterosexual opera queens I have known over the years have been either childless or terribly bad parents who didn't mind having the kids heat a can of Campbell's soup while Mom and Dad took in their umpteenth *Der Rosenkavalier*. (online)

It may be, too, that it's simply that this *particular* opera is not gay enough; *Streetcar* is one of the most important plays in contemporary

American drama and it may quite simply have been impossible for any version of it to compete:

> A play, by its continued popularity alone, can haunt the opera it prompted. If the opera is itself mediocre, the comparison will be devastating. Such is the case with André Previn's operatic treatment of Tennessee Williams's *A Streetcar Named Desire*, which received its world premiere at the San Francisco Opera on September 19[, 1997]. (Mermelstein online)

Mermelstein also found the music flat, adding that "[m]ore disconcerting, especially given that conventional narrative is slavishly adhered to here, is Previn's disregard for various operatic conventions. Instead of creating a score that includes repeated themes, Previn has written a through-composed text, and as a result, this *Streetcar* is far more a play set to music than an opera." Worse, some critics have argued that in making *Streetcar* into an opera, the very ambiguity that made its theatrical ancestor magical has disappeared:

> Seeming unable to recognize Williams' irony, Previn and Littell present Blanche as a diva, somewhere between [Puccini's] Tosca and [Strauss'] Marschallin. This is a parody of a parody—a sanitized appropriation of the homosexual opera fan's diva-goddess described by Wayne Koestenbaum in his revelatory *The Queen's Throat*. (Schiff)

Thus, the very act of adaptation that ought to have turned this version of *Streetcar* into even more of a queer entity than it is, failed to do so through a disregard of the very conventions that make opera such an obsessive and wonderful art form for gay men. Given the advances made in gay liberation in the fifty years between the premiere of the stage version and of the opera, and the position of both Tennessee Williams' plays and of opera in gay male culture, one would expect more, not less, of the homosocial to make its appearance. However, the production history of *Streetcar* finally shows an uneasy tension between the homoerotic and the heterosexual, in ways that remain ambiguous. Those tensions throughout the then fifty-year history of *A Streetcar Named Desire* become less conflicted and covert with each passing year and each new production, even with the return of the 1947 edition as the basis of the new opera. Perhaps the SFO didn't want to offend their richest patrons of all; perhaps there were legal issues with the production of an opera based on *Streetcar*. But the San Francisco production is awfully innocent, the final step in a long progression from 1947 to 1997. If so, it's only been faithful to its own past, as the homosocial gets stripped from this queerest of plays with each passing production in its fifty-year history.

Notes

1. Especially in his *Sexual Politics, Sexual Communities: The Making of a Homosexual Minority in the United States, 1940-1970* (1983, 1998).

2. Allan, "alone." This is a common pun: one thinks of Alan Strang ("alone strange") from Peter Shaffer's 1974 *Equus*.

3. I read advertisements from late 1946 to late 1948, the approximate period of the first edition's writing and production (as with all of Williams' plays, there are multiple versions of *Streetcar* written over a long period of time that precede the final version we know now); the ads cited here are very representative examples.

4. Stanley's red pajamas become red and white striped in the film version.

5. Most famously, of course, is the suppression of the motive for Allan Grey's suicide: Blanche's disgust at his homosexuality, one of the "sixty major or minor changes . . . including major omissions of any references to homosexuality or nymphomania . . ." required by censor Joseph Breen (Phillips 41), was apparently not minded by director Elia Kazan, who mentions only one "significant" cut in his film version in an interview taped in 1971 or 1972: "I felt very badly about it, and I still do, because it was a wonderful scene Kim Hunter had when she was responding to Brando calling her from the bottom of the stairs . . ." (Ciment 68-69).

6. In my own youth, I remember a beautiful woman racing up to me in a gay bar in Chicago. In a very inauthentic Southern accent, she exclaimed "You must help me! That person over there is trying to pick me up and he does not know that I am really a man!" (I had not realized it either but I was only 17 at the time.) It took me several

years and several readings of *Streetcar* later to realize that she was in fact performing a drag version of Blanche and depending on the "kindness of strangers" to get her out a tricky social situation.

7. In an interview from *Opera News*, *Streetcar* composer André Previn tells the story of his first opera performance: Strauss' *Salome*, thus making this circle of queer opera subjects complete (Myers 35).

Works Cited

Ames, Katrine. "Unstoppable 'Streetcar.'" Rev. of *A Streetcar Named Desire*. *Newsweek* 10/05/98, Vol. 132 Issue 14, p86, 2/3p, 1c. http://search.epnet.com/ direct.asp?an=1109360&db=aph *Academic Search Premiere*. EBSCOhost. ISSN 00289604. Accession Number 1109360. (07 November 2003).

Caplin, Alfred G. "Joe Palooka." Comic. *The Times-Picayune* 7 Oct. 1948, 26.

Ciment, Michel. *Kazan on Kazan*. New York: The Viking P., 1974.

Clum, John M. "From *Summer and Smoke* to *Eccentricities of a Nightingale*." *Modern Drama* XXXIX.1 (Spring 1996): 31-50.

Coulon, Claude. "Tennessee Williams: *A Streetcar Named Desire*." *Agrégation 2004: bibliographie sur A Streetcar Named Desire, la pièce*. 2004. http:// www.univ-pau.fr/saes/pb/concours/bibliconc/04/twilliams.pdf (29 October 2003).

Denton, William. "Twists, Slugs and Roscoes: A Glossary of Hardboiled Slang." *Miskatonic University Press*. 1993-2000. http://www.miskatonic.org/ slang.html (23 October 2003).

Dickson, Vivienne. "*A Streetcar Named Desire*: Its Development Through the Manuscripts." *Tennessee Williams: A Tribute*. Ed. Jac Tharpe. Hattiesburg: U.P. of Mississippi, 1977.

Gussow and Holditch. "Notes on the Texts." *Tennessee Williams: Plays 1937-1955*. New York: The Library of America, 2000.

Hofler, Robert. "The Myth of the Opera Queen." Article. *Advocate* 12 May 1998, p76, 2p, 1c. http://search.epnet.com/direct.asp?an=647565&db=aph *Academic Search Premiere*. EBSCOhost. ISSN 00018996. Accession Number 647565. (07 November 2003).

Keller-Zander. "They're smooth. They're cruise-styles. They're Keller-Zander's Jr.'s." Advertisement. *The Times-Picayune* 5 Jan. 1947, Sunday ed., sec. 3:7.

Koestenbaum, Wayne. *The Queen's Throat: Opera, Homosexuality and the Mystery of Desire*. New York: Poseidon Press, 1993.

Labiche's. "Sharkskin All-Wool Worsteds." Advertisement. *The Times-Picayune* 8 Oct. 1948, 4.

Mayer Israel's. "Bright Fashion 4-Star Basque Beret." Advertisement. *The Times-Picayune* 3 Jan. 1947, 25.

_____. "Mayer Israel's Kuppenheimer Worsted Flannels." Advertisement. *The Times-Picayune* 7 Oct. 1948, 3.

Mermelstein, David. "Derailed in San Francisco." Rev of *A Streetcar Named Desire*. *New Criterion* Dec 98, Vol. 17 Issue 4, p57, 3p. http://search.epnet.com/direct.asp?an=1339171&db=aph *Academic Search Premiere*. EBSCOhost. ISSN 07340222. Accession Number 1339171. (07 November 2003).

Myers, Eric. "Making Streetcar Sing." Article. *Opera News* Sep 98, Vol. 63 Issue 3, p34, 5p, 3c, 7bw. 34-6, 38, 40. http://search.epnet.com/direct.asp?an=1029914&db=aph *Academic Search Premiere*. EBSCOhost. ISSN 00303607. Accession Number 1029914. (07 November 2003).

Murphy, Brenda. *Tennessee Williams and Elia Kazan: A Collaboration in the Theatre*. Cambridge: Cambridge U.P., 1992.

Phillips, Gene D., S.J. "Blanche's Phantom Husband: Homosexuality on Stage and Screen." *Louisiana Literature* 14.2 (Fall 1997): 36-47.

Richter, Jay. "Sports Clothes Gaining Favor Over Suits." *The Times-Picayune* 5 Jan. 1947, Sunday ed., 2:4.

Ross, Marlon B. "The Making of Tennessee Williams: Imaging a Life of Imagination." *Southern Humanities Review* XXI.2 (Spring 1987), 117-131.

Savran, David. "'By coming suddenly into a room I thought was empty': Mapping the Closet with Tennessee Williams." *Studies in the Literary Imagination* XXIV.2 (Fall 1991), 64-65.

Schiff, David. "We Want Magic." Rev of *A Streetcar Named Desire*. *Atlantic Monthly* Sep 99, Vol. 284 Issue 3, p92, 5p, 1c. http://search.epnet.com/direct.asp?an=2248774&db=aph *Academic Search Premiere*. EBSCOhost. ISSN 10727825. Accession Number 2248774. (07 November 2003).

Sears Roebuck and Co. "Tuesday Wise Buys." Advertisement. *The Times-Picayune* 14 Jan. 1947, 9.

Sedgwick, Eve Kosofsky. *Between Men: English Literature and Male Homosocial Desire*. New York: Columbia U.P., 1985.

A Streetcar Named Desire. 1951. Screenplay by Tennessee Williams. Performed by Vivien Leigh, Kim Hunter, and Marlon Brando. Directed by Elia Kazan. Warner Home Video. ASIN: B000055XMH. Videocassette.

_____. 1997. Composed and conducted by André Previn. Libretto by Philip Littell. Performed by Renee Fleming, Elizabeth Futral, and Rodney Gilfry. Directed by Kirk Browning. Produced by San Francisco Opera. Kultur Video. ASIN: B000025RB9. Videocassette.

Tasker, Yvonne. *Spectacular Bodies: Gender, Genre, and the Action Cinema*. London: Routledge, 1993.

Williams, Tennessee. *A Streetcar Named Desire. Tennessee Williams: Plays, 1937-1955*. Ed. Mel Gussow and Kenneth Holditch. New York: Library of America, 2000.

_____. *A Streetcar Named Desire*. New York: Dramatists Play Service, Inc., 1953.

_____. *Not About Nightingales. Tennessee Williams: Plays, 1937-1955*. Ed. Mel Gussow and Kenneth Holditch. New York: Library of America, 2000.

"Tiger—Tiger!"
Blanche's Rape on Screen

Nancy M. Tischler

Tiger! Tiger! burning bright
In the forests of the night,
What immortal hand or eye
Could frame thy fearful symmetry?
—William Blake, 1794

When will the sleeping tiger stir
among the jungles of the heart?
I seem to hear the sound of her
gentle breathing in the dark.

O you that are deceived by this
apparent innocence, take care!
You know that storms are presaged by
such trembling stillness in the air.

And all that breathe have in their breast
capacity for certain flame.
Domesticated cats are merely
beasts pretending to be tame.

Not for the pelt but for the passion
would I track that tiger down,
to dwell with her more dangerously
beyond the lighted streets of town!
—Tennessee Williams, Acapulco, September 1940

"Tiger—tiger!" These are Stanley's words of recognition when Blanche challenges him to a brawl by breaking a bottle and threatening to twist the broken end in his face. Her practiced gesture validates his judgment of her as a temptress with round heels all too happy to be brought down off those legendary columns at Belle Reve. This scene, the foreplay for the rape, has an inevitability signaled by Stanley's words: "We've had this date with each other from the beginning!" (Williams, *Theatre* 402)

The preceding scenes foreshadow this moment in Blanche's invitations to sexual violence and in Stanley's brutal actions, gestures, words, and tone. When we first meet him, he throws a bloody package at Stella; later he bangs drawers and doors, smashes the radio, shouts at everyone, and demands repeatedly to be respected as the alpha male of this tribe. When Blanche laughs at him, spraying him with perfume, teasing him, treating him as a little boy, he responds with irritation and rising anger. She is flirting with him, a southern sexual ritual that he rejects: "I don't go in for that stuff," he asserts—perhaps without recognizing his own growing interest (Williams 278). As Elia Kazan has explained, "Nothing is more erotic and arousing to him than 'airs'. . . . she thinks she's better than me. . . . I'll show her" (Qtd. in Cole 377). Stanley senses in this woman a challenge to his authority and to his family. He must be rid of this meddlesome woman but finally realizes that he can be rid of her only by destroying her himself. Their fearful symmetry is at the core of the drama.

Audiences watching this play or film today accept the inevitability without contemplating the difficulties involved in articulating it some fifty years ago, when women were considered less sexual; on-stage lasciviousness and rape were forbidden, and a man capable of violating a woman was expected to be punished. The 1930 Motion Picture Production Code, which was still in effect at the time of the film, stated that there were to be no rape, no prostitution, no homosexuality, and no unpunished crimes. In dramatizing this powerful climax and the subsequent denouement in *A Streetcar Named Desire*, which he himself had revised over and over, Tennessee Williams was challenging the censors and the morality of the era. This first "adult" film to come out of

Hollywood presented a number of challenges to the code of the Motion Picture Association of America. These two final scenes were to become the crux of the conflict involving numerous individuals and organizations, from producers, directors, and advisers to the Hays office and the Roman Catholic Church.

In our era of open sexuality and violence-ridden entertainment, we are inclined to forget that halfway through the twentieth century, even Rhett Butler's famous final line in *Gone with the Wind* was a real shocker. In 1939, the producer of *Gone with the Wind* had to seek special permission from the Hays office for a breach of the Production Code in order for Rhett to say to Scarlett, "Frankly, my dear, I don't give a damn!" On the other hand, another sequence was apparently not contested—the conjugal rape scene, in which Rhett sweeps a protesting Scarlett into his arms and carries her up the grand staircase to unspoken delights of powerful sexuality. The following morning finds him chastened and her fulfilled but both unable to express their feelings openly. The scene was allowed because the couple were married, the language was not explicitly violent or sexual, and the action was off-camera.

This remarkable sequence lingered in the viewers' imaginations long after the actual plot line had dissipated. Molly Haskell (214) believes that Scarlett must remain silent to keep her power over Rhett. As a "superwoman" who seeks to adopt male characteristics in order to survive, she is obliged to refuse to acknowledge her bliss to this overpowering male, preferring the weak, unavailable, and easily dominated Ashley (166). Haskell, who apparently finds Scarlett's type of woman repellent, says, "She is a diabolically strong woman—deceptively so, in the manner of the southern belle—and she fears the loss of her strength and selfhood that a total 'animal' relationship with Rhett would entail" (167). Whatever the actual motivation, Scarlett's evident pleasure at the make-believe rape and the suggestive morning-after scene were in conformity with the rules of the Production Code.

When an older and more complex Vivien Leigh signed the contract to play the older and more complex Blanche DuBois in the film version of *Streetcar*, she once again assumed the role of a woman who sought control over a weak man (Mitch) while lusting after a strong, sexual brute (Stanley). Thus the rape scene and its aftermath in *A Streetcar Named Desire* retained an unspoken resonance of the earlier film. This time, implicit taboos intensify the conflict: the pair are in-laws, and Blanche's sister, Stella, is in the hospital having Stanley's child.

Both Tennessee Williams and Elia Kazan knew what they were doing here; they were also well aware of the spoken and unspoken rules of the theater and the cinema. Williams, who repeatedly demonstrated his taste for rough sex in his own life, was forced by theater conventions of the time to moderate his portrayal of sexual violence. Kazan, who relished the notion that sex for Stanley is a need to dominate, felt he should retain the hint of violent sexual battle in order to be faithful to the inner spirit of Williams's story. According to Michel Ciment, Kazan identified Blanche with Williams himself—"an ambivalent figure who is attracted to the harshness and vulgarity around him at the same time he fears it, because it threatens his life" (Ciment 71). As Kazan said,

Blanche Dubois [*sic*] comes into a house where someone is going to murder her. The interesting part of it is that Blanche Dubois-Williams is *attracted* to the person who's going to murder her. That's what makes the play deep. . . . So you can understand a woman *playing* affectionately with an animal that's going to kill her. So she at once wants him to rape her, and knows he will kill her. She protests how vulgar and corrupted he is, but she also finds that vulgarity and corruption attractive. (Qtd. in Ciment 71)

While Harold Clurman, who later directed the road version of the play, thought this conflict symbolic of a dying culture in America, Kazan thought it more explicitly autobiographical. This possibility is reinforced by Williams's own comment that he conceived Blanche as a very sexual woman: "In a small southern town like Laurel, Mississippi, to live such a life is totally revolutionary and totally honest. She was over-sexed, [and] dared to live it without harming anybody" (qtd. in Isaac 26).

For the play and the film, Kazan and Williams chose Marlon Brando for the role of Stanley as a debased Rhett, coaxing his wife down the rambling staircase rather than carrying her up the elegant one. When Kazan selected Vivien Leigh to play the role of Blanche, she was the only major actor replaced in the film version, taking the role created by Jessica Tandy. He made the choice partly because of her greater fame (derived largely from the earlier role), probably also because of recent gossip about her private life, and finally because of her proven experience: she had already played Blanche in the London production of *Streetcar*, under the direction of her husband, Sir Laurence Olivier. She struck Kazan as the ideal person for the part in the film, and according to Maurice Yacowar, the producers insisted on at least one box-office name (15).

The script itself was a larger problem for everyone concerned. The play had been a success from the moment it opened on Broadway at the Barrymore Theatre on December 3, 1947. As was usually the case when Tennessee Williams had a hit, his agent, Audrey Wood, immediately began to negotiate film contracts. Murray Schumach describes some of the preliminary exchange:

> Torn between the desire to produce a money-making and artistic movie and fear of offending powerful pressure groups, interested studios and producers sought the advice of [Joseph] Breen, who had not yet retired as administrator of the industry's self-censoring body. His responses were discouraging. Thus, he told Paramount that, if it tried to make *Streetcar* into a movie, the homosexuality and rape would have to be eliminated. More significant was his letter to Irene Selznick, who had produced the play and was interested in the movie prospects. "You will have in mind," Breen wrote to Mrs. Selznick,

that the provisions of the Production Code are quite patently set down in the knowledge that motion pictures, unlike stage plays, appeal to mass audiences; to the mature and the immature; the young and the not-so-young.

Because these motion pictures are exhibited rather indiscriminately among all kinds of classes of audiences, there is a frank acknowledgment on the part of the industry, of a peculiar responsibility to this conglomeration of patrons. Material which may be perfectly valid for dramatization and treatment on the stage may be questionable, or even completely unacceptable, when presented in a motion picture. (Schumach 73)

Here, clearly stated by the leading authority on movie censorship at that time, was a variation of the philosophy that movies are suited to the mentality of twelve-year-olds. Here was the conviction that some material is not for the American screen, regardless of its artistic merit or the taste shown in making the movie. The subject itself was censurable, regardless of the film's beauty or sensitivity. The concept of the adult movie was, obviously, not yet acknowledged by Hollywood's chief censor in 1950 (Schumach 73).

Before the purchase by Warner, Selznick had tried another strategy. After receiving the quoted message from Breen, she wrote Williams on July 1, 1949, that she was negotiating the deal for the film rights. She added this note to her letter:

Very, very confidentially, I have laid my hands on the Hays office report which is the factor, aside from generally poor business prospects, which has most seriously damaged us. The worst of it says, "The element of sex perversion would have to be omitted entirely. The rape scene is also unacceptable . . . but most specifically because in the play this particularly revolting rape goes unpunished. The element of the lead's prostitution should not be discussed in so much detail. (Selznick to Williams, n.p., July 1, 1949, 3 pp., typed letter, Boston University)

The censors also worried about the toilet gags, the other vulgarities, and so forth. Selznick admonished Williams to keep this quiet until after the property was sold. And then she added, "In any case, I think most objections can be met, others compromised, and withal, the flavor, essence and story retained."

As a possible solution, she says that she took a

bold step . . . , a personal gamble I feel justified. I engaged a writer to come here for discussion, conjecture and to work on a treatment. I chose someone with knowledge and feeling for the South and a writer with the most respect for your work and the greatest esteem for the play. I'll spare you further detail lest you expire meanwhile and advise you immediately that it is Lillian Hellman.

Selznick goes on to explain that Hellman is a "skilled scenario craftsman," one "resourceful at managing to meet the Code and yet not lose substance." She continues:

Lillian arrives here July 7th and will stay with me for the two weeks for which she has committed herself as I am just across the street, fortunately, from Willie Wyler who has agreed to sit in and work with Hellman. Willie has agreed to contribute his time, even though "on spec" because of his passion for the property and because the screenplays of three of his most successful pictures have been done by Lillian. If things work out on our two-week venture, then Lillian will agree to do the shooting script, and it is our hope that we can sell a shooting script to Paramount. . . .

Lillian has stated her position fully last night: she won't contribute anything of which you would not approve, she has no intention of distorting the play in any way, she is not going to superimpose her stamp, AND she wants very much to know, as does Wyler, your thinking in terms of screenplay. . . . I *cannot* tell you how valuable any ideas you have will be, both in regard to preserving content while meeting the Code as well as added material to compensate for losses which will be inevitable. (Selznick to Williams 2-3)

There must have been a flurry of activity at this point—probably telephone calls, delivery of bits of manuscript previously cut, and so forth. The other important document that I found in the Selznick file to testify to the fascinating work in these preliminary arrangements in anticipation of the sale of the "property" is a six-page, typed, double-spaced document that is unsigned. I assume it is the result of the work of Hellman and Wyler those two weeks in July and bears the unmistakable mark of Hellman—her clear view of human character, her disdain for fragile southern belles, and her firm judgments.

The Hellman typescript begins with what she labels the "FIRST PROBLEM: Blanche tells Mitch of her marriage to a homosexual."[1] The author then marches staunchly on to the SECOND PROBLEM: The Rape Scene. She acknowledges that any approach can prove "foolish and tricky." "It is the most common of Hollywood delusions that if a writer can describe a good scene he can also write a good scene. It is impossible to tell what will fit until you come to fit it; impossible to see a part without knowing the whole. The solutions put down here are practical and possible. It is hardly necessary to say that their worth—their "literary" worth can only be proved by a full and final script." This is the way she saw the problem at hand, and her solutions, neatly numbered:

One: The beginning of scene ten, as is. Scene ten opens as Stanley comes back from the hospital to find Blanche drunk and in a mood of hysterical exhilaration. Blanche flirts with Stanley. He is part tempted, part maliciously amused. But he decides not to sleep with her. Maybe he gets bored with her fancy talk and falls asleep from it, the beer and the heat. He did want her and would have taken her but her intensity, her high-flautin [*sic*] attempt to make the seduction into something else, is as alien to him as it must have been alien to many men from whom she had begged pretty decoration for sexual intercourse. (I have always seen her reading poetry in bed to a bewildered travelling [*sic*] salesman from Memphis, Tenn.) His refusal of her is horrible to her: she pretends to herself that *he* wanted her, that *she* is shocked, that she is frightened of him, that she cannot stay in the house with him, etc. The scene ends in a violent fight between them. She has now so twisted and turned that an already sick mind believes he did try to rape her. And by morning is convinced that she must tell Stella of Stanley's villainy. This is not a lie: it is a delusion. But the delusion-stage set long before—years before the play begins. (From Hellman typescript 2ff.)

This scenario, cast in Hellman's ironic voice, makes Blanche a more lascivious version of her own character Birdie, from *The Little Foxes* and *Another Part of the Forest*. But in actuality, Blanche has some of the strength of Regina as well. She, like Scarlett, enjoys both sex and romance. Her love of poetry is more important to Williams than simply class reinforcement. She peppers her speech with poetic allusions, as did he. She wants the romance of "Rosenkavalier" as part of her relationships; she sees herself as Camille, as he saw himself as Byron. I think it unfair to call this hunger a "high-falutin attempt to make seduction into something else" or "pretty decoration." It is more than a superficial ploy but rather the mark of a hunger for a deeper meaning to sexuality, the difference between animalistic coupling and romantic love.

Not only does this Hellman typescript scenario caricature the romantic nature of our heroine but it also diminishes her truth-telling. If this be delusion, then much of the remainder of the story is also problematic. This interpretation calls into doubt the whole of Blanche's judgments and narratives, an enormous price to pay for audience comfort.[2] Thus the climactic scene of the play is eviscerated, the ambiguities are eliminated, and the play is reduced to the unwelcome visit of a delusional sister-in-law.

Suspecting that this scenario may not prove satisfactory, the writer, who sounds more and more like Lillian Hellman, continues:

Two: The beginning of scene ten, as is. Blanche is closer to the edge of mental breakdown, perhaps because all through the script we bring her nearer to the edge. Perhaps because of Mitch's refusal to marry her. Stanley does try to sleep with her. She becomes hysterical, runs from the house. (Stanley doesn't give a damn: he falls asleep.) Blanche wanders around the district trying to find somebody to talk to, occasionally buying a drink or asking for one. The wandering becomes a nightmare: the streets are confused with Belle Reve; a passing young man with his girl fades into an image of herself and her husband; the music of a Quarter honky-tonk becomes "her" song; men at bars are men with whom she slept in Laurel, Miss.; an open window looking into a cheap Quarter bedroom fades into the bedroom she had as a child. She finds, at a bar, a bewildered man to tell about the cruel rape that did not happen; a bewildered woman to whom she explains that she never had anything to do with Stanley, that he is unworthy of her sister, etc. I think we could do an extremely effective night of the increasing darkness of a woman's mind: her lostness, her loneliness, her desire to go back to Stanley and her guilt in wanting to go to him. Perhaps she does return to the house expecting Stanley to be waiting for her, only to find that he is sleeping. She tries to wake him, tries to make him listen to her, realizes that he is bored, and cruel, in the face of her misery. And runs to Stella. (Hellman typescript 3-4)

Stanley sounds increasingly like Dashiell Hammett in this version, though Blanche sounds not at all like Lillian Hellman. The last sentences elaborating on the cinematography of the mad scene testify to Hellman's infatuation with this variation. She is expanding the play into a film, using the medium's possibilities of space and shading in ways denied the stage-bound playwright. Curiously, Williams is the one generally accused of diffusion and Hellman is praised for her efficiency, but this is an example of Williams accomplishing a host of outcomes in a handful of gestures and phrases while Hellman embroiders a whole series of gratuitous scenes.

The point at issue is still the same: to satisfy filming's constraints, the rape did not happen and Blanche is delusionary. In this ironic scenario, Stanley displays passing interest but is less sexy or violent than sleepy and bored. Hellman has reduced his brutality, has ameliorated his cruelty and his will to power, and has demonstrated her continuing disdain for weak-minded southern belles. For her, this forest of the night contains no powerful mystery worthy of exploration.

Hellman then tries a couple of shorter scenarios, building on ideas she has previously elaborated:

> Three: The beginning of scene ten, as is. Stanley has no interest in Blanche, and wishes only to be rid of her. She identifies Stanley's rejection of her with the bridegroom's rejection. He goes to bed. Blanche wants him, knows she does, feels intense guilt, begins to drink by herself, tries to wake Stanley on various foolish excuses, and grows more desperate and more frightened as the night wears on, and the drinks take effect. (I would also like to include in this plan the night-wandering which I have previously described.) By morning—the crack-up has come—she believes that he did rape her. And she runs to Stella. (Hellman typescript 4)

This version turns Blanche into a lusty dipsomaniac who is pestering poor Stanley; he, in turn, sleeps the sleep of the innocent. (Note that Hellman is still enamored of her earlier mad scene.) She must have realized that this scenario has slight hope of finding acceptance, for she moves quickly to the final solution: "Four: Beginning of scene ten, as is, very much as is. But an outside force interferes as the rape is about to take place. Maybe by Mitch reappearing, maybe by Eunice appearing. So that all intent, and all effect, is the same as in the play. Except the censor's forbidden act of rape. I don't like this solution but it could be done, and I put it down here because it is one of the ways" (Hellman typescript 4).

The deus ex machina is no solution for this troubled trio. Hellman had used the surprise and improbable intervention at times in her own plays, but they were well-made plays in which the scene could be neatly foreshadowed. *Streetcar*, unlike *The Little Foxes*, is a play of passion in which the tragedy moves inexorably toward the meeting of Blanche and Stanley. There must be a rape. The play demands it.

Hellman remains uncomfortable with all the solutions, realizing that "in so good a play the elements are so well blended that the choice [of the most important motives and the most important emotions] must be delicate and careful." She believes that Blanche has been headed for a mental collapse for years and that it could come at any time. "If this is true, then the sleeping with Stanley is of as much importance, and as little, as the desertion of the boy in Laurel, Miss. Stanley is guilty of his own act, he precipitates destruction of Blanche, but the actual destruction began years before he ever knew her name" (Hellman typescript 5). This puzzling statement would appear to make Stanley guilty with or without the rape, which seems to suggest that he is a symbol of those forces that will inevitably destroy the fragile and beautiful. This strikes me as more nearly true of her "little foxes" than of this more complex all-American Kilroy figure, who is trying to make a life for himself and his family. He may have no background, but Stanley Kowalski is certainly striving for a future. The writer acknowledges her own ambivalence about Stanley, attributing it to Williams and/or Kazan. This meditation on Stanley and evil is worth quoting more fully, inasmuch as the censors demanded that Stanley be punished for the rape, if the rape is to remain in any form:

There is a very interesting difference between Stanley in the book and on the stage. And because of this difference I know now why the last scene in the play always worried me. (It seemed hurried, as if a trick were being played on the mind and eye.) I think somebody—Kazan or Williams—was conscious of an unsolved problem. Was it this problem? What is Stanley, how "good" or "bad" is he meant to be, how responsible, how simple? Is he the victory of the low-down over the sensitive? Or is he like everybody else, no better no worse? (That is not possible because it would be a sentimental untruth.) Stanley cannot allow Blanche to be sent to an insane asylum if he thinks he alone caused the breakdown. This would make him a villain too large for life or art and I thus conclude that I am right in thinking the act of rape was only the shove over the dangerous mountain: the end act of what had begun years before, and the fall inevitable, whatever the nature of the shove.

If this is a true conclusion then the omission of the actual act of rape need not fundamentally change this play. (Hellman typescript 5)

The Hellman typescript may be referring to the way Marlon Brando played Stanley, with humor and irony, in accordance with Kazan's view of the character as a virile man who seeks to protect his family from the threats of Blanche and all she represents. Hellman is clearly distressed by the ambivalence that Williams frequently felt about his "villains" and his "heroes." He frequently blends inevitability with guilt, a complex theological mix not unlike Blake's recognition of beauty in danger, a common creator for both the tiger and the lamb. Nothing is ever as straightforward for Williams as for Hellman.

Williams must have been dismayed by this set of ideas. From his earliest letter to Audrey Wood, March 23, 1945, where he had set out the idea for "The Moth," "The Poker Night," "The Primary Colors," or "Blanche's Chair in the Moon"—all early versions of the play—he had affirmed that the attraction/revulsion between Blanche and "Ralph" (a.k.a. Stanley) is a "strong sex situation": "Ralph and Blanche being completely antipathetic types, he challenges and is angered by her delicacy, she repelled and fascinated by his coarse strength." This line of action moves along until Ralph/Stanley unconsciously falls in love with Blanche, uncovers her background and the scandalous reputation, and exposes them to his wife and Mitch. Having lost Mitch, Blanche sits alone in the flat (two rooms by the freight yards). Ralph enters. "There is a violent scene at the end of which he takes her by force." As Williams outlined the three possible endings, the madness is not inevitable but just one option: "One, Blanche simply leaves—with no destination. Two, goes mad. Three, throws herself in front of a train in the freight-yards, the roar of which has been an ominous undertone throughout the play" (TW letter to Audrey Wood, n.p., March 23, 1945, 2 pp., typed letter signed, Boston University).

Evidence that Brando is playing the role much as Williams had expected/hoped comes from his letter to Audrey, in which he says, "I know this is very heavy stuff and am writing it with as much lyrical and comedy relief as possible while preserving the essentially tragic atmosphere. The comedy comes mostly from Ralph's friends, and the sex theme dignified and relieved by a poignant characterization of Blanche."

In one early version of the play, called *The Passion of a Moth*, Stanley and Blanche are shown the morning after the rape, both admitting that it was the best sex they had ever had. Then comes word that Stella has had a baby girl. So Blanche prepares to leave, apparently to "get her lily white hooks" into someone else somewhere else, and Stanley takes the streetcar to the hospital.[3]

Dan Isaac (*Louisiana Literature* 10) describes a related scenario in an early draft that he convincingly dates as September 1946, in which Blanche and Stanley wake up together, discuss their sexual encounter, and describe Stanley's igniting of Blanche's violent sexuality as "putting dynamite under a teapot." "She depicts the sexual act as a contest—literally an agon, a wrestling match," which Blanche has won. Blanche plans to leave, and Stanley threatens to follow, "because I won't be able to help myself." The resulting child, because of the nature of their passion, will be an "angelic monster" (11).

Brenda Murphy also discusses *The Passion of a Moth* in her extended study *Tennessee Williams and Elia Kazan: A Collaboration in the Theatre* (21). She mentions that the anticipated son will "wash them all clean."

On the other hand, in *The Poker Night*, another version, Blanche becomes a victim, catatonic at the end of the play, crouching in a grotesque twisted position, screaming in a straitjacket. In what Murphy calls the "August version" of the play, the rape is emphasized; Stella subsequently discovers Stanley's pajama top "ripped to shreds," his shoulders and back covered with scratches.

Tennessee Williams was always ambivalent about his monsters.

They are rarely clearly good or evil. Stanley was never intended to be a stereotypical villain. He is a combination of Williams's "Kilroy" figure, the red-blooded American boy in *Camino Real*, and "One Arm," the gay sexual fantasy figure. Molly Haskell spoke of his flexing and posturing as an example of homosexual pornography aimed at a "repressed or 'closet' seductee."

> The feelings expressed by . . . Vivien Leigh . . . for the studs played by . . . Brando . . . are of lust, not love, a desire not for souls but for beautiful bodies; but it is lust pierced with bitterer emotions—with the pathos and vulnerability and the self-exposure of the woman/homosexual past her/his prime. The other undercurrent in these tortured relationships is the ambivalence, even self-hatred, of the cultured homosexual who is bound to be spurned by the mindless young stud he is compelled, often masochistically and against his "taste" to love. (Haskell 249)

Some of the correspondence appears to be missing at this point. There was apparently a great deal of negotiation, perhaps much of it by telephone. According to Schumach, *A Streetcar Named Desire* was to become Hollywood's first "adult" movie, primarily because of Charles K. Feldman. While others were clearly frightened of the censorship battles that such a film would invite, Feldman, a leading talent agent, persuaded Warner Brothers to join him in the project, with a screenplay to be done by Tennessee Williams and direction by Elia Kazan.

We assume that Williams contacted Selznick to reject most of these proposed changes to his play but without offering to write the film script himself. He knew from experience that he must maintain artistic control. Warren French describes the intricate process of negotiations this way:

> Tennessee Williams refused to write the script, but insisted on approving any changes. When Kazan took Oscar Saul's script to Joseph Breen's office, which administered Code, Thomas Pauly reports that he learned that

to get the seal of approval that most exhibitors required, 68 changes, including major omissions of any references to homosexuality, nymphomania, or the rape—the principal causes of Blanche's downfall, would have to be made. The first two big no-nos were handled by glossing over them with euphemistic references to "nervous tendencies" that many viewers already understood from widespread discussion of the play. Kazan insisted, however, that the rape was essential. Breen acquiesced, so long as there was no evidence of evil intention on Stanley's part, as leeringly suggested by the line in the play, "We've had this date with each other for a long time [*sic*]," and by merely suggesting what will transpire as Stanley advances on the terrified Blanche, brandishing a beer bottle which he smashes into a mirror. Since the Code also demanded that crimes could not be exonerated, Breen insisted that Stella must make it clear that she would not return to Stanley, even though many viewers would realize that in the still patriarchal South a woman with a baby might have no alternative. (French 966)

In his study of film censorship, Schumach notes that when he heard that the Hays office wanted the rape removed, "Williams, who had reluctantly agreed to other changes, decided he would not permit his play to be shattered or branded as smut. Williams wrote to Breen:

"Streetcar" is an extremely and peculiarly moral play, in the deepest and truest sense of the term. . . . The rape of Blanche by Stanley is a pivotal, integral truth in the play, without which the play loses its meaning, which is the ravishment of the tender, the sensitive, the delicate, by the savage and brutal forces of modern society. It is a poetic plea for comprehension. . . . Please remember, also, that we have already made great concessions which we felt were dangerous, to attitudes which we thought were narrow. In the middle of preparations for a new play, I came out to Hollywood to rewrite certain sequences to suit the demands of your office. No one involved in this screen production has failed to show you the co-operation, even the deference that has been called for. (Qtd. in Schumach 75-76)[4]

Maurice Yacowar says that Williams himself finally wrote the screenplay for the film with Elia Kazan. In their collaborative effort, "the film moves even more inexorably than the play toward the clash between Blanche's romantic illusions and Kowalski's brutish, though affable, realism." (Yacowar is convinced that Kazan's sympathy with Stanley's overbearing masculinity altered the relationship, making him somewhat more sympathetic. His notebook would seem to justify this conclusion.) Thus the rape itself is "Kowalski's physical triumph over Blanche's fragile dreams" (Yacowar 15-16).

Elia Kazan searched for means to make the play more cinematic but worried about weakening the drama in the process. He reports that he experimented with a process of "opening out" the script but finally discarded the idea as inferior to the original. Basically, Kazan decided to film the play rather than try for a radically different approach.[5]

Given the concern with the Hays office and the problems of making the rape scene conform to the Production Code, Kazan undertook interesting filmic strategies. He shot the struggle between Blanche and Stanley in reflection through a large, oval mirror: "Blanche's last defense, a broken bottle, shatters the mirror. The solid object (bottle, Kowalski) shatters the fragile image (mirror, Blanche). The mirror is an image of Blanche's shattered composure and self-respect. There is also a horror in the shot, as if it were too powerful to be viewed directly and needed to be deflected" (Yacowar 20).

The second shot Yacowar calls a visual pun: it is a fire hose that sprays the garbage off the street. As he explains, the image has been set up by Eunice's earlier line to Stanley: "I hope they do haul you in and turn the fire hose on you, same as last time." (20) Any close observer understands that this is a phallic image; it is so obvious that it usually elicits a gasp and a laugh. Yacowar explains the "multiple perspectives" of the pun:

As bawdry, it tempts us into Stanley's view, that the affected Blanche is trash, which needs to be washed away by his purifying, direct force. This sense agrees with the "raffish charm" that the screenplay . . . described in Kowalski's furnishings. From Blanche's perspective, however, the shot expresses her shame and the blow to her self-respect caused by the rape and then Stella's disbelief. Eunice's line gives the image yet another meaning: it suggests that Stanley, formerly a victim of the hose and treated as trash by the regularizing forces in society, is now enjoying a kind of revenge by bringing Blanche down to his level. Finally, the image relates to the succeeding scene, where we see the Kowalski baby in his carriage. From this perspective, the characters are washing aside the embarrassing past in order to begin life anew. At whatever cost to Blanche, of course. (Yacowar 20)

The other, related concern of the Hays office, as mentioned before, was the punishment of the rapist. By this time, the Catholic Legion of Decency had also entered the picture and was making further demands before the play could be cleared. Apparently, this body sought once again to remove the rape and change the ending.

Yacowar reports that Williams and Kazan labored to find an acceptable compromise while refusing to remove the rape scene, which they argued was "the crux of the action" (22). They finally agreed that the rape would remain but that the rapist would not go unpunished. Thus the film ends with Stella rejecting Stanley ("Don't you touch me. Don't you ever touch me again.") and assuring her baby, "We're not going back in there. Not this time. We're never going back. Never, never back, never back again." Although Kazan and Williams thought this sufficient to clear the film, Warner Brothers—without informing either the author or the director—made another twelve cuts to appease the Legion (22).

Apparently Kazan heard that cuts had been made during his absence and threatened to remove his name from the picture. A draft letter Williams apparently wrote to Charles Feldman ends with this plea: "I also feel grave mistake to exceed cuts we all agreed upon in New

York. A great picture can be botched by injudicious cutting. Don't let them spoil a great picture" (TW to "Charlie" n.p., n.d., 1 p., autograph letter, Columbia University). His emotional request was apparently ignored.

The cuts, which have been restored in the most recent release of the film, create a conclusion for the film that reverses the conclusion of the play. The play had ended with Blanche destroyed and Stella lying to herself. Yacowar describes this painfully realistic ending:

> Stella collapses into Stanley's arms "with inhuman abandon." . . . As the curtain falls, Stanley unbuttons Stella's blouse and his brutish friends play on ("seven card stud," aptly enough). But the film ends with Stanley isolated and rejected—at least for the time being. Even his card cronies turn against him. Blanche, then, would seem to have won, for she has exposed Stanley and kept Stella from "hanging back with the brutes." As Blanche is driven away, against the silhouette of the cathedral, we hear the bells that she earlier called "the only clean thing in the quarter." Where in the play it seems that Stanley has won, in the film Blanche seems triumphant. (22-23)

Yacowar acknowledges that the film's conclusion, which reverses the "externals of the play," does not change the "bleak vision beneath. To the questioning viewer, the film ends as negatively as did the play" (23). He attributes this compromise ending to Kazan, who believed that life can be sustained by a lie. Kazan rejected Williams's proposed ending with Stella crying. This action reflects his preference for truth-tellers, unlike Williams's sympathy for romantic dreamers.

All of these struggles with the censors, both secular and religious, the producer, the director, and a host of other people helped determine the actual product that we see as a completed work of art. The finished film—a "collaboration," according to Williams—stands along with *Gone with the Wind* as a screen masterpiece.

The artistic triumph is in no small measure the result of Tennessee Williams's constant insistence on the integrity of his own vision. In retrospect, we can see how intricate and nuanced his characterizations, how inextricably entangled his relationships and actions. Like the blues music that underscores the entire play, it is full of passion, laughter, brutality, and lyricism. And like Blake's tiger, Blanche and Stanley both stand before a backdrop that is dark and mysterious, not easily understood or domesticated, splendid and dangerous, the creations of an imagination that loved both tigers and lambs.

Notes

1. In an earlier paper, I covered this issue. See Nancy M. Tischler, "Sanitizing the *Streetcar*," *Louisiana Literature* 14.2 (Fall 1997): 48-56.

2. Dan Isaac has written at length on the significance of "truth-telling" as a factor in the tragic structure of the play. See "No Past" 8.

3. In a conversation in 1995, Allean Hale noted this scenario that she discovered in the Williams file at the Harry Ransom Humanities Research Center. It parallels one of the variant scenarios described by Vivienne Dickson 164, which she identifies as *The Primary Colors*.

4. Rev. Gene D. Phillips, S.J., also quotes extensively from this letter in *The Films of Tennessee Williams*, 81ff.

5. See his interview with Elia Kazan, reported in Gene D. Phillips's article, included in the Kolin collection *Confronting Tennessee Williams's "A Streetcar Named Desire,"* 225.

Works Cited

Ciment, Michel. *Kazan on Kazan*. New York: Viking Press, 1974.

Cole, Toby. *Directors on Directing*. New York: Bobbs-Merrill, 1953.

Dickson, Vivienne. "*A Streetcar Named Desire*: Its Development through the Manuscripts." In *Tennessee Williams: A Tribute*, edited by Jac Tharpe. Jackson: University Press of Mississippi, 1977.

French, Warren. "*A Streetcar Named Desire*." In *International Dictionary of Films and Filmmakers*, vol. 1, edited by Nicholas Thomas. Chicago: St. James Press, 1994.

Haskell, Molly. *From Reverence to Rape: The Treatment of Women in the Movies*. Harmondsworth: Penguin Books, 1974.

Hellman, Lillian (?). 6 pp. Typescript, Irene Selznick file, Boston University Library.

Isaac, Dan. "No Past to Think In: Who Wins in *A Streetcar Named Desire*?" *Louisiana Literature* 14 (Fall 1997): 8.

Kolin, Philip C., ed. *Confronting Tennessee Williams's "A Streetcar Named Desire."* Westport, Conn.: Greenwood Press, 1993.

Murphy, Brenda. *Tennessee Williams and Elia Kazan: A Collaboration in the Theatre*. Cambridge: Cambridge University Press, 1992.

Phillips, Gene. *Films of Tennessee Williams*. Philadelphia: Art Alliance Press, 1980.

Schumach, Murray. *The Face on the Cutting Room Floor: The Story of Movie and Television Censorship*. New York: William Morrow, 1964.

Selznick, Irene, to Tennessee Williams, n.p., July 1, 1949, 3 pp., typed letter, Boston University Library.

Tischler, Nancy M. "Sanitizing the *Streetcar*." *Louisiana Literature* 14 (Fall 1997): 48-56.

Williams, Tennessee. Tennessee Williams to Audrey Wood, March 23, 1945, 2 pp., typed letter signed, Boston University.

_____. Tennessee Williams to "Charlie," draft, n.p., n.d., 1 p. autograph letter signed, Columbia University.

_____. *The Theatre of Tennessee Williams*. Vol. 1. New York: New Directions, 1971.

Yacowar, Maurice. *Tennessee Williams and Film*. New York: Frederick Ungar, 1977.

RESOURCES

Chronology of Tennessee Williams's Life_____

1911	On March 26, Thomas Lanier Williams is born in Columbus, Mississippi, to Cornelius Coffin and Edwina Dakin Williams. His sister Rose was born in 1909.
1911-1918	While his father is a traveling salesman, Williams lives with his grandparents, sister, and mother; they move several times before settling in Clarksdale, Mississippi. Williams falls sick for a year with diphtheria and Bright's disease.
1918	Edwina, Rose, and Tom move to St. Louis, Missouri, to be with Cornelius.
1919	Brother Walter Dakin Williams is born.
1927	Williams wins a prize for his essay "Can a Good Wife Be a Good Sport?," which is published in *Smart Set* magazine.
1928	Williams's short story "The Vengeance of Nitocris" is published in *Weird Tales*. He tours Europe with his grandfather.
1929	Williams enrolls at the University of Missouri at Columbia.
1932	Williams withdraws from the university and begins working at the International Shoe Company; he writes stories and plays at night.
1935	Williams experiences a physical and emotional breakdown and then recuperates at his grandparents' home in Memphis. His one-act play *Cairo! Shanghai! Bombay!* is performed by the Memphis Garden Players, an amateur theater group.
1936	Williams enters Washington University, St. Louis. His one-act play *27 Wagons Full of Cotton* is published in *Manuscript.*
1937	Williams's first full-length plays, *The Fugitive Kind* and *Candles to the Sun*, are produced by the amateur group the Mummers in St. Louis. Williams transfers to the University of Iowa, where several of his short plays are produced. His sister is institutionalized for schizophrenia.

1938	Williams graduates from the University of Iowa with a bachelor of arts degree.
1939	Williams lives briefly in several different places, including the French Quarter in New Orleans. He sends four one-act plays to a contest organized by the Group Theatre in New York and travels to Mexico, then California, then New York. He meets Audrey Wood, who becomes his agent. He publishes the short story "The Field of Blue Children" in *Story* under the name Tennessee Williams. He is awarded a Rockefeller Foundation grant of one thousand dollars.
1940	Williams enrolls in The New School in New York for a playwriting seminar. He travels to Provincetown, Massachusetts, where he has first major love affair. His play *Battle of Angels* opens in Boston.
1941-1942	Williams lives in various locations, including Key West, New Orleans, and Georgia.
1943	Williams's sister, Rose, undergoes a prefrontal lobotomy. Williams signs a six-month contract to be a scriptwriter for Metro-Goldwyn-Mayer (MGM) in Hollywood. *You Touched Me!* opens in Cleveland.
1944	Williams's grandmother dies. Williams is awarded one thousand dollars by the National Institute of Arts and Letters. *The Glass Menagerie* opens in Chicago.
1945	*The Glass Menagerie* opens on Broadway and wins the New York Drama Critics' Circle Award. Williams starts writing *A Streetcar Named Desire*, and *27 Wagons Full of Cotton, and Other One-Act Plays* is published.
1946	Williams begins a relationship with Pancho Rodriguez y Gonzalez. He meets the writer Carson McCullers.
1947	*Summer and Smoke* opens in Dallas, Texas. *A Streetcar Named Desire* opens in New York and goes on to win the New York Drama Critics' Circle Award, the Donaldson Award, and the Pulitzer Prize for drama.

1948	A collection of Williams's short fiction, *One Arm, and Other Stories*, is published, as is *American Blues: Five Short Plays*. *Summer and Smoke* opens in New York. Williams begins what will be a fourteen-year relationship with Frank Merlo.
1950	Williams's novel *The Roman Spring of Mrs. Stone* is published. The film version of *The Glass Menagerie* is released. *The Rose Tattoo* opens in Chicago.
1951	*The Rose Tattoo* opens in New York and wins a Tony Award for best play. The film version of *A Streetcar Named Desire* is released and wins the New York Film Critics Circle Award.
1952	An Off-Broadway production of *Summer and Smoke* opens in New York. Williams is elected to the National Institute of Arts and Letters.
1953	*Camino Real* opens in New York.
1954	*Hard Candy: A Book of Stories* is published.
1955	Williams's grandfather dies. *Cat on a Hot Tin Roof* opens in New York; it runs for 694 performances and wins the Pulitzer Prize and the New York Drama Critics' Circle Award. The film version of *The Rose Tattoo* is released.
1956	*Baby Doll*, a film for which Williams wrote the screenplay, opens in New York. His collection of poems *In the Winter of Cities* is published.
1957	*Orpheus Descending* opens in New York. Williams's father dies. Williams starts psychoanalysis with Dr. Lawrence Kubie.
1958	*Garden District* (a double bill of the two one-act plays *Suddenly Last Summer* and *Something Unspoken*) opens Off-Broadway. The film version of *Cat on a Hot Tin Roof* is released.
1959	*Sweet Bird of Youth* opens in New York. Williams travels to Cuba, where he meets Ernest Hemingway and Fidel Castro. The film version of *Suddenly Last Summer* is released.

1960	*Period of Adjustment* opens in New York. The film *The Fugitive Kind* (based on *Orpheus Descending*) is released.
1961	*The Night of the Iguana* opens in New York, and Williams wins his fourth New York Drama Critics' Circle Award.
1962	The film version of *Sweet Bird of Youth* is released.
1963	*The Milk Train Doesn't Stop Here Anymore* opens in New York. Frank Merlo dies of cancer.
1964	The film version of *The Night of the Iguana* is released.
1966	*Slapstick Tragedy* opens in New York.
1967	*The Knightly Quest: A Novella and Four Short Stories* is published.
1968	*Kingdom of Earth* (also known as *The Seven Descents of Myrtle*) opens in New York. *Boom!*, the film version of *The Milk Train Doesn't Stop Here Anymore*, is released.
1969	Williams receives the National Institute of Arts and Letters Gold Medal. *In the Bar of a Tokyo Hotel* opens Off-Broadway in New York. Williams spends three months in Barnes Hospital, St. Louis, for drug withdrawal.
1970	*Dragon Country* is published.
1971	*Out Cry*, a revised version of *The Two-Character Play*, opens in Chicago. Williams replaces Audrey Wood, his literary agent for thirty-two years, with Bill Barnes.
1972	*Small Craft Warnings* opens Off-Broadway.
1973	*Out Cry* (a third revision of *The Two-Character Play*) premieres in New York. Williams is awarded the first Centennial Medal of the Cathedral of St. John the Divine. He gives what later becomes known as his famous *Playboy* magazine interview.

1974	*Eight Mortal Ladies Possessed: A Book of Stories* is published.
1975	Williams receives the National Arts Club's Medal of Honor for Literature. *The Red Devil Battery Sign* opens in Boston. Williams's *Memoirs* and his novel *Moise and the World of Reason* are published.
1977	*Vieux Carré* opens in New York.
1978	*Creve Coeur* opens in New York. *Where I Live: Selected Essays* is published.
1979	*A Lovely Sunday for Creve Coeur,* a revised version of *Creve Coeur,* opens in New York. Williams is honored at the Kennedy Center by President Carter.
1980	Williams's mother dies. He is appointed Distinguished Writer in Residence at the University of British Columbia, Vancouver. *Clothes for a Summer Hotel* opens in New York.
1981	*A House Not Meant to Stand* opens in Chicago. *Something Cloudy, Something Clear* opens in New York. Williams and playwright Harold Pinter are both presented the Common Wealth Award of Distinguished Service for the dramatic arts.
1982	Williams receives an honorary degree from Harvard University.
1983	On February 24, Williams dies at the Hotel Elysée in New York City.

Works by Tennessee Williams_____

Plays and Librettos (date shown is that of first production)
Cairo! Shanghai! Bombay!, 1935 (with Bernice Dorothy Shapiro)
Headlines, 1936
The Magic Tower, 1936
Candles to the Sun, 1937
Fugitive Kind, 1937
Spring Song, 1938
Spring Storm, 1938
Battle of Angels, 1940
The Long Goodbye, 1940
You Touched Me!, 1943 (with Donald Windham)
The Glass Menagerie, 1944
27 Wagons Full of Cotton, and Other One-Act Plays, 1945
Moony's Kid Don't Cry, 1946
This Property Is Condemned, 1946
The Last of My Solid Gold Watches, 1947
Portrait of a Madonna, 1947
Stairs to the Roof, 1947
A Streetcar Named Desire, 1947
Summer and Smoke, 1947
American Blues: Five Short Plays, 1948
The Rose Tattoo, 1950
Camino Real, 1953
Cat on a Hot Tin Roof, 1955
Lord Byron's Love Letter, 1955 (libretto)
The Case of the Crushed Petunias, 1957
Orpheus Descending, 1957 (revision of *Battle of Angels*)
Something Unspoken, 1958
Suddenly Last Summer, 1958
Talk to Me Like the Rain and Let Me Listen, 1958
I Rise in Flame, Cried the Phoenix, 1959
Period of Adjustment, 1959
Sweet Bird of Youth, 1959
The Night of the Iguana, 1961
The Milk Train Doesn't Stop Here Anymore, 1963
Eccentricities of a Nightingale, 1964 (revision of *Summer and Smoke*)
Slapstick Tragedy: "The Mutilated" and "The Gnädiges Fräulein," 1966

The Two-Character Play, 1967
The Seven Descents of Myrtle, 1968 (also performed as *Kingdom of Earth*, 1975)
Dragon Country, 1969
In the Bar of a Tokyo Hotel, 1969
Confessional, 1971
I Can't Imagine Tomorrow, 1971
Out Cry, 1971 (revision of *The Two-Character Play*)
The Theatre of Tennessee Williams, 1971-1981 (7 vols.)
Small Craft Warnings, 1972 (revision of *Confessional*)
The Red Devil Battery Sign, 1975
This Is (An Entertainment), 1976
Vieux Carré, 1977
Creve Coeur, 1978 (also performed as *A Lovely Sunday for Creve Coeur*, 1979)
Tiger Tail, 1978
Clothes for a Summer Hotel, 1980
Some Problems for the Moose Lodge, 1980 (also performed as *A House Not Meant to Stand*, 1981)
Will Mr. Merriwether Return from Memphis?, 1980
Something Cloudy, Something Clear, 1981

Screenplays
The Glass Menagerie, 1950 (with Peter Berneis)
A Streetcar Named Desire, 1951 (with Oscar Saul)
The Rose Tattoo, 1955 (with Hal Kanter)
Baby Doll, 1956
Suddenly Last Summer, 1959 (with Gore Vidal)
The Fugitive Kind, 1960 (with Meade Roberts)
Stopped Rocking, and Other Screenplays, 1984

Fiction
One Arm, and Other Stories, 1948
The Roman Spring of Mrs. Stone (novel), 1950
Hard Candy: A Book of Stories, 1954
Three Players of a Summer Game, and Other Stories, 1960
The Knightly Quest: A Novella and Four Short Stories, 1966
Eight Mortal Ladies Possessed: A Book of Stories, 1974
Moise and the World of Reason (novel), 1975
It Happened the Day the Sun Rose, and Other Stories, 1982
Collected Stories, 1985

Poetry

In the Winter of Cities, 1956
Androgyne, Mon Amour, 1967
The Collected Poems of Tennessee Williams, 2002

Nonfiction

Memoirs, 1975
Letters to Donald Windham, 1940-1965, 1977
Where I Live: Selected Essays, 1978
Five O'Clock Angel: Letters of Tennessee Williams to Maria St. Just, 1948-1982, 1990
The Selected Letters of Tennessee Williams, 2000, 2004 (2 vols.; Albert J. Devlin and
    Nancy M. Tischler, editors)
Notebooks, 2006 (Margaret Bradham Thornton, editor)

Bibliography

Adler, Thomas P. *A Streetcar Named Desire: The Moth and the Lantern.* Boston: Twayne, 1990.

Bak, John S. "Vestis virum reddit: The Gender Politics of Drag in Williams's *A Streetcar Named Desire* and Hwang's *M. Butterfly.*" *South Atlantic Review* 70.4 (Fall 2005): 94-118.

Blackwell, Louise. "Tennessee Williams and the Predicament of Women." *South Atlantic Bulletin* 35.2 (1970): 9-14.

Boxill, Roger. *Tennessee Williams.* London: Macmillan, 1987.

Crandell, George, ed. *The Critical Response to Tennessee Williams.* Westport, CT: Greenwood Press, 1996.

Duyvenbode, Rachel Van. "Darkness Made Visible: Miscegenation, Masquerade, and the Signified Racial Other in Tennessee Williams' *Baby Doll* and *A Streetcar Named Desire.*" *Journal of American Studies* 35.2 (August 2001): 203-15.

Fisher, James. "'The Angels of Fructification': Tennessee Williams, Tony Kushner, and Images of Homosexuality on the American Stage." *Mississippi Quarterly* 19.1 (Winter 1995): 13-20.

Fleche, Anne. *Mimetic Disillusion: Eugene O'Neill, Tennessee Williams, and U.S. Dramatic Realism.* Tuscaloosa: University of Alabama Press, 1997.

Fordyce, Ehren. "Inhospitable Structures: Some Themes and Forms in Tennessee Williams." *Journal of American Drama and Theatre* 17.2 (Spring 2005): 43-58.

Foster, Verna. "Desire, Death, and Laughter: Tragicomic Dramaturgy in *A Streetcar Named Desire.*" *American Drama* 9.1 (Fall 1999): 51-68.

Griffin, Alice. *Understanding Tennessee Williams.* Columbia: University of South Carolina Press, 1995.

Gross, Robert F., ed. *Tennessee Williams: A Casebook.* New York: Routledge, 2002.

Hirsch, Foster. *A Portrait of the Artist: The Plays of Tennessee Williams.* Port Washington, NY: Kennikat Press, 1979.

Holditch, Kenneth, and Richard F. Leavitt. *Tennessee Williams and the South.* Jackson: University Press of Mississippi, 2002.

Hovis, George. "'Fifty Percent Illusion': The Mask of the Southern Belle in Tennessee Williams's *A Streetcar Named Desire, The Glass Menagerie,* and 'Portrait of a Madonna.'" *Tennessee Williams Literary Journal* 5.1 (Spring 2003): 11-22.

Hurrell, John D., ed. *Two Modern American Tragedies: Reviews and Criticism of "Death of a Salesman" and "A Streetcar Named Desire."* New York: Scribner's, 1961.

Isaac, Dan. "No Past to Think In: Who Wins in *A Streetcar Named Desire?*" *Louisiana Literature* 14.2 (Fall 1997): 8-35.

Johnston, Monica Carolyn. *Tennessee Williams and American Realism.* Berkeley: University of California Press, 1987.

Kolin, Philip C., ed. *Confronting Tennessee Williams's "A Streetcar Named Desire":
Essays in Critical Pluralism.* Westport, CT: Greenwood Press, 1993.

_____. *Tennessee Williams: A Guide to Research and Performance.* West-
port, CT: Greenwood Press, 1998

_____. *Williams: "A Streetcar Named Desire."* New York: Cambridge Uni-
versity Press, 2000.

Leavitt, Richard F. *The World of Tennessee Williams.* London: W. H. Allen, 1978.

Londre, Felicia Hardison. *Tennessee Williams.* New York: Ungar, 1979.

Martin, Robert A., ed. *Critical Essays on Tennessee Williams.* New York: G. K. Hall,
1997.

Miller, Jordan Y., ed. *Twentieth Century Interpretations of "A Streetcar Named Desire": A Collection of Critical Essays.* Englewood Cliffs, NJ: Prentice-Hall, 1971.

Murphy, Brenda. *Tennessee Williams and Elia Kazan: A Collaboration in the Theatre.*
New York: Cambridge University Press, 1992.

Nelson, Benjamin. *Tennessee Williams: The Man and His Work.* New York: Obolensky, 1961.

Pagan, Nicholas. *Rethinking Literary Biography: A Postmodern Approach to Tennessee Williams.* Madison, NJ: Fairleigh Dickinson University Press, 1993.

Paller, Michael. *Gentlemen Callers: Tennessee Williams, Homosexuality, and Mid-
Twentieth-Century Broadway Drama.* New York: Palgrave Macmillan, 2005.

Roudané, Matthew C., ed. *The Cambridge Companion to Tennessee Williams.* New
York: Cambridge University Press, 1997.

Rouse, Sarah A. *Tennessee Williams.* Jackson: Mississippi Library Commission,
1976.

Schlueter, June. *Dramatic Closure: Reading the End.* Madison, NJ: Fairleigh Dickinson University Press, 1995.

Shackelford, Dean. "Is There a Gay Man in This Text? Subverting the Closet in *A
Streetcar Named Desire.*" *Literature and Homosexuality.* Ed. Michael J. Meyer.
Amsterdam: Rodopi, 2000. 135-59.

Stanton, Stephen S., ed. *Tennessee Williams: A Collection of Critical Essays.* Englewood Cliffs, NJ: Prentice-Hall, 1977.

Tharpe, Jac, ed. *Tennessee Williams: A Tribute.* Jackson: University Press of Mississippi, 1977.

Thompson, Judith J. *Tennessee Williams' Plays: Memory, Myth, and Symbol.* New
York: Peter Lang, 1989.

Vannatta, Dennis P. *Tennessee Williams: A Study of the Short Fiction.* Boston:
Twayne, 1988.

Voss, Ralph F., ed. *Magical Muse: Millennial Essays on Tennessee Williams.* Tuscaloosa: University of Alabama Press, 2002.

Williams, Tennessee. *Conversations with Tennessee Williams.* Ed. Albert J. Devlin.
Jackson: University Press of Mississippi, 1986.

Zhang, Xin. "A Comparison Between the Two Tragic Heroines: Miss Emily Grierson in William Faulkner's 'A Rose for Emily' and Blanche DuBois in Tennessee Williams's *A Streetcar Named Desire*." *Re-reading America: Changes and Challenges*. Ed. Weihe Zhong and Rui Han. Cheltenham, England: Reardon, 2004. 88-94.

CRITICAL
INSIGHTS

Brenda Murphy is Board of Trustees Distinguished Professor of English at the University of Connecticut. Her scholarly work, spanning more than thirty years, reflects her interest in placing American drama, theater, and performance in the broader context of American literature and culture. She has written numerous articles about American playwrights and other writers, but her most significant work is in the ten books she has authored on the American theater. Among Murphy's books are *The Provincetown Players and the Culture of Modernity* (2005), *O'Neill: Long Day's Journey into Night* (2001), *Congressional Theatre: Dramatizing McCarthyism on Stage, Film, and Television* (1999), *Miller: Death of a Salesman* (1995), *Tennessee Williams and Elia Kazan: A Collaboration in the Theatre* (1992), *American Realism and American Drama, 1880-1940* (1987), and, as editor, *Twentieth Century American Drama: Critical Concepts in Literary and Cultural Studies* (2006) and *The Cambridge Companion to American Women Playwrights* (1999). She has been recognized as breaking new ground through her synthesis of the study of the play as literary text and the play as performance in her books on Tennessee Williams, Arthur Miller, and Eugene O'Neill. *Congressional Theatre*, her study of the theater's response to the House Committee on Un-American Activities in the 1950s, was honored by the American Society for Theatre Research in 1999 for outstanding research in theater history and cognate studies.

Professor Murphy has been active in a number of international professional organizations throughout her career. She serves on the editorial boards of several journals and book series and on the boards of several societies that promote the study of American playwrights, and she has served as President of the American Theatre and Drama Society and The Eugene O'Neill Society. Her research has been supported by grants from the National Endowment for the Humanities, the American Council for Learned Societies, the National Humanities Center, and other sources.

About *The Paris Review*

The Paris Review is America's preeminent literary quarterly, dedicated to discovering and publishing the best new voices in fiction, nonfiction, and poetry. The magazine was founded in Paris in 1953 by the young American writers Peter Matthiessen and Doc Humes, and edited there and in New York for its first fifty years by George Plimpton. Over the decades, the *Review* has introduced readers to the earliest writings of Jack Kerouac, Philip Roth, T. C. Boyle, V. S. Naipaul, Ha Jin, Jay McInerney, and Mona Simpson, and published numerous now classic works, including Roth's *Goodbye, Columbus*, Donald Barthelme's *Alice*, Jim Carroll's *Basketball Diaries*, and selections from Samuel Beckett's *Molloy* (his first publication in English). The first chapter of Jeffrey Eugenides's *The Virgin Suicides* appeared in the *Review*'s pages, as well as stories by Edward P. Jones, Rick Moody, David Foster Wallace, Denis Johnson, Jim Shepard, Jim Crace, Lorrie Moore, Jeanette Winterson, and Ann Patchett.

The Paris Review's renowned Writers at Work series of interviews, whose early installments include legendary conversations with E. M. Forster, William Faulkner, and Ernest Hemingway, is one of the landmarks of world literature. The interviews received a George Polk Award and were nominated for a Pulitzer Prize. Among the more than three hundred interviewees are Robert Frost, Marianne Moore, W. H. Auden, Elizabeth Bishop, Susan Sontag, and Toni Morrison. Recent issues feature conversations with Salman Rushdie, Joan Didion, Stephen King, Norman Mailer, Kazuo Ishiguro, and Umberto Eco. (A complete list of the interviews is available at www.theparisreview.org.) In November 2008, Picador will publish the third of a four-volume series of anthologies of *Paris Review* interviews. The first two volumes have received acclaim. *The New York Times* called the Writers at Work series "the most remarkable and extensive interviewing project we possess."

The Paris Review is edited by Philip Gourevitch, who was named to the post in 2005, following the death of George Plimpton two years earlier. Under Gourevitch's leadership, the magazine's international distribution has expanded, paid subscriptions have risen 150 percent, and newsstand distribution has doubled. A new editorial team has published fiction by Andre Aciman, Damon Galgut, Mohsin Hamid, Gish Jen, Richard Price, Said Sayrafiezadeh, and Alistair Morgan. Poetry editors Charles Simic, Meghan O'Rourke, and Dan Chiasson have selected works by Billy Collins, Jesse Ball, Mary Jo Bang, Sharon Olds, and Mary Karr. Writing published in the magazine has been anthologized in *Best American Short Stories* (2006, 2007, and 2008), *Best American Poetry*, *Best Creative Non-Fiction*, the Pushcart Prize anthology, and *O. Henry Prize Stories*.

The magazine presents two annual awards. The Hadada Award for lifelong contribution to literature has recently been given to William Styron, Joan Didion, Norman Mailer, and Peter Matthiessen in 2008. The Plimpton Prize for Fiction, given to a new voice in fiction brought to national attention in the pages of *The Paris Review*, was presented in 2007 to Benjamin Percy and to Jesse Ball in 2008.

The Paris Review won the 2007 National Magazine Award in photojournalism, and the *Los Angeles Times* recently called *The Paris Review* "an American treasure with true international reach."

Since 1999 *The Paris Review* has been published by The Paris Review Foundation, Inc., a not-for-profit 501(c)(3) organization.

The Paris Review is available in digital form to libraries worldwide in selected academic databases exclusively from EBSCO Publishing. Libraries can contact EBSCO at 1-800-653-2726 for details. For more information on *The Paris Review* or to subscribe, please visit: www.theparisreview.org.

Contributors

Brenda Murphy is Board of Trustees Distinguished Professor of English at the University of Connecticut. Her books on Arthur Miller include *Miller: Death of a Salesman* in the Cambridge University Press series Plays in Performance and, with Susan Abbotson, the casebook *Understanding Death of a Salesman*, as well as a substantial portion of *Congressional Theatre: Dramatizing McCarthyism on Stage, Film, and Television*. She has published many articles on Miller and other American playwrights, as well as books such as *The Provincetown Players and the Culture of Modernity*, *O'Neill: Long Day's Journey into Night*, *Tennessee Williams and Elia Kazan: A Collaboration in the Theatre*, *American Realism and American Drama, 1880-1940*, and, as editor, *The Cambridge Companion to American Women Playwrights*.

Robert J. Forman is Professor of English and Classics at St. John's University in Jamaica, New York.

Catherine Steindler has directed at many theaters, including those of Trinity Repertory Company, the Oregon Shakespeare Festival, Williamstown Theater Festival, the Monomoy Theater, the Underwood Theater, and the Huntington Theatre Company. She is director of development and events at *The Paris Review*.

Camille-Yvette Welsch is a senior lecturer in English at the Pennsylvania State University. She is the director of Penn State's Summer Creative Writing Conference for high school students and the coordinator of the Red Weather Reading Series. Her work has appeared in *Mid-American Review*, *Barrow Street*, *The Writer's Chronicle*, *The Women's Review of Books*, and *Small Spiral Notebook*.

Kenneth Elliot has directed many Off-Broadway plays and musicals, including the original productions of Charles Busch's *Vampire Lesbians of Sodom* and *Psycho Beach Party*. He has also directed at regional theaters across the United States and in London's West End. His work has appeared in such publications as *Theatre Journal* and *Text and Presentation*. He is currently Assistant Professor of Theater at Rutgers University, Camden.

Neil Heims is a writer and teacher living in Paris. His books include *Reading the Diary of Anne Frank* (2005), *Allen Ginsberg* (2005), and *J. R. R. Tolkien* (2004). He has also contributed numerous articles for literary publications, including essays on William Blake, John Milton, William Shakespeare, and Arthur Miller.

Janyce Marson is a doctoral student at New York University. She is working on a doctoral dissertation on the rhetoric of the mechanical in Samuel Taylor Coleridge, William Wordsworth, and Mary Shelley.

Verna Foster is Associate Professor of English at Loyola University. She is the author of *The Name and Nature of Tragicomedy*. She has contributed essays to the journals *American Drama* and *Journal of American Drama and Theatre* and to the volumes *The Undiscovered Country: The Later Plays of Tennessee Williams* (ed. Philip C.

Kolin, 2002) and *The Influence of Tennessee Williams: Essays on Fifteen American Playwrights* (ed. Philip C. Kolin, 2008).

Britton J. Harwood is Professor of English at Miami University of Ohio. He is the author of *Piers Plowman and the Problem of Belief* (1992) and *Class and Gender in Early English Literature: Intersections* (with Gillian R. Overing, 1994).

John S. Bak is Associate Professor at the Université of Nancy in France. He has published many articles on Tennessee Williams and is editor of *Post/modern Dracula: From Victorian Themes to Postmodern Praxis* (2007) and Williams's *New Selected Essays: Where I Live* (2009).

Dan Isaac is author of *Form and Meaning in the Major Plays of Tennessee Williams* (1968) and editor of editions of Williams's plays *Spring Storm* (1999) and *Candles to the Sun: A Play in Ten Scenes* (2004).

Dean Shackelford taught at Southeast Missouri State University. He published articles on Tennessee Williams and Harper Lee.

Anne Fleche teaches in the Cinema Studies Program at Northeastern University. Her book *Mimetic Disillusion: Eugene O'Neill, Tennessee Williams, and U.S. Dramatic Realism* was published in 1997.

Linda Costanzo Cahir is Coordinator of Secondary Education at Kean University. She also serves as coeditor of the *Edith Wharton Review*. Her books include *Solitude and Society in the Works of Herman Melville and Edith Wharton* (1999) and *Literature into Film: Theory and Practical Approaches* (2006).

Keith Dorwick is Associate Professor of English at the University of Louisiana at Lafayette. He has published articles in a variety of journals, including *Computers and Composition Journal, Gender Blending, Kairos, Interdisciplinary Humanities*, and the *Journal of Bisexuality*.

Nancy M. Tischler is Professor Emerita of English and the Humanities at the Pennsylvania State University. Her previous books include *Student Companion to Tennessee Williams* (2000), *Men and Women of the Bible* (2003), and *All Things in the Bible* (2006).

Acknowledgments ━━━━━━━━━━━━━━━━━━━━━━

"Tennessee Williams" by Robert J. Forman. From *Dictionary of World Biography: The 20th Century*. Copyright © 1999 by Salem Press, Inc. Reprinted with permission of Salem Press.

"The *Paris Review* Perspective" by Catherine Steindler. Copyright © 2010 by Catherine Steindler. Special appreciation goes to Christopher Cox and Nathaniel Rich, editors for *The Paris Review*.

"Desire, Death, and Laughter: Tragicomic Dramaturgy in *A Streetcar Named Desire*" by Verna Foster. From *American Drama* 9, no. 1 (Fall 1999): 51-68. Copyright © 1999 by the University of Cincinnati. Reprinted by permission.

"Tragedy as Habit: *A Streetcar Named Desire*" by Britton J. Harwood. From *Tennessee Williams: A Tribute*. Jac Tharpe, ed. 104-115. Copyright © 1977 by University Press of Mississippi. Reprinted by permission.

"'Stanley Made Love to Her!—By Force!' Blanche and the Evolution of a Rape" by John S. Bak. From *The Journal of American Drama and Theatre* 16, no. 1 (Winter 2004): 69-97. Copyright © 2004 by Martin E. Segal Theatre Center. Reprinted by permission.

"No Past to Think In: Who Wins in *A Streetcar Named Desire*?" by Dan Isaac. From *Louisiana Literature* 14, no. 2 (Fall 1997): 8-35. Copyright © 1997 by Southeastern Louisiana University. Reprinted by permission.

"Is There a Gay Man in This Text? Subverting the Closet in *A Streetcar Named Desire*" by Dean Shackelford. From *Literature and Homosexuality*. Michael J. Meyer, ed. 135-159. Copyright © 2000 by Rodopi. Reprinted by permission.

"*A Streetcar Named Desire*: Spatial Violation and Sexual Violence" by Anne Fleche. From *Mimetic Disillusion: Eugene O'Neill, Tennessee Williams, and U.S. Dramatic Realism*. Copyright ©1997 by the University of Alabama Press. Reprinted by permission.

"The Artful Rerouting of *A Streetcar Named Desire*" by Linda Costanzo Cahir. From *Literature/Film Quarterly* 22, no. 2 (1994): 72-77. Copyright © 1994 by Salisbury State University. Reprinted by permission.

"Stanley Kowalski's Not So Secret Sorrow: Queering, De-Queering, and Re-Queering *A Streetcar Named Desire* as Drama, Script, Film, and Opera" by Keith Dorwick. From *Interdisciplinary Humanities* 20, no. 2 (October 2003): 80-94. Copyright © 2003 by National Association for Humanities Education. Reprinted by permission.

"'Tiger—Tiger!' Blanche's Rape on Screen" by Nancy M. Tischler. From *Magical Muse: Millennial Essays on Tennessee Williams*. Ralph F. Voss, ed. 50-69. Copyright © 2002 by the University of Alabama Press. Reprinted by permission.

Index

Davis, Walter A., 34, 107

Death, 17, 105, 112, 117, 165, 168, 171, 185, 232, 246; acceptance, 186; as opposite of desire, 45, 86, 102

Death of a Salesman (Miller), 41, 96; expressionism, 51, 54; point of view, 48

DeJongh, Nicholas, 194

D'Emilio, John, 256

Derrida, Jacques, 235

Desire, 27, 57, 128, 138, 204, 220; and incompleteness, 230; and loneliness, 102; nature of, 74; as opposite of death, 45, 86, 102, 113, 168; and repression, 62, 71; unconscious, 140

"Desire and the Black Masseur" (Williams), 230, 238

Dickson, Vivienne, 126, 265, 295

Doolittle, Eliza (*Pygmalion*), 155

DuBois, Blanche (*A Streetcar Named Desire*), 43; actors in role, 241, 250, 280; alcoholism, 99, 133, 159; and Allan, 47, 58, 69, 117, 186, 196, 245; aristocratic image, 50, 79, 127; audience responses, 97, 99, 102, 166; as comic character, 97, 101; guilt, 168, 172, 198; mental breakdown, 45, 105, 115, 231, 234, 248, 285; name, 43, 90; as outsider, 27; rape scene, 123, 125, 144, 224, 228, 246; relationship to Mitch, 99, 106, 119, 171, 210; relationship to Stanley, 41, 53, 59, 74, 96, 113, 131, 137, 151, 155, 157, 165, 167, 173, 188, 226, 277; relationship to Stella, 61, 99; as sexual predator, 104, 125; sexuality, 47, 113, 135, 160, 179, 284; speech patterns, 52; struggle between flesh and spirit, 64, 128, 133, 139, 144; as tragic heroine, 77, 87; as victim, 82, 174, 206

"Electric Avenue" (Williams), 127-128

Epigraphs, 130, 149, 257

Epistemology of the Closet (Sedgwick), 190

Expressionism, 30, 50, 53, 104, 219, 226, 229, 233, 238

Feldman, Charles K., 241, 250, 290, 293

Flamingo Hotel, 47, 104

Flanders, Chris (*The Milk Train Doesn't Stop Here Anymore*), 170

Flashback scenes, 29, 48

Fleche, Anne, 74

Flirtation, 61, 86, 101, 113, 277, 283

Forever Amber (Winsor), 128, 149

Foster, Verna, 85

Foucault, Michel, 220

Four Daughters (film), 161, 183

Gallaway, Dorothea (*A Lovely Sunday for Creve Coeur*), 127

Ganz, Arthur, 206

Garfield, John, 161, 183

Gassner, John, 73

Gilbert, Sandra M., 87

Glass Menagerie, The (Williams), 9, 12, 30, 66, 192, 214, 222, 225, 233

"Go, Said the Bird!" (Williams), 127, 129, 153

Goforth, Mrs. (*The Milk Train Doesn't Stop Here Anymore*), 170

Gone with the Wind (film), 147, 278

Great Depression, 42, 44

Grey, Allan (*A Streetcar Named Desire*), 29, 33, 47, 57, 69, 78, 82, 114, 117, 119, 123, 172, 186, 195, 199, 210, 245, 250, 256, 273

Group Theatre, 11, 23, 43, 161

180; early drafts, 4, 63, 86, 127, 130, 136, 139, 143, 148, 152, 160, 182, 266, 288, 295; feminist criticism, 88; film version, 3, 33, 57, 105, 122, 127, 147, 186, 241, 247, 266, 273, 277, 280; as morality play, 125, 130; names, 131; as tragedy, 83, 126, 166, 179; as tragicomedy, 73, 83, 85, 96, 107

Suddenly Last Summer (Williams), 188, 193, 252

Suicide, 29, 45, 50, 54, 70, 114, 119, 167, 172, 186, 197, 245, 253, 273

Summer and Smoke (Williams), 63, 160

Swindell, Larry, 161

Tandy, Jessica, 3, 53, 116, 241, 280

Tarantula Arms, 104, 119

Thompson, Judith, 152

Tischler, Nancy M., 122, 147, 214

Tragedy; action of, 111, 120; Aristotelian, 41, 85, 195

Tragic protagonists, 11, 41, 77, 87, 95, 97, 114, 116, 120, 179

Tragicomedy, 83, 95, 100, 106

Transformation, 30, 58, 66, 119, 234, 239

27 Wagons Full of Cotton (Williams), 126, 136

Venable, Mrs. (*Suddenly Last Summer*), 188

Venable, Sebastian (*Suddenly Last Summer*), 193, 252, 255

Vengeance, 120, 123, 293

Vidal, Gore, 36, 154, 180, 182, 204

Violence, 24, 27, 37, 58, 88, 107, 113, 138, 145, 181, 207, 223, 225, 233, 238, 247-248, 279

Vlasopolos, Anca, 89

Voyeurism, 34, 203, 220

Vulgarity, 32, 61, 75, 100, 115, 196, 264, 279, 282

Warner Bros., 32, 122, 250, 281, 290, 293

Wasserman, Lew, 162

Whitmore, George, 180

Wild Duck, The (Ibsen), 95, 98

Wilde, Oscar, 268

Will Mr. Merriwether Return from Memphis? (Williams), 188

Williams, Cornelius Coffin, 8, 165

Williams, Edwina Dakin, 8

Williams, Rose, 10, 42, 184, 239

Williams, Tennessee; on *Cat on a Hot Tin Roof*, 63; childhood, 8; compared to Arthur Miller, 44; death, 13; on desire, 102, 230; education, 9; epigraphs in plays, 130, 149, 257; on expressionism, 30; on film version of *Streetcar*, 146; on guilt, 17; homosexuality, 42, 160, 190; letter to Audrey Wood, 136, 141, 157, 288; *Memoirs*, 125, 239; on *A Streetcar Named Desire*, 41, 151; on tragicomedy, 95; writing career, 10

Winchell, Mark Royden, 34

Wingfield, Tom (*The Glass Menagerie*), 12, 192, 214

Winsor, Kathleen, 128

Wood, Audrey, 11, 95, 123, 136, 141, 157, 164, 188, 280, 288

Yacowar, Maurice, 280, 292, 294